More Praise for *Liti*

"*Liturgies from Below* has come to us at a time when racial violence, hunger, migration, and death is on the rise. Rather than rely on the traditional Western canons of liturgical practice and expressions, this book offers a needed corpus of liturgies that will reinvigorate communities of faith to respond faithfully and lovingly to the social and political injustices of this era. For Christian communities seeking to democratize their worship experiences with the voices of those rendered unseen by colonizing elite power, this book is essential."

    —Gregory L. Cuéllar, associate professor of Old Testament/Hebrew Bible, Austin Presbyterian Theological Seminary, Austin, TX

"*Liturgies from Below* unleashes the subversive and creative power of prayer that destabilizes dominant forms and acts of worship, by praying with the 'unwanted' people and the earth. The 'unwanted' people who cry out 'I can't breathe' invite us to breathe God's breath in the world to bring about healing, justice, and restoration. This book, with imagination and creativity, gathers and weaves these prayers from 'unwanted' locations and demonstrates that worship can be a system-threatening and therapeutic spiritual and political act that creates counter-imperial alternatives."

    —George Zachariah, Wesley Lecturer in Theological Studies, Trinity Methodist Theological College, Auckland, New Zealand

"This book confronts Empire, not only in its centering of voices, spaces, and places that are often unheard and marginalized but also in its clear acknowledgment that even Western dominant ways of doing theology do not have the last word. The prayers and liturgies contained in this powerful and useful collection embrace the pain and injustice and the joy and beauty of such voices, places, and spaces in a way that affirms and invites the shalom of a God who acts concretely in history. It invites us as readers to do likewise as we stand in prayerful solidarity and sing the songs of freedom together with all who yearn."

    —Nadine Bowers Du Toit, professor of practical theology and missiology, Stellenbosch University, Stellenbosch, South Africa

"What should prayer and worship look like in a world that is seeming more unjust and less hopeful each day? *Liturgies from Below* shows how worship that occurs in contexts of war, poverty, dehumanization, and hopelessness engenders courage and inspires resistance to oppressive structures. It demonstrates forcefully that worship should never be an exercise that lulls us into indifference, or even worse complacency, to injustices around us, but worship should inspire us to become catalysts for change. An essential resource for every Christian community that seeks to worship faithfully and live out its calling as people committed to justice."

    —Raj Nadella, Samuel A. Cartledge Associate Professor of New Testament, Columbia Theological Seminary, Decatur, GA

"*Liturgies from Below* touches the mind, stirs the heart, and ennobles the spirit within us all. With a myriad of liturgical styles and emphases, there is something for everyone in this impactful worship resource. Minority and poor communities will find words that leap from the heart of their very existence. Majority and affluent communities will find prophetic challenges so compellingly penned it will move them to examine deeply held assumptions of wealth and privilege."

—B. J. Beu, worship and preaching consultant, co-editor of *The Abingdon Worship Annual* from Abingdon Press

"The seeming ordinariness of a traditional book of prayers is quickly disrupted by the invasive smells, noisy hustle, fears and exuberance, cardboard houses, and ready-to-eat meals of global city streets. These street prayers reek of the aroma of Christ."

—Steed Vernyl Davidson, professor of Hebrew Bible/Old Testament, vice president of academic affairs, and dean of the faculty, McCormick Theological Seminary, Chicago, IL

"Christian prayer is a participation in the ongoing, eternal intercession of Jesus the Christ before his Father. As we participate in Jesus' prayer, we gain God's heart for the entire created order—and in particular for the poor, the marginalized, the innocent, the oppressed, the sick, the dying. But, as *Liturgies from Below* makes clear, we also come to the realization of our own complicity in perpetuating evil and oppressive systems of thought, politics, economics, behaviors, and activities that militate against the kingdom of Christ, and we are led to a place of metanoia, or repentance. That change of heart by the Spirit of God working in us, is the only real hope of the world, but a hope rooted in God's love for the entire created order. I commend these prayers as they participate in the prayer of the Savior for the 'least of these.'"

—James R. Hart, President, Robert E. Webber Institute for Worship Studies, Jacksonville, FL

"*Liturgies from Below* invites readers on a vital journey to pray with people 'at the ends of the world' and, as one of the prayers says, 'to step into their lives.' Continually yielding insight, often deeply moving, not always easy, and sometimes searing, *Liturgies from Below* powerfully implores that when we 'raise our hands in prayer' we need to 'use those hands to help.'"

—Stephen Burns, professor of liturgical and practical theology, Pilgrim Theological College, University of Divinity, Melbourne, Australia

"This is a priceless resource. We can no longer be satisfied praying the prayers that we know; we must instead begin to pray in a way that can 'heal, recuperate, reconfigure, restore, and restitute our communities, the earth, and our social-natural systems.'"

—Vinnie Zarletti, Director, School of Worship Arts, North Central University, Minneapolis, MN

"Cláudio Carvalhaes has gathered a great variety of prayers for many occasions. Some fit classical liturgical settings and are offered for specific concerns. The collection will inspire leaders to facilitate liturgical creativity and lament, and it will help people resist authoritarian cultures of repression and capitalist structures of exploitation."

—Marion Grau, professor of systematic theology, ecumenism, and missiology; research fellow, Norwegian School of Theology, Religion and Society, Oslo, Norway

CLÁUDIO CARVALHAES

LITURGIES from BELOW

462 acts of worship

Praying with People at the Ends of the World

Abingdon Press™

Nashville

LITURGIES FROM BELOW:
PRAYING WITH PEOPLE AT THE ENDS OF THE WORLD

Copyright © 2020 by Abingdon Press

Library of Congress Control Number: 2020941580

ISBN: 978-1-7910-0735-5

Interior illustrations are by Kate Morales.

The prayers and liturgies in this book were written in a collaborative process, with multiple people wor-shiping, praying, and sharing together. The process was facilitated by Cláudio Carvalhaes and others, and the spoken words were recorded and written out as part of these spontaneous sessions. There are very few direct lines of authorship in this work. It is the spirit work of the people. If we learn after publication of any alternative attribution for any part of this work, we will update the acknowledgments accordingly. Contact permissions@abingdonpress.com.

20 21 22 23 24 25 26 27 28 29—10 9 8 7 6 5 4 3 2 1
MANUFACTURED IN THE UNITED STATES OF AMERICA

CONTENTS

ix—Foreword by Collin I. Cowan

xi—Preface: Worship Creates Counter-Imperial Alternatives
by Sudipta Singh

1—Praying with Unwanted People: What It Means and
Why It's Important

7—Praying at the Ends of the World: The Locations and
Methods for Creating These Prayers

12—Praying in Your Community: What This Book Can Do,
and How to Use It

19—A Word of Gratitude

21—Participants List

THE PRAYERS

PART ONE: Prayers for the Beginning and Ending of Worship

31—Invocations, Calls to Worship, Gathering Prayers

46—Benedictions

PART TWO: Prayers of Confession, Thanksgiving, and Intercession

71—Prayers of Confession and Petition

86—Prayers of Thanksgiving

91—Prayers of Intercession

Contents

PART THREE: Liturgies of Baptism and Eucharist

   109—Liturgies of Baptism

   125—Liturgies of Eucharist

PART FOUR: New and Adapted Psalms

   151—New and Adapted Psalms

PART FIVE: Topical Prayers and General Prayers

   181—Anger

   198—Forgiveness and Repentance

   202—Resistance

   210—Hunger

   215—Mourning

   222—Healing

   228—Power/Oppression

   238—General Prayers

PART SIX: Prayers Based on the Liturgical Calendar

   279—Prayers Based on the Liturgical Calendar

PART SEVEN: Praying through Poetry

   295—Praying through Poetry

PART EIGHT: Praying through Scripture

   311—Praying through Scripture

PART NINE: Complete Liturgical Sequences

   325—Complete Liturgical Sequences

Please visit www.reimaginingworship.com, to find prayers and liturgies not included in this book. You'll also find reflections and testimonies from participants, visual art, songs, and theater compositions created as part of this project, plus photos and videos from the locations. You're invited to engage with all the content, to write your own prayers and liturgies, and to share them in your faith community and social networks.

FOREWORD

Worship is central to Christian discipline and service to God. According to William Temple (1881–1944), it is the sum total of our adoration, "the most selfless emotion of which our nature is capable."[1] In that sense, worship is counter to idolatry, the ultimate expression of loyalty, and an outright display of defiance to all "authorities" and "powers" (Eph 6:12)—all forces of domination and control, that which the Council for World Mission (CWM) labels as *Empire*. In other words, worship is subversive because, through the act of worship, the worshipper says *yes* to God and in so saying automatically says *no* to empire and all the "ungods" of our time, all the systems and forces that claim supremacy.[2]

In the book of the Revelation, worship is interwoven throughout the entire book in an uncompromising message to Caesar that the Christian community could and would pay homage and pledge allegiance to God and God alone. To heed the words "Be faithful even to the point of death" (Rev 2:10) was to declare and devote primary, unconditional, and selfless loyalty to God alone.

Then I heard every creature in heaven and on earth and under the earth
and in the sea—I heard everything everywhere say,

"Blessing, honor, glory, and power
belong to the one seated on the throne
    and to the Lamb
        forever and always."

Then the four living creatures said, "Amen," and the elders fell down
and worshipped. (Rev 5:13-14)

This was the shout of "many angels. . . . They numbered in the millions—thousands upon thousands" (Rev 5:11). Gathering to worship God was a direct defiance of

---

1. William Temple, *Readings in St. John's Gospel*, vol. 1 (London: Macmillan, 1939), 68.

2. See Burchell Taylor, *The Church Taking Sides: A Contextual Reading of the Letters to the Seven Churches in the Book of Revelation* (Kingston, Jamaica: Bethel Baptist Church, 1995).

Caesar's decree that everyone in Asia Minor worship him; and this was at a time when Christians were being persecuted, even killed, for disobeying this decree.

This volume on worship is a well-needed resource, and it is long in coming. It is the answer to a long-held dream of CWM. When CWM decided to name Empire as the context of mission, we agreed that we should develop worship material to enable and support the people of God to offer this "most selfless emotion" to God in the context of Empire. We said then that dispassionate, lifeless, and disinterested words will not embolden faith, expose false power, and embrace—with unmistakable and uncompromising clarity and devotion—the God of faithfulness and justice.

The content of this book reflects the people of God in their deep struggle and search to find meaning in "Unexpected Places." More important, the writers cause us to see the inextricable intertwining of worship with all of life. Here they present worship as wrestling with God in defiant determination. The writers confess their allegiance to God and God alone, baring their heart and soul in these litanies of lament, protest, and praise. The songs and prayers in this volume are meant to inspire "the eyes of [the] heart" of the worshipping community to be "enlightened" (Eph 1:18 NIV), to deepen our faith in the God of life, and to fortify our spirits for renewed commitment to justice and peace as the lived expression of worship.

Just as important as the content of this volume is the process that led to harvesting and producing the material for publication. Through a process of engagement with real-life situations, a group of worshippers, students, and leaders of worship spent time in contexts where people live in poverty and hopelessness. They listened to stories of suffering and pain, contemplated the presence of God and the meaning of hope, and out of that incarnational experience developed worship material to express true feelings of discontent with the world and conversation with God. This is true worship, the kind that springs from the bowels of discontent, anchors faith in the God of the risen Jesus, and calls forth commitment to resistance and transformative praxis.

I celebrate this long-awaited publication and commend it as a resource to further enhance our understanding and enrich our worship.

Collin I. Cowan

General Secretary, Council for World Mission, Singapore

The Council for World Mission is a worldwide partnership of Christian churches. The 32 members are committed to sharing their resources of money, people, skills, and insights globally to carry out God's mission locally. CWM was created in 1977 and incorporates the London Missionary Society (1795), the Commonwealth Missionary Society (1836) and the (English) Presbyterian Board of Missions (1847).

PREFACE

Worship Creates Counter-Imperial Alternatives

Worship is fundamental to the Christian calling and spirituality. Devotional surrender provides the basis for a spiritual life that instantiates life-giving bonds in the whole of creation that is continuously killed by Empire. Worshipping God is itself an act of rebellion, as Empire demands to be worshipped alone. In the context of Empire, it is not the absence of spirituality or religiosity per se that has become the challenge but a kaleidoscope of spiritualities manufactured by the hegemonic paradigm of neoliberal politics and economics in worship to Empire. As the book of Revelation shows, worship to "the Lamb who was slain" (13:8) subverts worship to the power and religion of Empire.

Worship is central to the calling and being of the church as faith community. Church is a community who gathers together in worship to affirm their faith in the Divine as well as the Divine mission of redemption and healing. Worship inspires and anoints the community to translate this mission into radical social transformation in the here and now by enabling their agency to turn the world upside down. In worship we celebrate the spirituality of resistance and reconstruction.

Prayer, according to Jewish theologian and rabbi Abraham Joshua Heschel, "is meaningless unless it is subversive, unless it seeks to overthrow and to ruin the pyramids of callousness, hatred, opportunism, falsehoods."[1] To put it differently, worship is a subversive activity that contests and overthrows the prevailing sinful order of injustice and inequality. For Moses, the burning bush experience at Mount Horeb was not only an alternative experience of theophany; it was also a tutorial for an alternative understanding of worship. The alternative experience of theophany enabled Moses to reimagine God as the vulnerable One, deeply affected by the scars of slavery. In the vision of the burning bush, Moses encountered God as a co-sufferer who was embodied in the life stories of pain and struggles for freedom and dignity of the enslaved communities. The sacramental and liturgical symbol of fire in the burning

---

1. Abraham Joshua Heschel, "On Prayer," in *Moral Grandeur and Spiritual Audacity*, ed. Susannah Heschel (New York: Farrar, Straus and Giroux, 1996), 262.

bush provided Moses with an alternative understanding of worship. Worship should instill in the enslaved community the audacity to believe that the blazing fire of the Empire cannot destroy the beauty of life. The green leaves in the liturgy of the burning bush empowered Moses to believe in the possibility of a beyond of Egypt.

Worship is therefore a life-changing experience where we are invited to realize and denounce our power and privileges in order to become credible and authentic comrades of the communities at the margins who are engaged in the salvific mission of turning the world upside down.

The dominant always uses religious institutions and rituals to create and legitimize new idols that ensure their prosperity and power. Idolatry is nothing but the fetishization of our imperial projects, and liturgy in the context of idolatry celebrates the sacrifice of the powerless and the voiceless in the altar of patriotism, progress, family values, racism, casteism, patriarchy, heteronormativity, and cultural nationalism. Ungods have been created in history to offer spiritual and theological legitimization to the pyramids of injustice and exclusion. We are more comfortable with depending on the mercy of the ungods who rule us than with the empowering presence of the liberating God. Religion—with its distorted theology, liturgy, and morality—continues to incorporate its followers into the band of idol worshippers. We have become devotees of the Golden Calves. This is the context in which we need to reimagine worship as rituals of defiance and alternatives.

So "Let my people go so that they can worship me" does not mean that God's liberative mission is to enable us to worship God in a safe and comfortable space; rather, the very struggle for liberation is the act of worship. Let us paraphrase Rabbi Heschel's interpretation of prayer contextually. Worship is our political engagement to overthrow and ruin the pyramids of economic injustice and social exclusion such as casteism, patriarchy, and heterosexism. Such discernment helps us go beyond our binary thinking of worship, social work, ministry, and social action.

Egypt is around us and within us, and we need to discern it and gather the prophetic courage to destroy the Golden Calves of our times. It is our faith imperative to occupy our churches, our spiritual practices, and our institutions so as to reclaim them from the worship of the ungods. It is in our unending journey toward freedom, dismantling the pyramids of systemic sin and evil, that we worship the God of life in truth and spirit.

Why Empire?

Fullness of life for all creation is how Jesus interpreted his mission in the context of the Roman Empire. This theme of life in fullness actually started with the then World Alliance of Reformed Churches, which at its 2004 General Council in Accra, Ghana, explored its meaning within the context of economic globalization and emerged with the Accra Confession, a confession that has had widespread transformative impact on the way churches and ecumenical organizations have understood and engaged God's mission since.[2] At the heart of the Accra Confession is the conviction that God is the "Creator and Sustainer of all life"; and that God "calls us as partners in the creation and redemption of the world."[3]

CWM, in response to this confession, observed that life is in danger and hence showed the prophetic courage to declare that the context in which we understand ourselves to be carrying out God's mission is Empire. And we used as a definition for Empire that which came out of the Globalisation Project—Uniting Reformed Church in South Africa and Evangelical Reformed Church in Germany:

> We speak of empire, because we discern a coming together of economic, cultural, political and military power in our world today, that constitutes a reality and a spirit of lordless domination, created by humankind yet enslaving simultaneously; an all-encompassing global reality serving, protecting and defending the interest of powerful corporations, nations, elites and privileged people, while imperiously excluding even sacrificing humanity and exploiting creation; a pervasive spirit of destructive self-interest, even greed—the worship of money, goods and possessions; the gospel of consumerism, proclaimed through powerful propaganda and religiously justified, believed and followed; the colonization of consciousness, values and notions of human life by the imperial logic; a spirit lacking in compassionate justice and showing contemptuous disregard for the gifts of creation and the household of life.[4]

The CMW Theology Statement 2010 provides the theological basis for CWM's existence today. It identifies Empire as the context in which we are called to be partners with God in God's mission to transform the face of the earth. Engaging in mission in the midst of the Empire is not a new slogan. God's mission has always taken place in the midst of the Empire. God became flesh in Jesus Christ in an imperial world. From the time of his birth Jesus's life was threatened by the Empire. We learn from the Gospel accounts that it is the Empire and its allies who eventually killed Jesus. So we are called to continue this missional engagement in the midst of the Empire. Here we need to understand and name the diverse manifestations of the Empire in our midst. And we need to contextualize the missional trajectory of Jesus in confronting the Empire as we engage in the mission of God.

We understand Empire as that which claims absolute lordship over God's creation and commodifies God's people, disabling their agency to amass wealth and exercise control and domination over them. Empire is hence an ungod that rejects God and God's plan for the world. So it is a faith imperative on all of us to resist all manifestations of Empire in order to protect and affirm life. When we resist the

2. http://wcrc.ch/accra.

3. "The Accra Confession," World Communion of Reformed Churches, accessed May 20, 2020, http://wcrc.ch/accra/the-accra-confession, article 17.

4. "WARC/Global Dialogue on the Accra Confession," accessed May 20, 2020, https://www.reformiert-info.de/WARCGlobal_Dialogue_on_the_Accra_Confession-4370-0-12-2.html.

power of Empire, we are reclaiming our agency to liberate our lives and our world. The hope that sustains us in the context of Empire is the possibility to live in opposition to the logic of Empire. When we live out our faith rejecting the claims of Empire on our lives and our world, we witness the God of life. So, mission in the context of Empire is our absolute allegiance to the blossoming of life, exposing and confronting the imperial forces of death and destruction. The politics of Christian witness in the context of Empire is to resist the temptation to be co-opted by the Empire, and to find the nerve to come out of the Empire. In that politics, we experience a profound spirituality. It is the mission of God in which we, the people of God, are invited to partner with God.

Why This Initiative?

We affirm that our worship should offer a distinct form of life-giving spirituality inspired by experiences of worship in the harrowing rupture of life amidst the hopelessness and death-dealing catastrophes of Empire. More than just a set of religious actions carried out within the context of the gathered community worship, at its very core worship speaks to a lifestyle involving every facet of daily living. Indigenous civilizations have continued to rival dualistic forms of spirituality and devotedness to God and offer us gifts that inspire our cost of discipleship, embodied in our whole lives together with creation as life-affirming worship and praise to the God of life. Council for World Mission's commitment to mutually challenge, encourage, and equip churches to share in God's mission beckons us to look again at the worship life of our churches and our obedience to the mandate given by Christ.

We must ask, in breaking the seals of Empire (Rev 5) does our worship life subvert Empire? Our worship should underscore the idea that all religions are dangerous, including the religion of revelation within Christianity. The history of religion in the whole world is disappointing, Christianity included. Yet religious consciousness in human beings is something we deny at our own peril. The body has its parts, the mind has its parts, and the soul has its parts too. The religion of Empire targets the soul of humanity and colonizes faith as the currency for its religious outlook. Empire engineers spirituality and harnesses our sources of spirituality to subject humanity and creation to its worship. The violent usurpation of God from God's throne and the defilement of God's holiness by the ideology propagated with clichés (such as "there is no alternative") by the current economic system requires not only devotional surrender of humanity, creation, and cosmos to Empire but also coercive and blind devotion to its antics against the good news of the gospel.

In engaging the priority of developing our congregations, we urge a reexamination of worship within our members. Christianity as a global faith is in perpetual danger of associating itself with forms of worship, surrender, and discipleship that bend to the religiosity of neoliberal economics and power. By constantly unveiling the distortions of worship in our gathered communities, we undertake to liberate Sunday from cultic forms of worship and prosperity, and develop material that will reenergize our worship to reclaim our spiritual resources from the temples of Empire. We affirm the symbolic and sacramental knowledge of indigenous peoples of the world in our quest for alternative life-affirming spiritualities.

This book will enable members of our local congregations to worship relevantly in their own context. It will help them to imagine and write worship resources from their daily experiences of pain and struggle. In that process, God will not remain a distant deity but a co-sufferer in their daily life.

We understand from all the participants that this enriching process transformed their view on worship. They mentioned that they won't be able to continue teaching in their class on worship in the same old way. We hope and pray that a new movement of liturgy from the margins will emerge and grow and this book will initiate that process.

This book is an invitation to resist the temptation to be co-opted by the Empire, and to find the nerve to come out of the Empire, creating counter-imperial alternatives.

Sudipta Singh

Mission Secretary, Research and Capacity Development,
Council for World Mission, Singapore

PRAYING WITH UNWANTED PEOPLE

What It Means and Why It's Important

Faced with pain that rips apart, we cry out in one voice,
>   **intercede with us,**
>   **oh solidarity Lord.**

Faced with death that wounds,
and marks with pain,
>   **give us the strength of an embrace**
>   **and the peace that your love gives us.**

Faced with injustice that kills
and cries out for conversion,
>   **move us to transform the world**
>   **and let all death become a song.**

In the face of desolation and crying,
faced with impotence and frustration,
>   **come to our side,**
>   **sustain us with your life, Lord.**

You are the God of the poor, the One who sows hope,
>   **you are the God of solidarity, the One who gives love.**

You are God with us, the Eternal, the Great I am.
>   **God of the embrace, God of song, God who caresses,**
>   **God who strengthens, God who surrenders, God of action.**

O Lord of Solidarity: Your kingdom come to the mourner,
lean your ear to the cry,
>   **your sons and daughters are coming**
>   **to show your great love.**[1]

---

1.   Find many additional prayers from this project at http://reimaginingworship.com.

1

Introduction

A diverse group of about one hundred pastors, theologians, students, artists, and activists from various Christians traditions, churches, and walks of life from about fifty countries gathered together during 2018–2019 in four different countries on four continents, blessed and supported by the Council for World Mission.[2] They gathered for a common purpose: learning to pray with local communities in order to create liturgical resources for Christian communities around the world. This project is rooted in God's demand for us to live a life of compassion, listening to those who are suffering and learning how to pray with them. We hope that, in the desire of God and the strength of our faith, we will respond to the challenges of our world today.

Challenges in Our World, Challenges for Our Praying

Many people are feeling, in one way or another, that the world is moving toward a difficult place, that we are moving toward an impending collective death. Inequality soars. The vast majority of people around the earth are getting poorer. As Oxfam says, "The world's 2,153 billionaires have more wealth than the 4.6 billion people who make up 60 percent of the planet's population."[3] We live in a slow-moving catastrophe that doesn't make headlines. Our era has been designated as *anthropocene, capitalocene, plantationocene,* or *chthulucene.*[4] Most of us humans, who place ourselves above any other form of life, are extracting more from the earth than it can offer, straining natural resources beyond the earth's sustainable supply. Our planet is losing its balance. Global warming, melting ice caps, erratic seasons, droughts, overpopulation, deforestation, the ocean's warming, extinction of species, death, and loss are showing up everywhere. Geopolitical configurations are marked by an expanding movement of migrants and refugees due to climate change and civil wars. Democracies are collapsing, social inequality is widening, nation states are dissolving into dictatorships with fascist leaders, public spaces are collapsing, fear is the political emotion of our time, various forms of destruction and violence are becoming normalized, and the consequences of an unrestrained neoliberal economy are thrusting us toward a place of no return.

What prayers are Christians called to pray during these times? How are we to pray as we are confronted by a world in collapse? While some Christians recite the

---

2. https://www.cwmission.org.

3. https://www.oxfam.org/en/press-releases/worlds-billionaires-have-more-wealth-46-billion-people.

4. Donna Haraway, "Anthropocene, Capitalocene, Plantationocene, Chthulucene: Making Kin," *Environmental Humanities*, vol. 6, 2015; https://environmentalhumanities.org/arch/vol6/6.7.pdf.

ancient prayers in the midst of a church burnt by wars, other Christians try to find words to pray that make sense of the absurdity of their conditions. For the ways of praying that we are proposing here, the condition of our world begs for different prayers and different forms of prayer. As we witness the pain of the poor, the collapsing of the world we know, and the natural disasters around the globe, there seems to be no prayer that can respond to it all. However, we must pray anyway, and the way we pray makes total difference! Where should our prayers come from? If our prayers come from places of collapse and the debris of horrors, then what prayers may Christians offer to God and the world? That is what this book is wrestling with.

Learning New Grammar for Our Faith

If we are to pray today from real historical and social locations, from places of deep pain and places that are entirely foreign to us, we Christians must learn a new grammar for our faith. We must learn new prayers and new ways to pray.[5] We will have to look at tradition differently. We will have to delve into a variety of prayer resources to engage with the earth and other people more fully. We will have to be willing to understand other people's lives, ways of being, and religions. Our prayers must learn how to speak of the trauma poor people face every day. Our prayers must teach us to reject altogether any historical construction founded in the unhappiness and oppression of others. Otherwise our prayers are something other than prayer.

As God's voice in the world is expressed in our prayers, we are called to be radically converted in our ways of praying, to go deeper within ourselves, and to relate more deeply with nature. We are called to be radically converted toward forms of action that heal, recuperate, reconfigure, restore, and restitute our communities, the earth, and our social-natural systems. May our prayers be anathema to any form of government that sustains war, that oppresses people, animals, mountains, oceans, and the whole earth! Instead of being apart, prayers can reconcile us back into a deep sense of communities. And blessed be those who understand that we live in *conjunto*, together, with the same rights and responsibilities.

---

5. Paul Holmer in *The Grammar of Faith* shows how prayer consists of structural languages that shape people's ways of being. The grammar of faith for him is marked by language *of* faith and not language *about* faith. Theology for him is done by the one praying and not a comment or reflection on proper theology done elsewhere. Theology is a personal event. He says, "Theology must always move towards a present-tense, first-person mood" (p. 24). Following Holmer, we believe that every individual prays from their own life experiences and through their own lives. Their prayers are the forms and contents of theology. In other words, theology happens in the moment when one is praying, with their self/collective presence, the conditions, quality, and limitations of their lives. When we pray in places of hurt and violence, our theologies pulse with sweat and blood, and a new grammar of faith ensues. See Paul L. Holmer, *The Grammar of Faith* (San Francisco: Harper and Row, 1978).

Composing a New Tradition to Breathe God's Breath in the World

It is within our "anathema" *and* our "blessed be" that we *compose tradition*. This entails betrayal, a break with that which is harmful, and a rupture in our longtime habits and assumptions. But it also entails moving along with that which is important to our living. This form of living tradition goes beyond texts. The group of pastors, theologians, students, artists, and activists who joined in this project decided to hear firsthand what was meaningful for people living at the margins of the world and to compose a bundle of resources for the rest of the world's Christians. In this way, this collection of liturgies is more a path, a journey into and from places where people are struggling, rather than a self-enclosed set of prayers.

Only a prayer that has its ear attached to the earth, its eye upon those who suffer, and its hands stretched out in solidarity can help us realize our distance from God and a world in flaming pain. If prayer is about loving God, then prayer is also about building a house for the abandoned, becoming a wall of protection for the vulnerable, and giving our life away for those who are at the brink of disappearance. This building of a common happiness and place of safety for those who are vulnerable is an absolute imperative in our world today. Fascism and white nationalism globally have become a fundamental power effect in our times. The *de-negration* of the world; of the poor; of brown, yellow, red, and black bodies; as well as of the natural world has become the global political process of necropolitics by and for the sake of white supremacy.

Against that daily threat to the lives of so many, Christians must build expansive practices of compassion and solidarity with those who have been deemed to die. We must realize our deep connections with all from the lower classes, all the poor—in whatever religion or color they come—and expand this solidarity to include animals, rivers, oceans, birds, and the whole earth. Only through that confluence of mutualities and belonging does our prayer become breathing God's breath in the world.[6] In that way, prayers become a continuation of Jesus's prophetic life, expressing a radical commitment with the poor.

Avoiding or Embracing the Poor

Many Christians have created a faith that avoids the poor. In the United States, for instance, Protestantism is often a church full of middle- and upper-class people anxiously wrestling with secularism and the decline of their church. Only a few of these churches can boast large memberships or bountiful resources. Instead, most Protestant churches are growing smaller and weaker. Just like the neoliberal economy of the world.

---

6. Cláudio Carvalhaes, *Praying With: A Christian Orientation of the Heart* (Eugene, OR: Cascade, 2021), forthcoming.

4

In other parts of the world, however, there is a Christian renewal thriving amidst the poor at the fringes of Empire. This Christian renewal is taking place fundamentally through the ritual of Christian worship and prayers. Christian neo-Pentecostalism is exploding everywhere,[7] offering a new grammar of faith that gives strength, mission, and purpose to those who are exposed to social threats, chaos, and loss. These churches are embracing the poor and speaking from places where abandoned people live. Many of these churches are giving people tools to survive in the midst of violence, social and personal trauma, illness, anxiety and depression, deep economic hardships, and death. While many of these churches do exploit people, they also offer sanctuary and hope to those who are suffering and impoverished by creating new songs and prayers, new ways to pray and listen to the word of God. While we must be radically opposed to their exploitive theologies, theirs is a faith grammar grounded in the hearts of those who are unwanted around the world but who *are* wanted by God.

How Are We to Pray?

This prayer book offers an alternative to both the traditional prayer books of Christian liturgies and neo-Pentecostal cultic prayers. It *intertwines* traditional Christian liturgies and neo-Pentecostal prayers. Based on a gospel insistence that we must get closer to the poorest and the abandoned in the world, this book is intended to help us pray with those who are suffering the psychological, social, economic, sexual, and racial violence of our times. Thus, the main question here is: **How are we to pray with the unwanted of the world?** How can our prayers not only address the disasters of the world and the killing of people everywhere but also, in God's love, offer hope and actions of transformation? And in that way of praying, how do we get to the point where we can see our own vulnerability, our own incompleteness, our own frailty, and our own shakable ontological structure and impossibility to deal with life itself?

Once in a worship class, a guest speaker told my students that we needed to pray the established, written prayers of the church for at least twenty years before we were able to pray our own newly composed prayers. Does such a rule still apply? I do not think so. A new movement is required for this time: not to abandon the prayers of the church but to also pray new prayers in new ways, for others and ourselves, in a constant movement of God's grace into an expansive mindfulness, transforming and recreating ourselves and the world. This will mean learning how to pray differently, to be faithful to Jesus in these devastating times by praying with and for the

---

7. Jung Mo Sung, *Desire, Market, and Religion* (London: SCM Press, 2012); "Christianity Reborn: A Century After Its Birth Pentecostalism Is Redrawing the Religious Map of the World and Undermining the Notion That Modernity Is Secular," *The Economist*, December 19, 2006, https://www.economist.com/special-report/2006/12/19/christianity-reborn.

unwanted—those who are the "undercommons,"[8] including not only humans but also the whole earth and other animals, because their conditions of living are also the conditions of existence for all of us.

Through our collective prayers, with those who we are called to listen to, serve, and fight for, God calls us to live our faith in much deeper ways, understand our world in broader ways, and make a radical commitment with the poor in the name of God. Through prayers, we can envision a radical moral imagination of new worlds! By the grace of God, we can birth these new worlds through *ora et labora*—our prayers and our work in solidarity.

A lost voice. Squatting in my little street corner this very dark night. It is cold and the darkness is scary. Who can hold me—the hand of God. Is there a God out there? God, if you are there—if you can hear me, hold me through the night. I really want to sleep, but my belly is rumbling. Please don't let them find me here, stop them from taking and hurting me. God—if you are there—hear my voice![9]

---

8. Stefano Harney and Fred Moten, *The Undercommons: Fugitive Planning & Black Study* (Durham: Duke University Press, 2013), Kindle Locations 26–30, Kindle Edition.

9. Find many additional prayers from this project at http://reimaginingworship.com.

PRAYING AT THE ENDS OF THE WORLD

The Locations and Methods for Creating These Prayers

This book is a collection of prayers, songs, rituals, rites of healing, Eucharistic and baptismal prayers, meditations, poetry, and art from four continents: Asia-Pacific Islands, Africa, Americas, and Europe. It is the result of a project called Re-Imagining Worship as Acts of Defiance and Alternatives in the Context of Empire, organized by the Council for World Mission (CWM) during the years 2018–2019.

The project gathered about one hundred people to serve as participants. They are scholars, pastors, artists, activists, and students from radically different ethnicities, races, sexualities, churches, and theological backgrounds. The participants traveled to four different cities in four different countries (Manila, Philippines; Johannesburg, South Africa; Kingston, Jamaica; and Scicli, Italy). At each location, they spent a week together in different local neighborhoods and communities, where they lived alongside people, breathing in the circumstances of extreme poverty, oppression, violence, and pain. These communities are coping every day with issues of state-violence, drugs, land grabbing, immigration, war, attacks on women, militarization, climate change, ecological disasters, unjust wages, unsafe working conditions, inhumane living conditions, abandonment, and more. These are people who are living at the ends of the world.

The participants spent time with the people who live in these places, and some worshipped and prayed with them in their own worship contexts. The people in each location accepted us and allowed us to be with them. They shared their lives, stories, food, wisdom, households, joy, struggles, dreams, demands for justice, and pain. After listening to them, we gathered together as a group and prayed together. In this praying together, we created new prayers and liturgies with and for the people in each place. The words you will encounter in this collection include words from the participants and the people living in the locations we visited.

After we lived with the people, we soon realized that we were actually learning how to pray. When we were praying, we were not only praying with those affected

7

by violence and poverty but we were also praying for ourselves. By praying with those living in inhumane conditions, we were challenged to change. Together, with contradictions, heavy and full hearts, bringing with us their struggles and the ones from our own communities, we created these prayers for *our own churches*, not for the poor, with the hopes that we might learn how to pray for ourselves and go into deep change. In a circular movement, we were also praying *with* those at the ends of the world.

We wrestle with the tension between witness and solidarity on the one hand and poverty tourism on the other. In these prayers, we profess and confess both. We were there to learn and change, undoing a mission model that goes to "provide" something. We hope this work becomes a gesture toward a necessarily long and deeper stay with those who are suffering. From there we will learn what needs to change in us and in our ways of being in the world, and how to make the change. From the ends of the world, we came out praying, singing, creating art, and crying out loud for the mercy and power of God. The experiences reflected in this resource aim to give churches and Christians a new methodology and a new vocabulary to pray, so that we might reorient ourselves in the world. Figuratively and concretely, this is a wave of liturgies coming from the bottom up.

The Locations

Manila, Philippines

In Manila we experienced how the world will become in the future. After many years of colonialism, Philippines is a fertile ground for fascism. The country is controlled by a few rich people, and neoliberalism is the preferred weapon of the state. A fascist government led by Rodrigo Duterte is in place, using martial law and extrajudicial killings as necropolitics, expelling indigenous people from their own lands and selling the country's natural resources to agribusiness. The government is in the hands of China's economy and US militarization, and it doesn't know how to address poverty. The top twenty richest men and women in the Philippines have more money than the entire national budget of the country.[1] There are no workers' rights, and most jobs offer low wages.

In Manila we visited four communities:

> **Indigenous people's communities** in the province of Rizal. The people we were with here are victims of militarization, forced evacuations, demolitions, and extrajudicial killings. They are continuously harassed by land grabbers, mining companies, and government military forces.

---

1. Jay B. Hilotin, "Meet the 20 richest Filipinos and how much they're worth," *Gulf News*, January 21, 2020, https://gulfnews.com/photos/news/meet-the-20-richest-filipinos-and-how-much-theyre-worth-1.1579603693637.

Workers' organizations in the province of Bulacan and Southern Tagalog areas. The workers are victims of unfair labor practices, and two workers' organizations located in different communities are on hunger strikes at the time of writing this book.

Urban poor communities, where people are victims of demolition because of development aggressions.

Peasant communities in Batangas or Kalinga areas, who are victims of land conversions, militarization, demolitions, and extrajudicial killings.

Johannesburg, South Africa

In Johannesburg, we experienced the wonderful development of South Africa in the midst of its still deeply entangled history of racism and colonialism. The brutal history of apartheid has racist historical consequences that continue to plague the country. Trapped in a deep wound opened by white settlers, South Africa is still wrestling to find ways out of this complex situation. Here, we questioned how we could help when the situation was so difficult and seemed to require years of knowledge. In spite of these challenges, we tried to learn both from our insurmountable limitations and our struggle to write something about experiences and events that seem indescribable. Holding on to these dilemmas, we gathered to make a composition of African spaces and situations and to pray from that complex web of issues, histories, pain, violence, and struggles.

In Johannesburg we visited four communities:

Marikana, where there is exploitation of the workers that resembles modern day slavery, as capitalist corporations profit at the expense of human dignity by taking away the communities' resources.

Soweto, which is a township of Johannesburg located along the mining belt to the south of the city. Soweto is synonymous with the South African struggle, and is the site of the 1976 Soweto uprising. It is also considered the home of the liberationist leaders. Here, Moroka has become Johannesburg's worst slum area, where residents have erected their shanties on plots measuring six-by-six meters with only communal bucket-system toilets and very few water taps.

Alexandra, a township in the Gauteng province of South Africa. A poor urban area in the country, Alexandra made news during xenophobic attacks in 2019.

9

Johannesburg CBD (Central Business District), where we were able to spend time with economic and political refugees. In Johannesburg we interacted with people who experienced the brutal effects of wars, economic looting, and political instability. We also engaged with the realities of displaced communities (local and international), mostly made up of undocumented local residents and refugees.

Kingston, Jamaica

The third leg of this global project took place in Kingston, Jamaica. In keeping with the model structures of the workshops held in Manila and Johannesburg, this workshop also had a variety of participants from American countries who formed an expansive ecumenical group of scholars, pastors, students, and church leaders who came with the desire to create something new. Several issues were considered: state violence, urban displacement, land grabbing, neoliberal policies, corruption, climate change, poverty, hunger, violence, and so forth.

In Jamaica, we visited the following communities:

Tivoli Gardens, where seventy-three people were shot in a massacre by the state in 2010. Local residents claim that it was more likely one hundred or possibly even two hundred people who were killed. All these deaths were forgotten by the state. We heard the searing testimonies of people who survived the shootings, and we visited communities abandoned by the government.

August Town and Trench Town, communities struggling with poverty and abandonment by the government. August Town is a local community finding ways to survive. Trench Town was the town of Bob Marley. Our people walked on the streets and through local marketplaces with pastors and local leaders, and we heard the people's stories. We also heard the heart-wrenching testimonies of workers who are going to be displaced from the market where they have lived for the last fifty-five years because the place was sold to the owner of a nearby shopping mall. We were able to have a worship service organized by Jamaica Theological Seminary with all of the evicted vendors.

Bobo Shanti Rastafari community in Bull Bay, a thriving community of Rastafarians in the woods. Our people were able to participate in worship services and learn about their life and beliefs and proposal for a new society.

Two rural communities in Low River and Manchester, small, rural farm communities who received our people with joy. They taught us

10

how to care for the earth, and they shared with us their struggles to survive against extractivism and big corporations.

Scicli, Italy

The fourth and last meeting of this global project happened in Scicli, on the island of Sicily, Italy. This small town on the shores of the Mediterranean Sea receives refugees and welcomes immigrants from Africa, Syria, Iraq, and other parts of the world. We were hosted by **Mediterranean Hope—Refugee and Migrant Programme**, a recent migration project conceived by the Federation of Protestant Churches in Italy, which is associated with Protestant churches in Europe. With them, we listened to refugees and immigrants. We ate with them, shared smiles, learned about their struggles, the ways they faced death in order to survive, the so-many losses along the way, and the fears and newness of life they experienced in a place where they didn't know how they would be received. These precious people went through unspeakable forms of trauma. With them, we started to understand the disastrous situations of migrants and refugees.

———— ———— ————

In all of these places, we heard testimonies about extremely difficult situations of people who are dealing with violence across the globe. In every community, we saw a multiplicity of wisdom, a variety of cosmologies, and the resilience, agency, subversion, and subterfuge in people's everyday lives. In the ways they keep going, in their resisting ways of smiling either to please or to dismiss, in moving with what they had, in praying and crying, in sharing, in being tricksters, in being bold in many forms of living and survival, in creating new forms of exchange and informal economies, in their struggles and fights, in their uses of religion and being religious, in their genuine hopes and trusts, in many forms of solidarity, in breathing life in the midst of suffocating death, in resisting the shadows casted upon them, and in calling themselves alive when they undergo others' endless attempts to bring their death.

Being with them gave us a sense that we were praying with those at the ends of the world. But also, with so much suffering, violence, and destruction, we felt that we are all at the end of the world as we know it. Hearing the call of God to live our faith in Jesus fully, we wanted to breathe with them. Because prayer is nothing more than breathing together.

11

PRAYING IN YOUR COMMUNITY

What This Book Can Do, and How to Use It

Prayer as a Circular Movement

Prayer does something; it is a potent ritual action! Prayer effects a deep circular movement within us, moving between our inside and outside without separation. When we pray to God, our prayer first changes us, and then, while the movements of our hearts go toward God, our prayers have ripple effects into the world, affecting the course of our individual and communal life. Prayer affects our personal and political thinking, feelings, actions, and ways of being. In the United States, when there are disasters or mass gun shootings that kill many people, including children, or even in the midst of COVID-19, politicians typically say they are sending "thoughts and prayers" to the victims. But, most of the time, that is empty rhetoric since nothing else happens, nothing really changes. The public quickly learns from the rote repetition of this expression that prayers do not really matter. In these cases, however, we can also see an evident circularity: prayers and thoughts unaccompanied by sociopolitical and economic actions and changes are not really genuine prayers. When we think of our prayers, we have to remember Jesus saying: "You will know them by their fruit" (Matt 7:16). When we pray, the fruits of gratitude, solidarity, justice, and compassion are seeds that, once planted in us, make the soil of our hearts and communities rich and grow into new gardens of collective harvest and bounty. When we pray together, no one should go hungry or be abandoned. When we pray, genuinely, for families who have lost their children to gun violence, to jail, or poverty, a whole network of life and solidarity should come to fruition and be turned into laws against guns, social disparity, and systems of death and exclusion. If prayer has indeed a live and full circularity within one's body and spirit, the whole community will breathe this prayer and be connected in love and true solidarity. Prayer can be the starting point for change.

12

Praying can bring people into re-existence. We are called to pray into reexistence those people who were hidden in a shadow of oblivion, hidden and forgotten in abject and obscure places, whose lives are considered disposable. To pray people into re-existence is to bring them closer to our hearts and neighborhoods, rewriting laws and offering a new way of organizing and living our social life. For those abandoned at the ends of the world, we pray to God to bring them into full existence, and we pray for an end to the necropolitics of Empire that tortures and exterminates the poor.

When we believe that, by the power of the Holy Spirit, demons of death that devour life around the world will be cast away, a light will shine where there was once only shadow. A new life, fully and morally imagined through prayers, can radically change our own hearts and neighborhoods. When we pray with those who were thrown into abandonment, we can draw closer to those who live at the ends of the world, like the people who participated in the project for this book.

We can develop new ways of praying in our own contexts. This book may be used in a variety of ways for that transformative purpose, according to the readers' context. In whatever way you choose to use this book, we hope it will help you pray with your community for a greater awareness of the forces of Empire all around us and for a new inhabitation of the Holy Spirit, self-transformation, conversion, and solidarity with the poor. May this book help you develop a new prayer language to live out the Christian faith more fully and to become a community of resistance and solidarity, where you are, with those who are suffering. We hope you will expand liturgy, worship, and prayers into transnational solidarity against Empire and on behalf of those who live at the ends of the world. Get to know their wisdom, call them by their names, listen to their stories, shift your gaze away from fear or condescending thought, and begin to hold them close to your heart as precious ones, as those who can actually teach you how to pray.

The language of prayer is the language of real people. We have kept the written texts mostly raw, as they were created. Since we have offered in this introduction information about each city where the workshops took place, we decided not to organize the prayers geographically. We wanted to avoid creating an Olympic contest of oppression. Each prayer shows a reality that is experienced everywhere. The globalization of Empire has created various forms of violence that are repeated globally but that need to be responded to with the particularities of each location and community. Many languages and colloquialisms are used, reflecting the language and environments of particular communities. We have left some of the language untouched, to honor it and keep the prayers "real." But we have worked to make the prayers clear enough for you to use in your own setting.

Prayer embraces the language of pain. The group was very diverse, and we expressed our prayers very differently. Some of the prayers written by participants were especially challenging. When these difficult prayers were first spoken, the group talked about how painful it was for some to accept them. Yet, even when participants disagreed with the theology and language that was used, everyone understood the pain that was present. We all had been together in very difficult places, and love for the people kept us alive and together! We realized that what united us was not doctrine, beliefs, or faith orientations but a spirit of compassion and loving-kindness.

What we realized is that when we pray together, we tap into a force that is within, around, and beyond us. Through that power, we learn to adapt and create unthought possibilities. The world as it exists is never the final answer. With God, the world is always open to becoming something else, always looping and circling into new ways of flourishing. Praying with one another teaches us that we are never done. Through prayers God changes us as we change the world, and God becomes more significant than we first thought. With God we move, we cry, we survive, we become, we organize, we struggle. Prayers remind us that, through God, we understand that to become human is far more than the indoctrination of any human dominion. Instead, we learn that we are always collective, in our own communities as well as our communities with other species and the earth. Our prayers are liturgies where God transforms the world through us.

Doing This Work Where You Are

We hope with this book to offer a new methodology for praying with those who suffer. We encourage you to adapt it to your own context. Find ways to use these prayers in your **worship services and other gatherings**, in your **small group meetings and classes**, in your **ministry team meetings**, and as part of the work you do **in your community**. And use them in your own **personal devotional times**, where you can quietly absorb and feel and express the pain and joy of these prayers, in communion with the people who created them.

Below is a list of considerations we made for the gatherings during this project. Adjust them for your own community. Perhaps you feel inadequate or anxious (as I did and still do), but I encourage you to do it anyway. What we have presented here is not complete—it is an opening and an invitation for you to expand this work!

1) **Teach your church to imagine.** Engage with art and artists, go to plays, watch movies, try exercises in imagining new forms of life. What are the symbols that keep your community alive? Songs, poetry, gestures? Imagine a life together with those we never thought we could/would/should live. What are the hardships, the difficulties in imaging that?

2) **Teach your church how to pray with the poor.** Use biblical and theological resources that can help you learn about God's preferential option for the poor. Engage your community to go out and do mission by praying with people. This work does not prioritize giving money to other organizations, and it is not intended to create an environment for others to come to church but rather to have people moving outside of the church building and into the places where people who are suffering live.

3) **Teach your community to think in border terms, within a plurality of ideas, views, and ways of living.** Keep checking on the places and forms of belonging, mutual otherness, differences, and possibilities of life together in communities, groups of peoples, species, animals, and nature.[1]

4) **Examine your community to see where people are hurting economically.** From this *economic* sense, you will see why a few people have so much and so many have so little. Become aware of the ways we establish the law of our living together, the eco-nomos. Witness the many forms of violence and hurt that are present. Attend to who/what you have not seen before.

5) **Choose one community or group of people with whom you want to connect.** Make contact, listen to them, identify their needs, and ask if you can be a part of their lives. However, only say that if you mean it, if you are open to your own transformation.

6) **Before you go, learn why they are there.** If you are engaging with people who are experiencing homelessness, learn the history of public policies in your city/state that has contributed to this situation. Is there a lack of medical assistance? Possibilities of jobs? Education opportunities? What is the agency of the people? Their forms of survival?

Check if there are other organizations working with them, and add your presence. See what they are doing for themselves and ask how to support them. Evaluate strategies of action: interview people, spend time with them, and learn what they eat, what they celebrate, and how they struggle. A pastor friend once told me about a church who wanted to welcome people in experiencing homelessness. When coffee hour came, the children ate all of the donuts immediately. The church was outraged by their "lack of manners," not understanding their hunger and fear of deprivation. The children were devastated by the church's judgment. Good intentions are never enough. We must change ourselves. We must become flexible enough to understand through other people's experiences.

7) **While there, learn how people think, feel, imagine, and resist.** Try to think from their perspective and learn their traditions and resources of wisdom, immersing yourselves in their worldviews.

---

1. Search your own community for thinking together. Here are some suggestions: Gloria Anzaldua, *Borderlands/La Frontera: The New Mestiza* (San Francisco: Aunt Lute Books, 2012); Robin Wall Kimmerer, *Braiding Sweetgrass: Indigenous Wisdom, Scientific Knowledge and the Teachings of Plants* (Minneapolis: Milkweed Editions, 2015); Walter D. Mignolo and Madina V. Tlostanova, *Theorizing from the Borders: Shifting to Geo- and Body-Politics of Knowledge*, May 1, 2006, https://journals.sagepub.com/doi/10.1177/1368431006063333.

8) **Bring people of other knowledges to work with you.** Artists, lawyers, farmers, teachers, and others help imagine new forms of life and create resistance within the community.

9) In John 10:10 Jesus said that "The thief enters only to steal, kill, and destroy." **Search for what has been stolen or destroyed in your community** over the years, and learn about the policies of death that are prevalent in your communities. Do the research, find the policies, name the injustices, and go after them to make change. We must stop the theft, the destruction, and the killing. Jesus calls us to abundant life—which must include our neighbors!

10) **Imagine strategies for communities to get to know each other.** Listening deeply is paramount. What is at stake here? Are there class divisions? Racism? Sexism? Differences of beliefs? How can we learn together to engage injustice? We do not seek to save anybody, we are simply reaching out to learn about life, to be with and to be transformed.

11) **Every time you meet with those "outside the gate," start praying and naming the real, concrete situations of those you are gathered with.** May your prayer be an opportunity for conversion and transformation. Continue to pray and meet with the community. Invite them in, create opportunities for more gatherings, and find ways to promote inclusion and the revamping of the entire community.

12) **Imagine ways for common prayers to go beyond the worship space.** See how prayers can change the way the church creates the budget. How can this new community be central to the ways the church worships and exists in the world? What needs to be changed? Use of the space? Mission provision? Offerings? What are the church's priorities now? How can you make sure that each person who is experiencing homelessness can have a house to live in?

13) **Imagine new rituals, prayers, and spiritual practices.** Imagine fasting with those going hungry until we all can eat. Create rituals of mourning with people and species and the earth who are dying. *¡Presente!* Make rituals of cleansing bodies and spaces for new moments and meanings, rituals where a plethora of voices is present, rituals of healing amidst the diseases created by the Empire, and rituals of unloading bad practices, ideologies, and destructive theologies.

14) **Continue to write your own book of prayers with the prayers of your own tradition.** What prayers can be prayed? With whom? In sum, who do your prayers say is your God?

16

15) **Evaluate what is missing in this project, path, or imagination.** What haven't you prayed yet? Who still needs a blessing, an anointing, or a presence? What needs to be changed, rethought, or critically accessed?

Please visit www.reimaginingworship.com, to find prayers and liturgies not included in this book. You'll also find reflections and testimonies from participants, visual art, songs, and theater compositions created as part of this project, plus photos and videos from the locations. You're invited to engage with all the content, to write your own prayers and liturgies, and to share them in your faith community and social networks.

⸻ ⸻ ⸻

We hope this book will help you to pray, to find other forms of life together, and to receive visions of a new world. These prayers enable us individually and collectively to excavate ourselves, heal our colonial wounds, and understand what we have refused to explore within ourselves. To pray is to learn what to reject and what to welcome, always having in mind those who are suffering as the criteria for our collective decisions. When we pray with people who live at the ends of the world, drawing closer to people in borderlands and on the fringes, we can begin to imagine a *new* world, right there, where we live. When we gain the courage to begin denouncing and announcing, we learn that we can work together to make change. We find that we can open spaces for other people to *live*. We receive visions! When your community receives a vision, write it down so you won't forget. Then, keep praying and keep working. As Habakkuk 2:1-5 reminds us:

> I will take my post;
>> I will position myself on the fortress.
>> I will keep watch to see what the Lord says to me
>> and how he will respond to my complaint.

Then the Lord answered me and said,

> Write a vision, and make it plain upon a tablet
>> so that a runner can read it.
>>> There is still a vision for the appointed time;
>>>> it testifies to the end;
>>>>> it does not deceive.
>> If it delays, wait for it;
>>> for it is surely coming; it will not be late.

17

Some people's desires are truly audacious;
        they don't do the right thing.
        But the righteous person will live honestly.
Moreover, wine betrays an arrogant man.
        He doesn't rest.
        He opens his jaws like the grave;
            like death, he is never satisfied.
He gathers all nations to himself
        and collects all peoples for himself.

A WORD OF GRATITUDE

The project. I am thankful for everyone from the Council for World Mission, each local community that received us and spent time with me, and every person who agreed to come to be part of this project. I must thank Maria Peachy Labayo who prepared the way and worked to provide the structure for us all to do this work. My special gratitude goes to Sudipta Singh who, on behalf of the Council for World Mission, made this dream work possible. Mr. Singh found people to talk to local communities, offered generous assistance to those who had difficulties traveling, helped us when we had troubles, and was always there with us. I am grateful for his compassionate heart, his visionary mind, his constant support of this project, and his heart, so close to the poor. I am also grateful to president Serene Jones and the board of Union Theological Seminary in New York for giving me a full-year sabbatical so I could do this work.

The participants. Everyone who participated gave their time, love, and wisdom to this work. To each one, I am immensely grateful. This introductory material might not reflect all of the thoughts and perceptions of the participants, since I am not able to reflect fully their experiences here. Surely, they would offer very different reflections and would have many criticisms as well. Nonetheless, I am grateful to all of them. Without them, this work would not have come into fruition.

The production of this book. I must name a few of the many who made this book possible: Adam Vander Tuig, my precious PhD candidate at Union Theological Seminary, for his labor typing almost every prayer of this book and offering excellent comments and suggestions; and pastor Katie Mulligan, who is a brilliant scholar and a fantastic editor. When I couldn't see the forest for the trees, she came along and helped organize the entire material, giving it shape and focus. She edited everything, and her work of wisdom, patience, and love empowered this work immensely. I also thank Professor Mayra Picos Lee, who first read everything and gave me fundamental comments and kept my spirit going, and pastor Rachel Srubas, whose close reading of this introduction was amazing. Paul Galbreath, Chris Elwood, Gregory Cuellar, Janet Walton, Yohana Junker, Nancy Cardoso, and Ivone Gebara read drafts of this book and helped me think and write better. Emily Everett has a gift with many languages and provided wonderful translations of several prayers. And finally, my thanks go to Connie Stella, the editor at Abingdon Press.

Without her diligent work, patience, wisdom, editorial abilities, pastoral care, and brilliant vision, this book would never be ready. To you all, my deepest gratitude.

My family. For my precious family: Katie, Libby, Cici, and Ike, who loved me and supported me even when I was away to do this work. They were patient with me, and would keep me company when I was anxious or afraid. Katie was my daily companion. She listened to me deeply, and I would not have been able to process so many aspects of this project during this time if it was not for her deep listening. Her caring and loving presence was God's breath in my life. And I offer gratitude to my kids, the most beautiful prayers I have in my life, and with whom I continue to learn to pray.

And finally, for my mother, Esther Carvalhaes, who taught me how to pray.

Shall we pray?

PARTICIPANTS LIST

Locations, Organizations, and People

Manila, Philippines

National Council of Churches in the Philippines
Minnie Anne Mata Calub, acting general secretary
Rommel F. Linatoc, Christian Unity and Ecumenical Relations program secretary
Hannah Santillan

Partnership of Ecumenical Religious Leaders And Solidarity (PERLAS) Bataan
Genesis Antonio

Church People Workers Solidarity
Antonio Balbin

Rise Up for Life and for Rights
Rubylin Litao

Promotion of Church People's Response
Nardy Sabino

Katribu
Pya Malayao

Ecumenical Voice for Human Rights and Peace in the Philippines (Ecuvoice)
Anie Bautista
Rebecca Lawson

Johannesburg, South Africa

Marikana
Jeff Batselakng

Soweto
Khanyiswa Minya

Alexandra
Nomvula Nkonyane

Johannesburg CBD
Mamodise Morobe

Kingston, Jamaica

Tivoli Committee
Lloyd D'Aguilar, Convenor
Marjorie Hinds
Marjorie Williams
Nicola Bryce Wilson

Rastafarian Bobo Camp or Black Liberation Congress
Ras Marcel Kelly
Ken Wilson

Sizzla Youth Foundation
Jango

Agency for Inner City Renewal
Henley Morgan, Executive Chairman

Bryce United Church
Dionne Harriott
Gary Harriott, Minister
Lembe Sivile

Scicli, Italy

Casa delle Culture
Antonia, Casa delle Culture volunteer
Mauro Covato, staff member of Casa delle Culture
Ron Dauphin, American pastor, United Church of Christ
Ivana De Stasi, staff member of Casa delle Culture
Clarissa Di Quattro, staff member of Casa delle Culture
Redouane El Khadiri, staff member of Casa delle Culture
Elisa, Casa delle Culture volunteer
Emilia, Casa delle Culture volunteer

Francesca, Casa delle Culture volunteer

Gerardo Filippini, staff member of Casa delle Culture

Gioia, Casa delle Culture volunteer

Luisa, Casa delle Culture volunteer

Alberto Mallardo, operator of Mediterranean Hope in Lampedusa, Italy

Teresella Mania, director of Opera Diaconale Metodista

Marine, Casa delle Culture volunteer

Ziri Salem, Imam of mosque of Scicli

Giovanna Scifo, director of Casa delle Culture

Francesco Sciotto, pastor of local Church

Piero Tasca, in charge of communications area of Casa delle Culture

Padre Gianni Treglia, Caritas Diocesana Modica

Franzo Trovato, president of local council of the church

Bartolo Ereddia, staff member of Casa delle Culture

Zaela, Casa delle Culture volunteer

Artwork

Miyoung Kim, artist; master of divinity student, McCormick Theological Seminary, Chicago, IL (artwork featured online)

Quantisha Mason, master of divinity, Presbyterian Church (USA), Louisville, KY (artwork featured online)

Kate Morales, scribe and visual facilitator, As the Crow Flies Design (artwork featured in book)

Participants

Participants listed are those who gathered in the four locations at the 'ends of the world' to live and learn from the people and communities in each location, and then collaborated in the writing of the prayers. They are listed in alphabetical order by last name. Descriptions supplied by the participants themselves.

Faafetai Aiavā, ordained minister, Congregational Christian Church, Samoa

Julio Cezar Adam, professor of practical theology, liturgy, homiletics, ministry and spirituality, EST University, São Leopoldo, Brazil

Eliseo Pérez Álvarez, associate professor of systematic theology, United Theological College of the University of the West Indies, Kingston, Jamaica

Ferdinand Anno, Union Theological Seminary, Dasmariñas, Cavite, Philippines

Berenike Neneia Biiko, Tangintebu Theological College and Kiribati Uniting Church, Kiribati

Fitzroy Blackman

Shirley Bong, parish worker, creative arts ministry, Chapel of the Resurrection, Singapore

Andy Braunston, United Reformed Church minister, Scotland

Mark Cezar "Wesley" Carbonell Cabansag, pastor of the United Methodist Church, Philippines

Amy Casteel, PhD candidate, Katholieke Universiteit Leuven, Leuven, Belgium

Nguyen Kim Chau

Sophia Chirongoma, senior lecturer in the religious studies department, Midlands State University, Gweru, Zimbabwe; academic associate/research fellow, the Research Institute for Theology and Religion, the College of Human Sciences, University of South Africa, Pretoria, South Africa

Joseph Chita, lecturer, Department of Religious Studies, University of Zambia, Lusaka, Zambia

Rahel Sermon Daulay, lecturer of church music, Jakarta Theological Seminary, Jakarta, Indonesia

Julian Ebenezer

Christopher Elwood, professor of historical theology, Louisville Presbyterian Theological Seminary, Louisville, KY

David Elliott, third year bachelor of theology seminarian, Seth Mokitimi Methodist Seminary, Pietermaritzburg, South Africa

Karl James Evasco-Villarmea, associate professor, Silliman University, Dumaguete, Philippines

Mickesha Fearon

Giulia Dalmonte Feliz, World Student Christian Federation, Italy

Rohan O. Forrester, United Church in Jamaica and the Cayman Islands, Jamaica

Johanna Boitumelo Gaborone

Thomas R. Gaulke, pastor; PhD candidate, the Lutheran School of Theology, Chicago, IL

Doug Gay, principal, Trinity College, Glasgow, Scotland; lecturer in practical theology, University of Glasgow, Glasgow, Scotland

Daniela Gennrich, lay canon, Anglican Diocese of Natal, South Africa, and coordinator, We Will Speak Out South Africa, Durban South Africa

Roshanna Gillis, pastor, Immanuel Congregational Church, Guyana

Dan González-Ortega, president, Theological Community of Mexico, Mexico City, Mexico

Canon T. J. Gumede, Anglican Church Diocese of Natal, South Africa

Dorothea Haspelmath-Finatti, researcher and lecturer for liturgical studies and ecumenism, University of Vienna, Vienna, Austria

Mauleen R. Henry, regional deputy general secretary, United Church in Jamaica and the Cayman Islands, Montego Bay, West Indies, Jamaica

Ann Hidalgo, Mary P. Key Diversity Resident Librarian, Ohio State University Libraries, Columbus, OH

Ralph Hoyte

Ching-Yu Huang, PhD student, Emmanuel College of Victoria University in the University of Toronto, Toronto, Ontario, Canada

Pichet Jantarat, lecturer in church history, mission and evangelism, McGilvary College of Divinity, Payap University, Chiangmai, Thailand

Jingyi Ji, lecturer, Yanjing Theological Seminary, Beijing, China

Tércio Bretanha Junker, dean of the chapel, Garrett-Evangelical Theological Seminary, Evanston, IL

Yohana Agra Junker, faculty associate of theology, spirituality, and the arts, Pacific School of Religion, Berkeley, CA

Samuel Mhone Kalopa, lecturer, Zomba Theological College, Zomba, Malawi; PhD candidate, Mzuzu University, Mzuzu, Malawi

Gertrude A. Kapuma, senior lecturer, Zomba Theological College, Zomba, Malawi

Nonhlanhla Kunene, Seth Mokitimi Methodist Seminary, Pietermaritzburg, South Africa

Annabell Lalla-Ramkelawan

Rommel F. Linatoc, program secretary for christian unity and ecumenical relations, National Council of Churches in the Philippines

Maria Ling, lay pastor, postulant in the Diocese of Toronto, Anglican Church of Canada, Canada

Violet Cucciniello Little, pastor, developer, The Welcome Church, Philadelphia, PA

Gerald C. Liu, assistant professor of worship and preaching, Princeton Theological Seminary, Princeton, NJ

Mceven Lulama

Enolyne Lyngdoh

Mamolotje Charles Magagane

Nyaradzai Mandevhana

Xolani Maseko, pastor, part-time lecturer, Catholic University of Zimbabwe, Bulawayo Campus, Bulawayo, Zimbabwe

Clement Matarirano, United Theological College, Harare, Zimbabwe

Staples M. S. Mazizwa, senior lecturer, Zomba Theological College, Zomba, Malawi

Dummie Gabriel Mmualefe

Ximena Ulloa Montemayor, Red Crearte; Iglesia Bautista Shalom, Mexico City, Mexico

Doran Munsimbwe, the United Church of Zambia, Zambia

Nelly Mwale, lecturer, Department of Religious Studies, University of Zambia, Lusaka, Zambia

Cecilia Castillo Nanjarí, Pentecostal feminist theologian, Santiago de Chile, Chile

Cristopher Joseph Navas-San Jose, Open Table Metropolitan Community Church, Mandaluyon City, Philippines

Kim Chau Nguyen

Moe Nilar, master of theology (mission) thesis, Myanmar Institute of Theology, Yangon, Myanmar

Carleen Nomorosa, HIV program coordinator, National Council of Churches in the Philippines

Mzwandile Patrick Nyawuza, doctoral student, University of Pretoria, Hatfield, South Africa

Gerardo Oberman, coordinator, Red Crearte liturgical network of music and liturgical resources, Buenos Aires, Argentina

Beatrice D. Okyere-Manu, University of KwaZulu-Natal, Durban, South Africa

Carl Petter Opsahl, musician and associate professor, MF Norwegian School of Theology, Religion and Society, Oslo, Norway

Kakay M. Pamaran, Union Theological Seminary, Dasmariñas, Cavite, Philippines

Daylíns Rufín Pardo, professor of ecumenics, faith and society, Evangelical Theological Seminary and Oscar Arnulfo Romero Center, Havana, Cuba

Alfred Randriamampionona

Silvia Rapisarda, Unione Cristiana Evangelica Battista d'Italia, Italy

Lala Rasendrahasina, full-time teacher of church polity and liturgy; former president, the Church of Jesus Christ in Madagascar, Madagascar

Samsonraj Chinnaiyan Rathnaraj

Ulrich Schmiedel, lecturer in theology, politics and ethics, University of Edinburgh, Edinburgh, Scotland

Christoforos Schuff

Lordwell Siame, minister, St. Andrews, the United Church of Zambia, Lusaka, Zambia

Dennis Mbita Sikazwe, synod communications and media relations secretary, the United Church of Zambia, Lusaka, Zambia

Lilian Cheelo Siwila, associate professor of systematic theology and gender studies, the University of KwaZulu-Natal, Durban, South Africa

Margaret Ssebunya, postdoctoral scholar, Univeristy of KwaZulu-Natal, Durban, South Africa

Suk-Yi Pang, honorary minister, The Church of Christ in China, Hong Kong

Carlos Omar Tapia Leyva, MA student, Theological Community of Mexico, Mexico City, Mexico; candidate for ordained ministry, The Evangelical Covenant Church of Mexico

Sajeev Thomas, Mar Thoma Church, India

Miranda Threlfall-Holmes, team rector, St Luke in the City Team Parish, Church of England Diocese of Liverpool, England

Angelica Tostes, MA in Religious Studies at Methodist University of São Paulo, São Bernardo do Campo, São Paulo, Brazil

Lindah Tsara, PhD student, University of Kwazulu-Natal, Zimbabwe

Adam Vander Tuig, Union Theological Seminary, New York, NY

Heather Walton, professor of theology and creative practice, University of Glasgow, Glasgow, Scotland

Janet Walton, Professor Emerita of Worship, Union Theological Seminary, New York, NY

Thomas R. Whelan, associate professor of liturgical theology; visiting lecturer, St Patrick's University College, Maynooth, Ireland

Ging Chai (Irene) Wong

YongJiang Zhou, East Theological Seminary in Shanghai, China

Reach Toward One Another
See page 31 to read *We Extend Our Arms to One Another*, which inspired this artwork.

PART ONE

PRAYERS FOR THE BEGINNING AND ENDING OF WORSHIP

INVOCATIONS, CALLS TO WORSHIP, GATHERING PRAYERS

Come If You Are Willing

Come, if you are willing.

Come into this place, but be prepared to find yourself sitting next to your worst enemy.

Come into this place, but be prepared to find yourself offering prayer with someone whose values and way of life revolt you.

Come into this place, but be prepared to find yourself.

Be prepared to find in yourself dark places, dark thoughts, that you would prefer to remain unacknowledged.

Be prepared to live in a world that can never match your memories of what it used to be, or dreams of what it might be.

Be prepared to know you are loved, but be prepared also for the outrageous news that every other human being is loved no more and no less, no matter what you or they do.

Come, if you will, but be prepared for an uncertainty that will not quickly be resolved, for a discomfort that will not easily be salved, for a hunger that will not willingly be satisfied.

Come, if you are willing.

We Extend Our Arms to One Another

Leader: consider inviting participants to extend their arms to God and one another.

The grace of God be with the oppressed, the poor, the marginalized, and the groaning creation.

We open our arms, for it is right and good to extend our arms to one another.

Come Unto Me

Consider adding a trumpet sound before each stanza.

> Come unto me you who are depressed
> And you who are oppressed
>
> Come unto me you who are hungry
> And you who are angry
>
> Come unto me you who are unemployed
> And you who are underemployed
>
> Come unto me you who are anxious
> And you who are bitter and frantic
>
> Come to the place of blessings
> Where you will find respite, peace, and joy

Call to Worship as Asylum-Seekers

We gather to seek asylum from a world that sets neighbor against neighbor.

We gather to seek asylum from the temptation to draw and enforce boundaries that mean we can describe other people as not our problem.

We gather to seek asylum from a worldview that values us primarily as consumers, as wealth-generators, as units of production and consumption.

We gather to seek asylum from the binaries that bind and constrain us.

We gather to seek asylum from the very church(es) in whose name we gather, in which orthodoxy and hierarchy have been tools of oppression and abuse.

We name ourselves as asylum-seekers.

We pray that in our seeking, we may create that asylum for which we yearn.

We pray that, starting here, starting now, our seeking may crack open the empires that we resist and turn away from so that the whole world may be transformed into a place of safe asylum for all.

Sacred Wind, Come Blow on Us

Sacred wind, come blow on us
Let us feel your presence

Holy Earth anchor us
Nourish our frames

Illuminating fire burn ever brighter
Reflect your truth

Life-giving water
Restore and baptize us

Amen

Out of the Depths We Cry

The Lord calls us to worship.

Come!

Remember the cries of those who come from the depths of the sea.

Leader: Out of the depths we cry to you, oh Lord!
Join your hearts with God's people
    who have had to pay their
    way toward freedom.

Leader: Out of the depths we cry to you, oh Lord!
Let your ears be attentive to those who have drowned,
those who have escaped from violence, and
those who have fled discrimination.

All: Out of the depths we cry to you, oh Lord!

—Adapted from Psalm 130

Calling Together

Hear God's people!
You shall love God with all your heart,
with all your soul and with all your might.

Hear God's people!
Love God truly. And your neighbor as yourself.

Hear God's people!
God is great.
There is no God but God.
God has spoken through the prophets.

But We Are . . . Kyrie Eleison

We praise mammon with shouts of joy
But we are mute for justice
kyrie eleison

We see the color of currency
But we are blind to the pain of the poor
kyrie eleison

We hear the gospel of prosperity
But we are deaf to the groans of the earth
kyrie eleison

Come All of You

Come all you who are widows, lonely, orphans, divorced, downtrodden,
homosexuals, unemployed, oppressed, and children.

Come everyone to have fellowship and socializing with God.

The God who bandages the wounded, heals the sick, feeds the hungry,
provides for the orphans and widows, raises up the downtrodden, and
gives hope to the hopeless.
A God who is a mother to the motherless and a father to the fatherless.

The God of nature who provides rain at the right time and blankets
the soil, which is the source of our physical life.

Water and Light: Invitation to Adore

We have come together to praise God to whom we have belonged since the creation of the world, when water was created. We heard God's voice ordering chaos with the Word of life, illuminating the darkness of an eternal night that saw light for the first time.

We come to thank God for being the water that purifies us and seals us in an eternal covenant, and to give all the glory to our creator who has always sustained us, even now.
God is our light.

May the whole creation adore him. Hallelujah. Amen.

Jesus Calls Us from the Market Stalls

Jesus calls us from the market stalls
Not to leave our livelihood behind

Jesus calls us from the market stalls
To fight the empire moving us out

Jesus calls us from the market stalls
To bring us to a home that cannot be
Bought or sold

Jesus calls us from the market stalls
To stay and work together in faith
And to turn the tales of greed

Proclaim the Dawn of God's Reign

This is what the Lord, the God of Israel says: "Let my people go so that they can hold a festival for me in the desert" (Ex 5:1).

Out of the house of slavery, through troubled waters, into the wilderness
a new people is born;
you are God's own.

Put your trust not in powers nor in wealth
but in the One who is creator, sustainer, and liberator on heaven and on earth, and called out to celebrate the breaking of every chain.

We are here to proclaim the dawn of God's reign.

35

Call to Adoration

The leader may include as many languages as possible or as many as exist in the community.

- The person leading moves to the center and looks around until the community is silent. This gesture reminds us that silence is a fundamental part of adoration.

- The leader starts clapping, creating a bridge between rhythm and silence. The clapping reminds us of the beating of the heart, because from the silence of our hearts and the rhythm of our heartbeats comes, "The Word."

- The leader begins to say, "come," alternating with "*ven*" and then "*vem.*"

- The leader stops clapping and with his or her hands expresses an invitation to come to our space, which is directed toward four cardinal points: in the first invoking "*Dios*"; in the second invoking "God"; in the third "*Deus*"; and when he or she reaches the fourth, the invitation is made without words to include any name of the Transcendent.

- At the last cardinal point the leader claps three times and makes the gesture of a broad embrace that welcomes the community, ending at the heart.

Bless Us

Bless us in your divine grace.

Bless us in your divine grace,
bless us in your love,
and bless the bread on the tables,
the hands of those who work,
the dreams of those who resist,
who still sing and hope.

Bless us as we walk in your ways,
give us your strength and vision,
may your peace give an end to death,
to hate, and to all injustice;
bless us as we seek an abundant life.

Bless us.

Advent God

For over two thousand years, Advent God, your blessings have been flowing. A river of grace and love and mercy has flowed through the desert of our lives, watering our souls, and satisfying our thirst. For two thousand years and more, we have recognized your Emmanuel presence, bringing light and life to your world. Many of us have experienced the miracle of rebirth and recreation and so once again, at this Advent season, we sing our thanksgiving anthem: "Joy to the world, our lord is come!"

But in the midst of our celebrations, Dear God, we have to admit that after two thousand years, the curse can still be found. Our lands are still infested with the thorns of injustice and unrighteousness. The briers of hatred and discrimination despoil our social and spiritual environment. In our frustration and irritation, we cry, "No more!"

Grant us the wisdom and the courage to make "no more" a reality. Even if the weeds and the wheat are to grow together, we pray for the boldness to keep on sowing good seed. We pray for the courage to confront the "enemy" with love and compassion until he or she changes from evil to good. In the meantime, healing God, we pray today for your children crying in the wilderness of oppression and dehumanization.

Help us to listen with you, as they cry, "No more!" and "Enough is enough!" Help us to share your concern for their suffering, and then empower us as we embark on a divine mission of renewal and transformation. Perhaps then our joy will be intensified this Advent season as we celebrate again the glories of your righteousness and the wonder of your love. We pray in the name of him who came and made his dwelling among us. Amen.

God Is Here Too

Come!
Come into the place where God listens!
Where you need no money, no status, no fine clothes!
Come as you are
Broken, whole
Sick, well
Satisfied or with deep needs
Come to sing
Come to cry
Come to hear
Come to see
Come and be ready or
Come to be made ready
We are here
God is here too

Call to Worship for the Weary and Wary

Jesus said, "Come to me, all you who are struggling hard and carrying heavy
    loads" (Matt 11:28).
So we come, with all our weariness and wariness.

Our weariness with injustice,
our weariness with fake news,
our weariness with a world that seems determined to be hostile rather than
    welcoming.
Our wariness of what it might mean to truly live out our call,
our wariness of how vulnerable our desire for openness might make us,
our wariness of how safe it is to trust where trust has so often been misplaced.

Come, and find not just rest for your souls but channels for your rage.

So Come

Jesus said: "Come to me, all you who are struggling hard and carrying heavy loads, and I will give you rest" (Matt 11:28).

So come, in your need and your pain,
in your anger and your powerlessness.

So come, those of us subject to immigration controls,
and those of us seeking to overthrow them.

So come, those of us who live with the bittersweet experience of exile,
and those of us who long for our true home in the Kingdom, which is to come.

So come, those of us who despair at the politics of our age,
and those of us who seek to resist them.

So come, and find not just rest for your souls,
but a channel for your rage;
not just healing for your pain,
but love in your loneliness and alienation;
not just God's loving kindness,
but energy to resist Empire's cruel curse.
Come.

All This Is You, God

God who created the Kiers River—all the rivers—from the greatest rivers to the smallest stream. From these you feed the land, the plants, and the seas, as you give life to us. We wonder as we behold the majestic Kilimanjaro and the great open range. All this is you, God. The forest, the living lion with his great roar, and even the little hare with lightning speed—all these are your concern.

Our ancestors were blessed as they saw you in nature, as they worshiped under the African skies, you are God of all, eternal.

39

Invocation from Everywhere

Leader: consider underscoring with a percussion instrument or clapping to simulate the rhythm of the heart or of the road.

From the ports on our coasts
Memory of unwanted arrivals
We search for you and we invoke you
Divine partner of tired lives

From the coffee plantations and mountains
From knowledge starting to be born
We make space for you and dedicate our time
Divinity without beginning and without end

From our damaged cities
Where misery and opulence coexist
We confess that we need you
Fresh source of renewal and hope

From the heart of the earth
With our calloused hands
We invite you to share the day
Creator of all that is good and that which gives life

Come, we are your people!
Come, we need you!

God You Are

People: God you are our refuge.
Leader: You are the shore in sight,
you are hands that reach out,
you are the ground on which to rest.

People: God you are our strength.
Leader: You are the life we long for,
you are the refusal to give up,
you are the keys of home we carry with us.

People: God you are our help in time of trouble.
Leader: We call on you from the ruins and the rubble,
we call on you from the wildness and the deep,
All: We call on you to meet us in this place!

40

Mother Africa

Leader: Come all people of mother Africa,
come as you are;
come from your desperate situations of
hunger, exploitation, and spiritual thirst.

Your God, the creator of the whole universe
is waiting for you.
He is full of truth and grace
to meet your needs.

**People: We come to cast all our care and burdens
upon the Lord our God.**

**We know she is our refuge and fortress,
a well that never dries up of life and salvation.**

Come, All of You

Come, you who are forgotten, for today your Lord has remembered you.
God bids you come today; your name is on the lips of the Almighty
Himself.

Come, you who labor, you who are breathless, come and be refreshed.
Come and find rest from your labors.
Come, you who are frightened, there is peace enough. Come, for He has
grafted you into the palm of His hands.

Come, you who are oppressed, depressed, homeless, hungry, and you who
feel no one understands you. You who can't voice your sicknesses, for your
tears are invisible.

Come to the God who sees you.
Come to the God who will go with you into that deep dark night.

Come, for you are loved.
Come, for you are valued.
Come and be cared for.
Come, let us worship.

People of Africa

People of Africa, daughters and sons of African soil
We call you to worship in the name of our African ancestors
Ancestors who have gone before us
Ancestors who have shaped our history and
Given us rich heritage to cherish and treasure
As Africans we walk tall and proud of our identity
Because we walk on the shoulders of our ancestors

Come and let us celebrate who we are
In the face of the world that is different from us
An African way of worship, we affirm who we are
People of Africa welcome to this fellowship that
Will take you out of colonial captivity
And set you free to worship God in a manner
That is truly inspiring and meaningful

The God That Provides

Hallelujah Hallelujah
Praise be to God

To the God of land
God of the sea
God of the sky
God of the mountains,
The God of rain
The provider of manna
God of our mothers and fathers

Come and be with us this
Morning as we bring our
Hearts to worship you
We come to you with our
Hearts that are dry, hopeless and heavy
With hope that you are
The God that provides,
You are the God of yesterday,
Today and tomorrow

Africa Is Calling

Leader: consider adding a drum beat or the sound of a horn to begin this call to worship.

Come! People all over the world.
Come! Africa is calling!
Respond to Africa, the mother of life.
As a mother calling her children back home,
so too Africa is calling.

Come out of your bondage and slavery;
come out of your oppression and exploitation;
come out of human induced poverty and disease;
come to the God of life.
Come Nkulunkulu, the God who is high up above all.
Come to Modimo warona, God who dwells high above.

Together we shall praise the name of the most high God;
God will hear us, as God heard Kwama Nkrumah of old.
The undying Spirit that fought until the door of liberation was opened for
    Ghana
and revived hope for Africa.
God will hear us as He/She listened to Haile Selasse
and restored Ethiopia, the home of Africa.
The God of Nelson Mandela will hear us
as we steadfastly strive for peace and reconciliation.

Daughters and sons, Africa calls us home
to invoke God's love, power, sustenance, strength,
our ancestors, *ubuntu*, unity, and love.
Come divine God, come!

Your God Is Present

Come, our Lord, our God is here, for the people of God are present here.
Come out of a world of hunger and degradation into a world of abundance.
For your Lord, your God is present.

Come out of the world of violence, degradation, and dehumanization
into the world of peace, comfort, and security.
For your Lord, your God, is present.

Ubuntu

Leader: Come, brothers and sisters in the Lord.

We invoke God's power, sustenance, and strength,
the God of solidarity, the God of Fihavanana.

God who taught us (*Ubuntu*),
help us to respond to the struggle of those
who lost their homes.
Without land, where they can grow crops?

Today we are called to worship God,
to lift up the pain of all who are oppressed
by those who hold the power.

People: By God's mercy, let us—all of us—be the hope in the world.

Come Let Us Worship

Come let us worship the Lord with gladness, let us raise our voices to the God who is the refuge of the humble and the lowly, the God of justice and righteousness.

The God who opposes the ritual and worship of the oppressor of the poor. He is the God of the destitute and the homeless.

He is the God who affirms the rights of the needy and the marginalized sections and despises the burnt offerings of those who promote injustice.

Come let us worship the Messiah, Jesus Christ, the champion and the liberator of the poor and the outcast.

He is a poor peasant like us.
He was homeless and rejected like our peasant community.
He is a fisherman and many of his disciples were fishermen.
He understands our struggles and our pain.

Come let us beseech him to deliver us from the snares of our oppressor and let us seek his presence in our midst.

—*From Isaiah 59, Amos 5:21-24*

44

Invocation: God of Our Ancestors

We invoke God, the Holy Spirit, and Jesus
We invoke God's love, power, strength, sustenance
The God of our ancestors
God of Africa
God of Chaminuko
God of Mackimahave
God of Nehanda and Kaguis

BENEDICTIONS

May the One Who

May the One who

    freed the people from slavery,
    led them dry-shod through the sea,
    suffered Empire's torture and execution and
    defeated the Powers—even the Power of death!

Free you,
lead you,
suffer with you,
and raise you;

that you may use:

    your weakness to be a blessing,
    your hope to be a force of change,
    and your audacious determination to usher in the New Age

and the blessing of Almighty God,
Father, Son, and Holy Spirit
[Creator, Redeemer, and Sustainer]
be with you,
and all whom you love
now and always,
Amen.

A Celtic Blessing for People On the Move

May the road be smooth under your feet
and the trees shade you on your way.
May the desert be smooth under your wheels
and may your water be enough.
May the sea be smooth under your boat
and the winds blow you gently across the borders.
May kindness be your companion and your guide.

May We Receive

Oh God may we receive your blessing,
through sharing your blessings beyond borders.

May we receive your gifts,
from those who carry nothing.

May we recognize you,
in people we don't know

and may we all find a safe home and peace in you
who had no place to lay your head.

Believe, Behave, and Belong

May the peace you experience here silence the sounds of conflict and weapons of warfare. May the joy of knowing you are loved conquer hatred and mend broken relationships in the community. May the love that surrounds you break down walls and barriers of political, social, and physical indifference. May the Creator bless you richly with healing grace. May you be a blessing to others, showing acts of kindness to your neighbor and all you encounter. Believe, behave, and belong!

Benediction with Bells

Worship leader uses bells to mark the sections of the benediction prayer.

* bell rings

> For God has made us by the labor of forming us from the red soil and it was good,
> MaUa lelei.

> Bless the hands of all those who work and toil, especially the hands of peasant laborers in factories, sweatshops, and mining sites,
> Faamanuia mai le atua.

* the bell rings and silence

> Please rise as you are able,
> for God heard our wailing and the sound of bones being broken, fingers cut, and skins being burned. God stands in our midst. For the workers in the condiments factory, the workers in the Philippines, and throughout the world.

> Bless the feet that resist and the hearts that find courage in each other,
> Faamanuia mai le atua.

* the bell rings three times

> Please raise your left hand, closed fist,
> for God has saved the lowly by the might of God's arms! Arms held together in picket-lines bless the strength of our resistance and the courage of our hearts,
> Faamanuia mai le atua.

> *Samoan Amen:* Amene! Amene! Amene!

A Benediction for Standing Firm

God sees you and calls you by name.
He calls you to stand firm in the face of oppression and injustice, to stand.
May you stand firm then as the Holy Spirit enlivens your hope, as Jesus Christ
    renews your faith, as God enfolds you in love.

May God Bless You

May God The Creator take away
    your pain and loss.
May Christ shield you in your
    sorrow and fear.
May The Spirit carry you each
    day of your life.
And may blessings lead you to the
    fulfillment of your dreams
    and give you peace in your heart.

Go Forth with Hearts That Move Us

Go forth with hearts that move our bodies to express a love that knows no boundaries, displaying the kindness of God's care for all.

May you experience honor and dignity,
may you see your dreams realized,
may you feel the power of your body to guide your choices.
I bless you, our bodies joined together to live justice realized;
you bless me with love, joining me in pain, birth, and possibility.

Many Out of One

God we are many out of one and so we pray to you, the one almighty, asking for you to bless all and each of us, your sons and daughters. May your breath be spread and felt from the inner cities and towns, from the mountains, the hills, and the downtowns, and garrisons. May your breath displace us in mind and heart and bodies far away from the many places of empire. Keep us all alive in justice, fight, and dreams. And send us forth all over this earth, out to the many places we have come from as one out of many. Amen.

Rescue

May God bring you rescue in us.
Amen.

Somewhere There Is a Home

Somewhere there is a home
A place of return
Of reunion
Safety and security
Of peace
A communion of friends, equals
Not only in God's eyes
But ours too

Believing in that home
Gives us hope and strength

I will work to make that home
A house for you, for we
For us
I want to live there
With you
My children and yours
My parents and yours
My ancestors and yours

I will work to make that home
Today, tomorrow,
And in the days to come
Join me when you can

Blessing from the Depth of Mary's Eyes

And now, when we return to life with all its circumstances and uncertainties, let us be affirmed and strengthened, knowing that there is much to be done, but that we are not alone. Let's go with hope, filled with the Spirit of Jesus, who nests among humble people and brings peace and certainty to poor homes. Let us go with the power of his love that heals and transforms everything and with empathy and the solidary gestures of ones who know we are loved by God's very self. And let us go with faith, with compassion, and with the depth of the gaze of a good mother and a loving father who look for their most needy children. And so, God will go with us. So be it. Hallelujah. Amen.

Blessed Are the People

Blessed are the people to whom the doors of the kingdom
are wide open
because in their poverty they have been able to make a reality
the solidary project of Jesus,
because they have understood the "our bread,"
because they live in worlds without doors or ceilings
but at the same time, without walls or exclusions.
Blessed are people who are hungry
and that, from that place of dissatisfaction,
protest, resist, march, protest
before the injustices of a cruel and perverse world.
In their search for dignity and equity
they will be satiated by the grace of a God
that has chosen to walk beside them.
Blessed are people who mourn
the pains that hurt their neighbors
and that, even in their own anguish,
have learned to smile and sing,
to embrace and take care of each other.
Blessed are people who are hated and despised
by those who claim to love and be faithful to their faith,
but who only care about their small spaces,
their exclusive privileges, their selective morality,
and their destructive theology of merit and prosperity.
Blessed are people who are insulted and persecuted
for sharing the liberating and inclusive message of Jesus.
There are insults that are a wonderful gift!
Blessed are people whose wealth is not a possession
but know how to share, extend the table,
make spaces bigger, build bridges, and
make holes in the walls and plant flowers in the cracks.
Blessed are the people who have learned to laugh,
who discover beauty in simple things,
who do not know rancor,
and who sleep peacefully.

The Lord Bless You and Keep You

The Lord bless you and keep you,
the Lord is a shadow on your
right hand,
so that the sun may not burn you
under the wide sky.

It is not that we understand
our God. So often there is just no answer
for a long, long time.

It seems that God has forgotten,
it seems that his arm is not
    long enough, simply not
        long enough.

But then some have told us
    that all of this light
    has sprung up from
        the depths of the sea.

This is the light of our God,
so may his face lighten
your way.
    Go in peace and bless them,
    Father, Son, and Holy Spirit.

Bless Us in Your Divine Grace

Bless us in your divine grace,
bless us in your love,
and bless the bread on the tables,
the hands of those who work,
the dreams of those who resist,
who still sing and hope.

Bless us as we walk in your ways,
give us your strength and vision,
may your peace give an end to death,
to hate, and to all injustice;
bless us as we seek an abundant life.
Bless us.

May You Stand Firm

God sees each of us and calls us by name.
Calling us to stand firm in the face of
oppression and justice.
May you stand firm then as the Holy Spirit
enlivens your hope, as Jesus Christ
renews your faith, as God enfolds you
in love.

Go Out to the World #1

Go out to the world and minister life in the context of pain and suffering,
starvation, unemployment, drugs and alcohol, abuse, and greed. Preach in
deed and word, love and serve the people of God without any discrimination. Be good servants and stewards of Lord Jesus Christ, and the blessing
of God Almighty, the Father, the Son, the Holy Spirit be with you and
remain with you always. Amen.

A Blessing for Those Who Mourn

May the One who makes all things new
hold you in loving arms.

May the One who overthrows religion
transform your anger into an energy of change.

May the One in whom the dead find their peace
wipe away every tear from your eyes.

And the blessing of Almighty God
[Father, Son, and Holy Spirit]/[Creator, Redeemer, and Sustainer]
hold you
and all whom you have loved and lost,
until the day comes when all shall be made new. Amen.

Run Free

Run free, you are the desire of God.

Give Us the Blessing

Give us the blessing of an open mind,
without imposed borders, without acquired prejudices.
Give us the grace of deep breath,
able to inhale all the pains and all the hopes of your suffering people
and exhale new life that is shared, generous, supportive.
Give us the impulse of an embrace that unites memory with promise,
history with project, enhancing the present with the flavor of full life.
Give us the certainty of a just earth
with space and opportunity,
food and dignity,
work and rights,
for each human being
and their rich and valuable diversity.

Solitary Embrace, Constant Presence

May the solitary embrace of God envelop us
and return to us our lost or stolen dignities;
may the grace of Jesus liberate us, heal us,
restore us, put us on our feet, and propel us to the new,
beyond all limitations and all forms of marginalization.
And may the constant presence of the divine Spirit animate us
to walk the paths of a shared life,
testifying to the plenitudes that are possible.

A Benediction for Boundary-Crossing

As you cross the boundaries that fight against people humbly serving each
other, you will face conflict. You will be tempted to focus on protecting
yourself. But putting on heavy armor forces you to stand still. Instead, set
your feet on the goal of peace. As for how you interact with others, make
it come from peace. Then you will be walking by the Spirit. As you walk
in peace, then comes kindness and goodness on the journey, small but
powerful acts of resistance in a world that nurtures conflict. May the hard
work of forbearance and gentleness be made possible by the exercise of
self-control. Choosing to continue in peace, may genuine joy make you
glad. And in all these things may the love of God so fill your soul that you
experience the profound power of peace.

Blessing for My Sisters

My sister, may you be blessed this morning with a bucket of water, that
you may wash your body and some of your pain away.

My sister, may you be blessed this noon with some rice, one cup for each
of your children and one for you.

My sister, may you be blessed tonight with a safe rest, that no captor will
sell you to his friends to quench their malevolent desire.

My sister, may you be blessed when they will put you on a rubber boat,
may the waters be kind to you, and may rescue come fast, that none
of your children shall lose their life, nor you.

My sister, may you be blessed when you make it to the other side, blessed
with water, rice, safety, and rights.

Final Prayer for Crossing Boundaries

Our God, we thank you for loving us. Knowing that you understand the
thoughts and cries of our hearts is comforting. Jesus, you know the pain of
rejection, of hate, of suffering, of torture. God, you know the anguish of
broken relationships and betrayal. You demonstrated the power of crossing boundaries over and over again. We learn from the stories of Adam
and Eve, the children of Israel, Ruth and Naomi, Esther and Mordechai,
and the exiles with Daniel that it is better to cross borders in the company
of others. You promise, "I am with you." Thank you for being with us as
we have already crossed so many borders. You promise, "I will keep you
wherever you go." We declare with them: "Our God is able to deliver us."
Knowing that whatever happens, just like those in the fiery furnace, your
presence is with us. Holy Spirit, fill us with courage, even as we pour out
our lives to be present in the lives of other border-crossers.

Go Forth!

Go forth!
Agitated, yet blessed!
Challenged, but determined!
Energized, but also fatigued!
Gifted too! Hallelujah!

I, the God of Life

I, the God of Life,
I bless you with life.
And because I give you life,
I bless you with uneasiness,
questions, and uncomfortableness, mainly
in relation to the lack of life for others.

And because I cause you trouble,
I bless you with food, water,
a bed for sleeping, friends, and
family, so that you find for yourself
shelter and comfort along the way.

And because I bless you with people and love,
I bless you with feelings,
passions, desires, and vitality,
so that you can relate
with the world, create, and generate
life, give and receive affection, and
distribute carefully.

And because I give you
life, I bless you with
courage and indignation, but
also with dreams, visions,
struggles on behalf of a better
world, more just, more dignified, and
peace-giving for all breathing beings.

Blessing for Building a Home

This can refer to an actual residence, or to a metaphorical home being built by a congregation, group, or individual.

If you will
Building that home
Is God's blessing today
Whether that home is finished
Or just begun

May that home come to be
Soon
And may we live there together

May God Keep You

May God keep you safe
May your bellies be full
May your thirst be quenched
May your hearts be blessed
With knowing you are loved
And may you share that love
With all who come your way
Amen

It Is Me and God Too

May God bless and keep you
May God's face shine upon you and be gracious to you
May God look upon you with favor and grant you peace

Know that someone sees you
It is me

Know that someone values your work
It is me

Know that someone prays for you
It is me

Know that someone is with you always
It is me
And God too

Amen

Benediction for Stepping Out into the Empire

And now, even as you step out into the Empire,
be not of this structure, but be:
the light that liberates
the salt that savors
the hand that heals
the water that washes,
until all have access to God's great and beautiful creation.
Amen.

Go Out, Children

Leader: Go out with rejoicing, safe in the arms of Jesus.
Have no fear of want, we feed each other.
The Spirit empowers you to do what you must do to live another day.
All: We are not afraid.

Leader: Do no hanker for the Empire.
All: We resist the Empire.
Leader: Go in peace.
All: We go with peace.

Children of the earth, God blesses the soil
Children of living water, God cleanses you
Children of blessing, God embraces you

Keep Your Eyes Wide Open

Keep your eyes wide open,
your hands willing,
your hearts generous,
your ears attentive,
your senses awake,
your feet light,
your hope alive,
and your faith on fire.

Go and shine wherever you may be.
Go and embrace with tenderness
all of life
with its sorrows and joys.

Go and know what divinity expects
and what your brothers and sisters seek.
May the creative force bless you.
May the divine solidarity sustain you.
And may you be encouraged and enveloped by
the tender breath that brings freedom.

God, Journey with Your People

God of the outcast, marginalized, and downtrodden,
journey with your people
on the road of persecution, victimization, aloneness, and hopelessness.

Breathe new life, courage, and strength for the fight.
God, be with your people until justice covers the earth
and all is at peace.
Amen.

The Revolution of Love and Justice

For God did not give us a spirit of timidity but of power, love, and self-discipline. For God did not gives us a spirit of docility, but of defiance, resistance, and revolution. Go out into the world and defy the powers, resist the enemy, and join the revolution of love and justice.

Go in Peace

Go in peace, be of good cheer, may Mother Earth smile at you, may the Almighty God bless you with a spirit of *Ubuntu*. Shalom! Shalom! Amen.

Blessing of Children

God bless your children with heroes
Not the kind that wear capes
But those that love even when it hurts
Not the kind who beat the baddies
But those who still shield others from harm
Not the kind who fight for themselves
But those who raise up others to be heroes too
Amen

Satan Prowls Like a Roaring Lion

Satan prowls like a roaring lion
Seeking whom he may devour
Death is near us; blood is on our floors

But even we sheep
Sent out among the wolves
May we be wise like serpents
May we fly with doves

May love guide our feet
When there is no way
May love be our lamp
When we go astray

God bring us together
When we can't go on
We'll rise up together
We'll sing a new song

The powers who crush us
Are torn from their thrones
Our hearts burn within us
My love for the poor

May You Stand and Raise Your Head

May you stand and raise your head in the fullness of dignity
Knowing that you are precious in God's heart
May you know courage when the road is hard
Consolation in your times of grief
Healing for the traumas you have suffered
Strength to continue on your journey

May this community be for you a place of comfort and support
Where you are fed and in turn where you feed others
May the love of God go with you and accompany you
As a tangible presence in your life as you bring God
To all you meet

Now unto Him

Now unto Him who is able to sympathize with our sorrow and to bring His blessings before His glorious throne; to Him be the glory, honor, and adoration. Now go in the spirit of our great ancestor, Jesus Christ. Fight for equal justice for the victims of oppression. The blessings of God the Father, the Son, and the Holy Spirit be with you. Amen.

May God, the Source of Life, Bless You

May God, the source of life and blessing, bless you so that all suffering—disease, famine, political conflict—would end. May God bless you so that you experience *ubuntu*, peace and solidarity. In the name of the Father, and the Son, and the Holy Spirit. Amen.

The Gift from Africa

With the gift of love and hospitality that God has blessed us with, go out there and share the love you have experienced so that, with those whom encounter, you may bear witness to the gift from Africa. Amen.

Liberator and Transformer

Now may the grace of our Lord Jesus Christ, the liberator and transformer, the love of the God of our ancestors, and the fellowship of the Holy Spirit, the comforter and restorer of our African Pride and dignity, be with us all now and forevermore. Amen!

Be His Witness and Light

May the God of love keep you in his grace through Jesus Christ, our savior and eternal life, and comfort you in the Holy Spirit that you will be his witness and light in this world. Amen.

God of Africa, Bless Your Children

The God of Africa, the God of mercy,
the God of love, the God of the oppressed,
the God of the heartbroken,
may you bless your children of Africa to regain what has been taken away from
   them by the empire. Bless Africa to live in peace and harmony among
   themselves.
Bless the people of Africa with wisdom so that they will preserve their resources
   and protect Africa from the invasion by the forces of empire. Amen!

God Protect Africa

God of all ages, bless and protect Africa.
May you bless all her children.
May you cause your face to shine upon her land and be gracious to her rivers.
May the children of Africa continue to live together in peace and harmony
   with each other. Amen.

Promote, Preserve, and Defend Life

As we come to the close of our service, fellowship, and meeting, may the
God of our ancestors, the God from whom all African beauty emanates,
the God who has taught us *ubuntu* and extended relationships, even the
father of our Lord Jesus Christ, bless you with all things perfect and grant
you happiness with others. Now go into the world and promote, preserve,
and defend life. Amen.

Go Out to the World #2

Go out into the world. It is full of pain and suffering, starvation,
unemployment, drugs, and alcohol, abuse, greed. Go out to love and serve
the people of God without any discrimination. Be good servants and stewards of Lord Jesus Christ, and the blessing of God Almighty, the Father,
the Son, and the Holy Spirit be with you and remain with you always.
Amen.

The Abundant and Unending Grace of God

May the abundant and unending grace of God, the love of God that doesn't tire, that was shown to our forefathers and the whole generation of the whole clan, and the fellowship of the Holy Spirit be with you.

Sons and Daughters of Africa

Sons and daughters of Africa, go ye therefore and continue in the spirit of *ubuntu* to do good. Loving thy neighbor and doing unto others as you would have them do unto you. May the eternal spirit of Nkulunkulu envelop you now and forevermore. Amen.

The Dynamism of Africa

In the name of God who created the dynamism that is Africa, go forth as the life-givers that you are, from the cradle of life, go and be a blessing to others. May your warm smile radiate the generosity of the rich African skies that house the brightest sun. And the most incredible stars that shine even throughout the darkest nights. Go forth and be that moon that gently brightens the night without displacing the night. Go, holding your head high as you give others the right to do so in the spirit of *ubuntu*, which you inherited. Make your ancestors proud. Make God visible. Be human. Amen.

Be Light-Bearers

And now go out into the mission world, be light-bearers, uplift the down-trodden, preserve creation, and be committed to bringing hope to the hopeless in the name of the creator and mother of all life. Amen.

Go with the Blessing of Your Fathers

Now go with the blessing of your fathers, to subdue the earth and not each other. Be fruitful and enjoy the fruit of your labor. Do not repay the humility and kindness of others with arrogance and exploitation. Rather, fight for the cause of the poor and vulnerable among you. Ensure that justice is done and that God's preferential option for the poor is seen through you.

And now, let the grace of the Son of God, which preserved your great leaders of Africa until the end of colonialism and Apartheid, preserve for you economic freedom.

May the love of God that led South Africa to choose reconciliation over revenge strengthen you and bring about a just world order.

And may the fellowship of the Holy Spirit and the undying spirits of the sons and daughters of Africa be with you, both now and always.

Having received freely and deeply from the living Mother of Africa, having been made right by Her beloved Son, having been renewed, challenged, and restored by Her reviving Spirit, go out into the world, walk in your Mother's footsteps, and do the same. Amen.

Now people of God, go out into the world. Be a blessing to those that need blessings, touch those that need your touch, and bring hope to the hopeless. Bring healing to those who are sick, love to those that feel they are alone, and comfort to those in despair. May we see you, Jesus, at the point of our need, assuring us that you are our source of hope in this broken world. Amen.

The Living, Disturbing God

Let us go in peace with the living, disturbing God:
to disrupt those who are comfortable,
comfort those who mourn,
and walk alongside those who suffer.

Now receive the blessing of God all-loving:
God our Mother who holds us in our pain,
God our brother, Jesus the Christ, who gives us courage to resist,
and God the Spirit who binds us together
in all that is free.
Amen.

Be a Blessing to Africa

All has been said and done; therefore, go forth and be a blessing to
Africa. Give hope to the hopeless, care for the sick, encourage those
who are despairing, give voice to the voiceless, feed the hungry. May the
great God of our ancestors be with you now until he calls you to join the
ancestry. Amen!

Go Home in Peace

Go home in peace. Return no evil with evil but with the good that is in
you. Conquer evil. Amen.

The God of Our Ancestors

And now may the God of our ancestors, God of Africa, who through
ages carried us on his shoulders and brought to life again from the dead
our Lord and King Jesus Christ, the great liberator of the oppressed
through the blood of the everlasting covenant, free us from hunger and
poverty and make us perfect in every way to do his will; work in us that
which is gratifying in his sight, through Jesus Christ to whom be glory
forever and ever.
Amen.

The Blessing of God

*To sing with the melody "May the Blessing of God," by Christopher Joel Brown,
Cody Carnes, Kari Brooke Jobe, and Steven Furtick.*

May the blessing of the God of yam, sugar cane, and earth,
may the blessing of the son born to Nurse Kelly,
may the blessing of the Spirit, the harvest, and the fruits
come over the earth, with rain, sun, and wind,
now and forever and ever. Amen.

Continuous Blessing

May bread never be lacking on the table,
for here you will find it.

May Jesus embrace you when hope is gone,
through our bodies.

May Grace blow the winds of Justice,
together with our voices.

Amen.

May God Wipe Away Your Tears

May God wipe away your tears,
may the wind, the breeze of the Spirit
take the violence away from you,
and like salt, protect us
as your sons and daughters;
may the divine guidance divert
bad men from your paths.

You Who Hold Us Tenderly

You who hold us tenderly like a long, beautiful, warm dress,
you who awaken our spirit in the movement of the waves in calm, quiet, and
    rhythms,
you who manifest through our minds, understanding, and spirit with the
    breath of life . . . in love . . . and visions . . . infinite.
You who encourage us deeply with tenacity and . . . anyone . . . your life and
    existence,
humiliate us, wake us up, manifest us, orient us in . . . entangle.

Let it be, for it is so!

Love Is God's Name!

May Jah look at you with a tender smile and from now on, may you always be seen as happy— happy because a tender deity has embraced you with sweetness.

Love is God's name!

May Jah always come to your aid, for Jah always acts with compassion and justice; Jah knocks down the powerful from their thrones and walks hand in hand with those who suffer.

Love is God's name!

God of the Bodies
See page 92 to read *God of the Bodies*, which inspired this artwork.

PART TWO

PRAYERS OF CONFESSION, THANKSGIVING, AND INTERCESSION

PRAYERS OF CONFESSION AND PETITION

I'm Trying, God

I'm trying God
But they keep pushing us out
I'm trying God
But can we really be safe?
I'm trying God
But they keep murdering our children
All I ask for is you
To let us live in peace
Amen

Reform Us

Lord have mercy, have mercy on us
for not loving our undocumented neighbors
like we love ourselves.

Christ have mercy, have mercy on your undocumented children.
You said that everything we do for the least of our brothers and sisters
we do it for you.
Lord have mercy, and by the power of your Holy Spirit
reform us in your merciful image
so that we might reflect You and save the immigrants.

71

Confession of the Oppressed

Lord, we confess that in our ignorance of the power structures of the rich and the powerful, our children are now suffering and we pray that you grant us wisdom and discernment.

We confess that we have literally taken your word for granted, and the saying, "Happy are you who are poor, because God's kingdom is yours," has in fact misled us (Luke 6:20). The powerful ones encourage us to be meek and obedient to you, but they have created for themselves an empire and have exploited our honesty and ignorance.

We confess that we have not earnestly stood in unity as the oppressed peasant community, and some of us are being enticed by the power of wealth to betray the community.

We confess that we have not seriously raised our voices to the injustice done against us because of fear and the feeling of rejection.

Forgive Us #1

For the roads that we have blocked,
For the bridges that we didn't build,
For the empty table that we didn't fill,
Forgive us.

For Our Dumagat Brothers and Sisters

God, we pray for those who have suffered the loss of loved ones from the conflicts in the midst of the Dumagat tribe. May you usher in your justice and peace, comforting and healing the afflicted, wiping away their tears and granting them courage to walk in your light.

God, we pray for our Dumagat sisters and brothers who are now imprisoned in oppression. Grant them courage to overcome the harsh physical and mental conditions. May your peace and comfort be with them.

We Come Against It

Leader, raising hands:

> As we lift up our hands toward where home is . . .
> we know that you are with us
> in the wilderness and on our journey.
>
> God who causes wars to cease,
> we come against gun violence
> in the entire community of Chicago.
>
> God who casts out fear,
> we come against imposed terror
> on immigrant, undocumented families
> that may be deported or separated.
>
> God who hears our hurts,
> we come against those in
> Winston, North Carolina,
> who ignore institutionalized oppression.
>
> Liberate us from death,
> liberate us from fear,
> liberate us from rampant racism
> that seeks to dehumanize, divide, and dismiss us.
> In Jesus's name we pray, Amen.

Prayer for Mothers Who Lost Their Children

> Come Holy Spirit, our Counsellor,
> Comfort the mothers who lost their children in miscarriages, sickness, violence
> Dry up their tears
> Alleviate their pain
> Give them Your strength to live in hope

A Place for Everyone

Heavenly Father and Mother, we pray for the
immigrant families, those who have built
their lives outside of their homeland;
those who had to run from their cities,
leave their homes, and their environments because of death threats,
dangers, natural disasters, or for better economic opportunities
because they could not see another possibility, because they had no other
    possibility.

Let the utopia of the gospel become real
in our communities.

Let us be the table that receives all
ethnic groups, races, languages, cultures, and families.

Let us be the banquet that receives those who have been excluded, so we may
    all be
invited to sit down and share with Jesus.

Let us be the place of protection, place of peace, of food, of fostering, of family,
    cities of refuge and care.

A place without borders, without stigmas, without xenophobia, without
    homophobia, without racism, without machismo.
A place for everyone.

God of Life

God of Life, You own our lives but as human beings we do not respect life.
Life is so easily being taken by our hands. We don't live as how you want us to
live, as how you create the clouds in the sky. They may have different shapes,
different directions, but they live in harmony and fulfill the sky beautifully.
That is how we are supposed to live. We come from a different part of the
world, different directions of life. Forgive us, God of Life.

They Do Not See the Ways They Hurt Us

God of hope,
God who opens hearts,
our people are suffering
because they don't have documents,
they have been oppressed, abused,
hurt, scared, despised.
They live in anxiety every day.

Our people are suffering
because of lack of confidence,
strength, courage, support.
They have been isolated,
detached from society.
Our people are suffering;
they suffer from the sin of indifference.

Others are ignorant to our pain.
They do not see the ways they hurt us.

Living Water

You invite us to ask for living water,
water that satisfies our thirst. You are
that living water poured out for us.
We confess that we seek to quench our
thirst in other ways.
We drink deeply, choosing these sweet waters
that turn to fear in our bellies.
We confess that rather than turning to you,
we set out to be brave.
Seeing the fear outside ourselves, we try
to force out fear by casting out others.
Lord help us to drink deeply of your love
remembering it is perfect love that casts
out fear.
Strengthen us to practice love to ourselves,
those close to us, and those we overlook.
Fill us with living water until it
overflows.

For People in the Land of Philippines

Lord have mercy on us.
Many people in the land of Philippines
    are disconcerted by the violence,
        poor living conditions,
        no human rights,
        and harsh oppositions.

As your chosen people,
You asked us to hold your people in our heart,
    but we chose to neglect their pain and sorrow;
You command us to love and care for the least among us,
    but we are too self-concerned to love others;
You send us as the comforter to be with your people,
    but we try to walk away from those people who are in suffering and
        despair;
You send us as the bearers of justice and peace,
    but we do not dare to confront and to stand against imperious rulers
        (foes).

Renew our hearts, O Lord,
    and touch our hearts,
    soften our hearts to feel and care;
Strengthen us, O Lord,
    enable us to be the voice of the voiceless.
Guide our feet, O Lord,
    to prepare us to be bearers of your truth and love,
    justice and peace wherever you place us
So we can make of this old world a new world.
May your justice and praise spring up before all nations,
    for the zeal of the Lord God will accomplish it.

On Behalf of Mothers

As mothers enraged and in anguish over the murder of another woman's child,
we plead with you, O God,
on behalf of the earth, our mother, to console that mother.

76

Have Mercy on Us All

For the defenders of the earth, the indigenous communities of the Philippines—the Dumagats of Rizal Province, the Aetas of Central Luzon, the Lumads of Mindanao, and the Igorots of the Northern Mountains. May we all stand with them with courage and commitment to protect and defend their sacred lands.
Let us pray to God, the creator of all things:
Diyos kaawaan mo kami (God, have mercy on us all).

For the innocents killed by the false war on drugs in the Philippines, together with their mothers, widows, and orphaned children—we cry out with them for justice.
We pray to Christ who grieves with us:
Kristo Kaawaan mo kami (Christ, have mercy on us all).

For the peasant workers in the Philippines and of the world—living and struggling under slave-like conditions—as with the slaves of Egypt, Rome, and throughout the ages, rise up God of the burning bush and unite the peasant workers to free themselves from the chains of slavery. Unite them to fight for their rights and the produce of their labor.
Let us pray to the God of the slaves:
Diyos kaawaan mo kami (God, have mercy on us all).

For the peasant farmers of the Philippines and the world—for those who feed us yet could not feed themselves because of corporations and landlords who take their land and their labor—unite them and give them strength to claim their rights to land and farming labor. By their dirt-filled hands and the sweat of their brow, may they be filled as they fill us all with good things.
Let us pray to the Christ who told parables about them:
Kristo kaawaan mo kami (Christ, have mercy on us all).

All: God of flames and of Spirit, the tiller of the earth and Spirit that brings life to all. Sacred One of the rivers, the mountains, and the sea who heard the cries of the slaves in ancient days. Prince of Peace who became flesh through a peasant mother and became one of us in every way, except in our sinful and selfish ways, we pray for the Philippines and their oppressed and marginalized peoples. United with them in prayer and action, we seek justice, equality, and peace for them, and we pray that we become the answer to our collective prayer. In the name of all that is holy and loving, we pray. Amen.

I Pray

Loving Parent God, forgive us for the many times that we cannot see and feel.
I pray for all of those who cannot pray and for those who don't know how to
    pray.
I pray for those who do not believe. I also pray for my unbelief.
Forgive us for the many times we depend so much on praying that we forget to
    actualize our prayer.

I pray, O God, for the unheard voices of our LGBTQ+ in our pews, inside our
    churches and places of worship, our communities and homes, may they be
    heard.
Instead of praying for them, I pray for us who treated them unjustly
by not allowing them to participate in our ministries and by spreading hate.
Help us, O God, to see them as you have created them.

For Peasants:
A Reverse Creation Story

God created life
And the killing of the poor is being experienced every day
    (in shanty places)
The mothers wailed in pain and anger
The loved ones are grieving
God created the heavens and the earth, the sun and the moon
And we have allowed earth to be built with dams
We have allowed the communal life to be trespassed to private ownership
We have allowed the rich to be rich and the poor to be poor

God created humans to be free, to be stewards of life, to enjoy the fresh water
    from the streams, the fish in the oceans
But we have caged them, we have exploited and polluted the water and earth
Forgive us

78

Prayer for Peasants (Fisherman)

Dear Lord,
Have you seen Your people who are lonely and faced with oppression?
Have you seen Your flock who are lost without a shepherd?
Have you seen Your sheep in danger?
Have you seen Your children whose faith is being challenged?

Send a good shepherd who leads them with Your heart;
Send a good shepherd who is willing to be with them;
Send a good shepherd who will protect them;
Send a good shepherd who will sacrifice for them.

We pray in the name of Jesus, our Good Shepherd.

Prayer for Workers on Strike

Merciful Lord,
turn your eyes
to the workers who work under unfair labor laws,
the workers who live in poor living conditions,
the mothers and fathers who have to leave their families behind to work
     abroad.

Lord, have mercy;
Christ, have mercy;
Lord, have mercy.

Righteous Lord,
we pray for the workers who are fighting for their rights to get a better life;
give them strength and wisdom to fight against the evil rulers of this world.
Put your justice and mercy in the hearts of the rulers and leaders,
that they will act for the benefit of the people.

Victorious Lord,
you who won the victory over darkness through our Lord and Savior Jesus
     Christ,
lead your people into the land of light, peace, and justice.

Lord, have mercy;
Christ, have mercy;
Lord, have mercy.

Courage to Fight

Dear God, bless the oppressed with courage to fight.

Bless us with courage to stand in solidarity with them and to work with them,
for them.

We pray for those who hear but cannot understand,
those who see but cannot comprehend.

May our solidarity with others give birth to justice and peace
in the land and to the people.

Every Time

Loving Parent God, forgive us for the many times that we cannot see and
feel.

Every time we close our eyes in prayer, help us to open them again to see
the many injustices and oppression around us.

Every time we raise our hands in praise to God, help us to stretch them
out once again that we may help those who are in need.

Forgive us, and every time we kneel in prayer, help us to stand again
with our brothers and sisters in struggle; help us to stand in solidarity
with them.

For the Dalits

Dear God, I pray for the Dalits in India;

I pray for those people who don't have identity as human beings.

I pray for the Dalits who are exposed to torture and attacks by the upper-class
people due to the caste system in our country.

I pray for peace and harmony among Hindus and Christians.

We Take Refuge

O Lord,
we pray for rest,
for the thousands of lives unjustly murdered in the name of war on drugs;
we pray for a cure,
for the mothers and wives whose hearts are being torn apart by the loss of their
    beloveds;
we pray for peace,
for the communities traumatized by random killings, not knowing if they will
    be the next tomorrow;
we pray for repentance,
for those who are powerfully armed yet point their guns at the poor and
    powerless.
Lord, hear our prayer as we take refuge in you.

We Pray for Justice

We pray for Justice, for the church is in silence, speechless, deaf to the
voice of the poor, while Christians in better situations enjoy themselves.

Lord of all mercies, encourage those in power to be in solidarity with the
unfortunate, to share with them, to hear them, to see them, to speak for
them, and to feel them.

Dear Parent God

Dear Parent God,

I met people in the village. All are less fortunate. They are fishermen, have
no health center, no school in the place. Some richer and fortunate people
claimed this village to be theirs and they blocked their ways, demolished
some permanent houses. The situation is terrible.

I believe that you have all the power, so I ask and plea that you come to
these people and help them. Talk to your people on earth who have the
power to assist and lend hands to these people so that they can be liberated from their situation.

Your loving daughter.

The "War on Drugs"

Lord of justice and hope, may you remember those who are unjustly killed by the government under the name of the "war on drugs."

We lift up their families and friends to you. May you be with them when they grieve and mourn for their beloved. Answer their cries when the world is so unfair to them.

Bring to justice those who sin against them through the structural evil of oligarchy. May their anger be your wrath, and their tears yours.

O Lord, we pray and cry out to you because the capitalist world would not let us rest. Workers, bus drivers, tricycle drivers, and peasants are made to work as hard as they can, yet their right to rest is denied.

We remember Wayne, O Lord, whose father died when he was young, who wished only for his mother to quit her job washing clothes and rest . . .

May we remember to pray: "Come to me, all you who are struggling hard and carrying heavy loads" (Matt 11:28).

Ahhh!!! Not Alleluia

Mary mother of the murdered—pray for us
In our grief—pray for us
Among our dead—pray for us
In the blood of the innocent—cry with us in our prayers

Ahhh!!!
And not alleluia
Grrr!!!
And not sanctus

How can we sing of praise?
How can we proclaim glory?

In the midst of blood on our streets
In the darkness of the night
In the cold of the pavement

Send a Shepherd

Dear Lord, our shepherd, please send a good shepherd to your flock in
_____. They are your sheep but are without a shepherd. They're lonely
facing oppression without a leader. Your sheep there are in danger, their
faith in you is being challenged. Please send them a shepherd to lead them
with your heart, to care for them, who is willing to be with them, to protect them, to sacrifice for them, to shepherd them.

Your people in _____ need your care through a good shepherd; someone
who resembles your ministry, love, and care.
In Jesus's name, Amen.

For the Fishing Community

God, we intercede for the fishermen at sea, whose lives are obstructed by
the unseen hand of capitalists, expanding their market economy by deplet-
ing the seas, using their power to take the fisher community away from
the sea, displacing them and taking away their resources.

Restorer and sustainer of the weak and the poor, we intercede for their
health and education so that the fishing community will be able to enjoy
their lives to the full, with dignity, love, and respect. We intercede that you
provide for them their daily bread, and that you will let the rich forgive
their debts and remember them no more.

A Bully-Ridden Land

God of mercy and justice, we come before you; we are crying out in a
violent and bully-ridden land in the Philippines, crying and asking for
peace. Our brothers and sisters are suffering under the drug war unjustly;
we share their pain and suffering.

Lord, have mercy on them and restore the victims their dignity. These people have no hope for the future, yet there is hope for them, and you can
grant them their hope and a peaceful life. Lord, hear our prayer. Amen.

For Those Who Labor

For those who labor, twelve hours with little rest and meager pay, whose children are left on their own to fend for themselves,

For those who labor, without promise of security for tomorrow, whose sweat makes our lives comfortable,

For those who labor for the rich and are treated without respect, without safety, without basic rights,

Sharanam Sharanam Sharanam

For those who labor in pain,

Lord, hear our prayer as we take refuge in you.

A Serenity Prayer for the IP Dumagat Community

God, grant us the serenity to accept the things we feel we cannot change,
like a violent and corrupt government and its desire for power.
We bring ourselves to you in silence. *(Keep a moment of silence.)*

Grant us the courage to change the things we can,
to protect our heritage and identity; our lands and our future; to defend our
    livelihood, to preserve our culture.
We bring our gifts to change ourselves and our world,
we bring ourselves to you in silence. *(Keep a moment of silence.)*

And grant us wisdom to know the difference.
Teach us to be resilient, against the power of empire, like Christ.
Amen.

Confession of Faith for Homeless Africa

Homeless and destitute as we are, we still believe that you have created us in your image.
Day and night, we are exposed to the anguish of the extreme weather of the seasons; but God commends God's love toward us and protects us.

Always, we are suspected of being criminals by those who have no idea of our history; but only you Lord, keep our lamp burning.

We are looked down upon because of our status as homeless; but you, gracious God, turn our darkness into light.

Every day we are the victims of unspoken and cruel judgments.

Some make us the objects of their charity and others put our pictures and misery on the front cover of their grant proposal requests; but you, oh Lord, are good and your love endures forever.

True Judge and Redeemer

Dear God, the true Judge and Redeemer of all, we pray against the discrimination and unfair treatment of the poor and oppressed in _____ [*country*]. See the plight and suffering of your sons and daughters. Hear their cries. Alleviate their pain and suffering. Bring justice swiftly to the oppressed and the oppressors. Deliver them from the systemic power of evil. Like Moses, we say to the oppressors, the powers of evil, the forces of darkness: "Let your people go, you have no right and authority over God's people." And may your healing and restoration come upon this land, so that your people can live in freedom, love, peace, and justice.

PRAYERS OF THANKSGIVING

NOTE FOR THE READER: Prayers of thanksgiving are traditionally included in the service of the Eucharist. When planning Holy Communion, consider using one of the prayers here as a prayer of thanksgiving. See Part Three, page 125 for Eucharist liturgies.

For Water

We thank you for enabling us to hear the gushing of the rivers, the lapping of the waves as they rejoice. We thank you for the water that runs from deep within the earth that fills our well that never runs dry. (*While this is read, someone continuously pours water to make the sound.*)

We remember that you journeyed with your people, bringing them through dangerous waters on their way to liberation. But we also remember those who did not survive, who perished in perilous journeys across the waters.

We remember the farmers whose wells have run dry. We remember all creatures who depend on clean water, who suffer because we pollute your precious gift. As we come to the waters of baptism, we confess that these waters are your gift to us.

The waters of hope,
The waters of peace,
The waters of joy,
The waters of death and rebirth.
Help us to understand that all water is holy.

For Children

Thank you, Lord, for the fruit of the womb
Thank you, Lord, for the material provision for our children's upkeep
Thank you, Lord, for the grace you provide them
Thank you, Lord, for the capacity to nurture and love them
    unconditionally

Thank you, Lord, for the communal solidarity
Thank you, Lord, that our children do not live in isolation
but they have a sense of belonging
Thank you, Lord, for the blessed assurance

Thank you, Lord, for charity and compassion toward the needy
Thank you, Lord, for opening our hearts and minds to the reality of your pres-
    ence that brings liberation and salvation.
Glory and honor be unto you, Amen.

For Gifts of Food and Those Who Provide It

Loving God, we call to mind the heavenly banquet revealed to us through
Jesus, in whose life of communion we have been invited. So, before we
dine and fellowship, we give thanks for your invitations and for your gifts
each day. Bless the hands that cooked and prepared this meal, remembering also the hands doing the work we cannot; the hands of fishers and
farmers; of those who till and harvest the land, of laborers who pack,
stack, and deliver; as well as the empty hands of the hungry. While we eat
and drink, we count our blessings, as we receive them all in your name.
Amen.

For the Gifts

Thank you, God, for the air
Thank you, God, for families that we can share with in good times and bad
    times
Thank you, God, for the gifts of other families, friends, visitors,
    strangers

For Opened Eyes

Lord, thank you for opening our eyes to see the needs of our neighbors in our community. You have inspired us to live and identify with the struggling peasant and fishermen community. You have shown us the consequences of the acts of selfishness and taught us to examine our greed. We thank you, for we have learned to be more human and to be in solidarity with the poorest of the poor. Thank you for softening our hearts to feel the pain of the oppressed and opening our ears to hear their cries for help. Thank you for moving us to stand against injustice and to promote justice in the community.

Thanksgiving

For tears, water of life that runs down our faces and connects our lives
for the burden of God's creation
for the spirit of solidarity
for when we are welcomed
for the hospitality of indigent people
for God's goodness running through the natural resources
for the ability to listen to wounded people
for the chance to becoming better humans
for the activists, community workers, and prophets who give their lives, gifts,
     and labor to the people of the world
for being together here
for the noise of children
for the spirit of resistance and rebellious people
for clean water
the strength and courage to live on in spite of loss
for the gift of the others, the families with whom we live
for maternal rage
for hope that comes from smiles and laughter
for faith and patience in the midst of suffering

For Farmers and Fisherfolk

God of the farmers and the fisherfolks, we thank you for the gift of fellowship. We thank you for the rice, for the fish, and for the coconut juice that
we have shared with one another. We thank you for this Holy Communion,
for in our sharing we remember your saving act through the life, death, and
resurrection of Jesus Christ. Enable us, with your Holy Spirit, to continue to
extend our arms to the poor, the oppressed, the marginalized, and the groaning creation so that the hungry will be fed, the thirsty will be given water,
the blind will see, and the captives will be set free. You will reign here on
earth now and in the coming days. Amen.

For the Opportunity to Live
with Poor People

Dear Lord:

Thank you for giving me the opportunity to live with poor people, to eat
with them, to sing with children, to listen to their stories, their struggles,
and their pain. Also to experience their love and hospitality.

But at the same time, it makes me feel shameful and guilty. I used to
compose prayers for the poor, for those who are in suffering, for justice
and peace prevailing in this world. I have taught lots of hymns about social
concerns and human rights, but I have never stepped into their lives. I have
always looked at these people and their oppressed situation from a distance.

I once heard, but now I have seen.
I once read, but now I have experienced.
I once was senseless, but now I have sensed their grief and despair.
I once looked at them from a distance,
    but now I am living with them and holding them in my heart.

For Sending the Soldiers

Today, my mind is consumed with grief, the sadness of a young life taken away. I am tired of the crime. We all struggle with situations in our lives that are painful experiences. I am bitter with very few words. I am angry, but the problems will not define me. I am overwhelmed; I want to run, I want to hide, to escape. But God is my refuge and strength and I know that I will make it. I am determined that the God I serve will see me through. Lord, watch over our country. I have hope that God will bring the culprits to justice. My circumstances will change one day. I am learning how to grieve. Thank God for sending the soldiers. We now can walk. Master God is not sleeping.

PRAYERS OF INTERCESSION

NOTE FOR THE READER: Prayers of Intercession are traditionally part of the service of the Eucharist. When planning a service of Holy Communion, consider using one of these prayers for a time of intercessory prayer. See Part Three, page 125 for Eucharist liturgies.

For All the Children

God of mercy, love, and justice,
In this prayer, we bring all children in our community,
Whom we as the society overlook in their pain of poverty,
God have mercy

Whom we as the society deny all human rights and dignity,
God have mercy

Who continue to suffer abuse silently,
And yet sometimes we deny a hearing ear when they cry,
God have mercy

As we continue to pray for the poor, we remember our own children
Who are more privileged, and yet we are sometimes ungrateful and oblivious;
Lord, grant them consciousness of your blessings to them,
Guide them in all decisions they take in the journey of life,
God have mercy

But all children in the society, those of the affluent, those of poor backgrounds,
Those with privileges of education, those in and without the church,
Grant them to have your salvation and blessings, good and perfect health,
Have hope in the midst of pain, and grant them to see your face in all your
    people
Amen

God of the Bodies

O God that became body and presence,
that wanted to share the path, the bread and the cup,
that loved and embraced, that dreamed and suffered,
that assumed the pain and stored up hopes.
Bring yourself today to those who feel pain in their bodies:
the pain of an unwanted absence,
pain that like a dagger cuts the soul
and rips open the bowels.

O God, you touched injured bodies,
you stretched out your hand to the despised bodies,
you embraced the ignored bodies,
you put on a body that struggled alongside the most humble,
you felt in your own flesh the brutality of oppression,
so lend your shoulder today to those who cry,
to those who need to know themselves as loved and content
because torturers and murderers
continue to steal the lives of loved ones' bodies.

Naked God, exposed, trophy of genocides,
your body crucified on a whim by the power of the day
and ignored by the lukewarm complicity of so many.
God, whose dead body was seen by the morbid
and cried helplessly in silence for the persecuted.
God, whose body was buried and guarded, out of fear . . .
Become a body in the midst of our fears,
liberate us, just as you freed yourself on the third day,
from the sadistic omnipotence of those who carry the sword.

God of the transcendent body,
of the body that makes us one body, community, people.
God of the body that remains, present
in every search for justice and fulfillment,
in each act of resisting the perverse,
in each table where shared bread reaches and remains,
and where wine is a transforming sacrament.
Rescue us from the waters of resignation,
give us your hand of solidarity and walk with us
to places where bodies can live and dance and be free,
without appropriators, without repressors, without mercenaries of death.

Father and Mother of the Dirt

Father and Mother of the Dirt,
The sun shines another day.
It is time to rise again
Though my feet are tired
My hands are cracked
My body is aching
The soil is hard
And the rain never came this month.

I pray for your grace to moisten us.
You know my children are hungry
For dumplings and plantains
For yams that, though I plant and
Reap, are too expensive to eat.

You also know my husband is sick—
My body is all I have to give.

Please keep our souls from breaking
Our bodies from aching

Please pour water down the trenches
May your abundant love turn the earth red again
May your blessings well up in the earth
May they bloom and produce fruits for our reaping.

May my fork and machete be
As kind to the earth as you have been to us

May this prayer sink into our being,
Mind, and the earth's one breath be deeper
Please remember us in all your glory, God

For the Weak and Poor in the Philippines

Leader: We intercede for the weak and the poor, the peasants, and fishermen in the larger part of the Asia Pacific region, whose land and lives are at risks at the hand of the capitalist and the ruling government.

People: Lord, in your mercy, empower the poor peasant and fishermen community with wisdom and discernment.

Leader: We intercede because the document produced by the rich capitalists to claim the land of the fishermen and peasant at the sea course of Bataan, Manila, and in the developing and underdeveloped nations is false.

People: Lord, in your righteousness and justice, let their plan be devastated and nullified by the ruling government.

Leader: We intercede for the sick in the absence of health care and a clinic at Morong village, Philippines, and in many villages in the different corners of the world, who need help and assistance.

People: God, in your faithfulness, we pray for health care programs to be established in the neglected places, which often feel like despicable and horrendous places in the Asian Pacific region.

Leader: We intercede for the children who are deprived of having access to education, and for those who have to face hardship and hindrances in the absence of roads and nearby primary education.

People: Rescue us, O Lord, from the greedy and selfish ruler who lacks concern for the poor, uneducated children. Confuse the plan of the rich and the powerful who thwart us from having access to education.

God Who Hears the Prayers of the Oppressed

Dear God,

You are the God of love, mercy, peace, and comfort. The God who gives hope for those who are hopeless. The God of liberation for those who are in bondage of sin of loneliness, poverty of oppression by the historical and present empire. Deliver us from all forms of oppression, past and present. Thank you for the hope we have in you because without you we will be dead. You are our only source of hope, even in times of suffering, poverty, loneliness, and sickness and all forms of injustice caused by the empire. The God who hears the prayers of the oppressed, hear our prayer.

Kyrie

Christ, Lamb of God,
who taketh away the sin of the world,
have mercy on us.

Christ, Lamb of God,
who taketh away the sin of the world,
have mercy on us.

Christ, Lamb of God,
who taketh away the sin of the world,
please don't grant us your peace until there is peace for all.

Amen.

Dry Bones #1

Dry bones, dry bones burned to dryness
Days seem desolate, dirt all around
The Devil prowls around seeking to devour
Dreadful cry, devastating damage, dead children.

Deliver us, deliver us, our Divine Strength
Draw us to freedom and delight in You
Desire for Your recompense moves us to
Devote our lives to Your will here on earth.

Prayer for Haiti

Faced with a pain that rips apart, we cry out in one voice:
Intercede with us,
Oh, Lord in solidarity.

Faced with death that wounds,
And marks with pain,
Give us the strength of an embrace
And the peace that your love gives us.

Faced with injustice that kills
And cries out for conversion,
Move us to transform the world
And let all death become a song.

In the face of desolation and crying,
Faced with impotence and frustration,
Come to our side,
Sustain us with your life, Lord.

You are the God of the poor, the One who sows hope,
You are the God of solidarity, the One who gives love.

You are God with us, the Eternal, the Great I Am.
God of the embrace, God of song. God who embraces,
God who strengthens, God who surrenders, God of action.

O Lord of Solidarity: Your kingdom come to the mourner,
Lean your ear to the cry,
Your sons and daughters are coming
To show your great love.

Prayer for the Poor

God of the destitute,
We are living under the Empire of cruelty and exploitation,
Which feasts on the toil and sweat of the African people.
We pray that under the Spirit of resilience and our lives together,
We can revolt against this tyrannical empire
So that we can regain our humanity
In the name of our revolutionary Lord,
Our redeemer Jesus Christ.
Amen.

Where Are You, Lord?

We have Heard it with our own ears, oh God,
Our ancestors have told us
What you did in their day
With your hands you smashed their enemies
You trampled their foes
But today, where are you Lord?
Awaken Lord! Why do you sleep? Awaken!
Slaughter our foes and let us rise
Show your face
Deport your enemies to the pits of hell,
And allow us to flourish.

Prayer for the People of Zimbabwe

Gracious Lord, Lord of Africa, Lord of the oppressed and downtrodden, may your grace shine upon the people of Africa, Zimbabwe, the landless and the disadvantaged. We ask the love of God the creator, giver of life and resources to continue to journey with the people of Zimbabwe in all their difficult circumstances created by the empire. And may the communion of your spirit, which surpasses all understanding, the comforter of the oppressed and segregated, continue to abide in African nations and your people. Amen.

Awaken Us to *Ubuntu*

God of mercy and forgiveness, we come to you with brokenness, asking that you forgive us for being negligent, selfish, fearful, and being of indifferent attitude to others who are in different situations. We confess that because of our lack of exercising *ubuntu*, we have left the responsibility of caring for the elderly and the sick under the care of a fourteen-year-old child. The poor, migrants, and the homeless are on the streets and yet we have not attended to them. They are dying of hunger, lacking basic needs such as food, shelter, and health. We pray that, Gracious Lord, you awaken our senses to exercise *ubuntu*, so that we can be moved to help the needy, sick, suffering, homeless, unemployed, and foreigners. We pray that you give us a heart to love them practically, just as we love ourselves. For we are all made in your image. Lord, hear our prayer. Amen.

For Their Heartfelt Needs

God of life
God of justice
God of love and mercy

God the provider
God our refuge and sustainer
God our comforter

Hear the plight of those living in squalid conditions
We present the vulnerabilities of the widows,
orphans, sick, the aged, and unemployed
We present their needs before you
We appeal to you to meet them at their point of need

Give them hope and faith in you
Give them courage to soldier on
Give them resilience and tenacity

We pray that while the powers that
have tended to ignore their plight,
you will be the eyes and ears that see and listen
to their heartfelt needs

We pray that you make us the instrument
and the channel of healing love and source of comfort;
We appeal to you to make us relevant and effective
to those in need.
Amen.

God of Mary and Joseph

God of Mary, who was found to be pregnant before marriage and probably faced shame from her peers. God of Joseph, who had to struggle with a
pregnant fiancée whom "he knew not." We pray for the girl child and the
boy child who are vulnerable to child trafficking, which is the tool of the
empire. We pray that you send the angel Gabriel once more, whom you
sent to Mary and Joseph, to bring good news to the lives of our children.
Help us mothers to be the Elizabeth of our time, who will give wisdom to
our children in this troubled world.

A Child's Prayer

Dear God, thank you for my mummy, daddy, grannies, teachers, friends, and pets. I pray for peace in my home that mummy and daddy may stop fighting. Also help mummy and daddy get money to pay for my field trip. I pray for my friends, Joshua and Martha. Help them to get what they need. I also pray for those children on the streets who have no home, no food, and no clothing. Dear God, please provide for them a nice home, nice food, clothes, and shoes.

I pray for grandma and grandpa. Help them to live forever so that I can continue to play with them.

I pray for my teachers. Help them to be good to all the children at school.

I pray for Aunt Kate and her children who are sick. When they are not here, I feel like a part of me is missing.

I pray for my dog, Spanky. He is a good dog and I love him so much. Help him to live forever and ever.

Prayers of Intercession That Were Answered

Dear God, thank you for giving dad a new house, please provide money so that he can buy enough chairs for all of us, and then we can all sit comfortably when we are having our meals. (The house had only one chair for the father and no sooner had the girl prayed then the family had received nice chairs.)

Dear God, please help mum and dad to buy a car so that we stop walking to Sunday school every Sunday and arrive late because it is embarrassing, and I always feel bad. (In a few weeks' time, the family was blessed with a car as a gift.)

God of Freedom

We are living under the empire of the devil that uses its powers to destroy your creation by stealing, using all sort of oppression and temptation.

We pray that, under the power of the Spirit and our lives together, that you will free us from all sorts of empire. We pray for the empire that they know and understand that You are the Lord of all and that everything is yours, so that they confess their sins and repent.

Do let us, not only resist the oppressors, but also help them be free from their evil manners,

So that all people in this world live in freedom and peace, the shalom that Jesus has already given us.

In the name of Jesus, our only savior and liberator.

May We Encounter You Today

Loving God, our faithful father, you who created us in your image and likeness, [and] are willing to meet with us here, as market vendors, barbers, mothers, and fathers.

We confess that in our sweat and toil, we often forget your presence. In our struggles and weariness and frustration we are often lukewarm. Forgive us.

Tabernacle with us.
We need you now more than ever. Drained of strength and energy we come, that we might be re-energized and filled.

So, come Lord.
Come as the wind, blow your breath gently over us, blow the dust off our lives. Come as the fire, burn out all hate and anger we feel toward those who oppress us and treat us unfairly. Come as the water, wash the dirt of poverty off our stalls, the marketplace, and our lives.

Come as the dove—settle all matters concerning us. Let peace reign.

May we encounter you today. Ignite our hearts to worship and serve you. Take your place and rule and reign in Jesus's name as we leave our struggle at the foot of the cross and liberate us to worship you. Amen.

With All Our Being, Our Voice Implores Today

For the families who have lost sons and daughters, who walk without ceasing in their search for justice and peace.

> Dm   Bb   C   Dm
> "With all our being, our voice implores today." *(sung chorus)*

For those who have lost their jobs, frustration and discouragement abounding in their lives.

Chorus

For displaced persons
Who have been expelled from their land, source of life, and work.

Chorus

For those who have had to leave their homes and go on uncertain and dangerous roads in search of a better life.

Chorus

For those who suffer from physical pain due to illness and try to maintain strength and courage.
Chorus

For the childhood that has stopped playing because of abuse and lack of freedom.

Chorus

I Ask These Things

God,
I ask that you stabilize the market, that you hold the powerful to their words.
I ask that you fortify us in community, that you make us out of many, one.
I ask that you provide us tools, that you give us what we need to steward and till.
I ask that you relieve our fatigue, that you grow our strength and resolve.
I ask these things in your Christ child's name.
Amen.

Guide and Empower Us

You who shepherd the lost and comfort the afflicted
Guide our hands to touch the untouchable
Our ears to listen to the hopeless
Our eyes to see the misery of others
Our hearts to feel the pain of prisoners
Empower us to take risks to be channels of healing and mercy
So that this world may be a better place
Amen

We Seek Your Face

God, we come before you in brokenness. We seek your face, a face with eyes that see our pain, with ears that hear our cries, with hands that touch our scars and open wounds. We remember those who suffer the effects of economic injustice; especially those who are homeless or living without the basic amenities for health and survival.

We pray for those whose voices are suppressed because of their sexual identity, gender, and religious affiliations.

We pray for those who tend the earth and struggle to feed others while sustaining themselves when the earth has been poisoned and the climate confused. Turn your face to those suffering ones, the face of your justice, your truth, and the transformative power of your love, acting through our own acts of courage and resistance. Amen.

Raise Them Up

Father I come to you in the home of our Lord and Savior, bring to you the poor, the weak, the hungry, the wounded, the oppressed.

I ask you to cover them with your anointing, glory, and tangible presence.

Give them food, justice, a fresh new release and flow of rivers with living waters springing forth abundantly with life.

Give them eyes to see spiritually, and a heart to understand and be led by your Holy Spirit.

I ask you to let your love and the Holy Spirit shine through them, raise them up in your precious work.

Amen.

O God of Transformation

O God of Transformation,
Use us to embody your love in the world
May broken hearts be embraced by our love
May grieving mothers find us willing to share their tears
May lonely elders find our community attentive
May despairing teens feel encouraged by our support
May displaced migrants be welcomed into safety here
May unemployed workers find connections to stable work

O Spirit, empower us to uphold the vulnerable
Through our prayers and our actions
Enable us to live into your deepest longing for us and for your precious world

Fall Over Me

Dear God,
I am in pain; I fear I'll lose it all.

Fall over me.
Cover me with your love. Massage me with your transforming current.

Fall over me.
Unravel the stressed knots in my shoulders.

Fall over me, drown my sense of despair.
Betwixt the rocks in the mountains YOU flow, sometimes thunderous,
    sometimes slow.

Fall over me NOW!
Show me YOUR way somehow.
Amen.

Until Justice and Peace Kiss

God of the earth, of heaven, and of all that we see around us,
allow us to learn to live together, and together with creation.
May the peace that is the fruit of justice
be a reality for every corner of the earth.

Give us strength, faith, and hope
because until justice and peace kiss
we will die plowing our fields,
waiting for new fruits of the earth
and new sunrises.

Heal Our World

Merciful God,
You hear the cries of your people
Put an end to all that divides us
For you call us to be one
End gang violence
Mend the broken hearts of mothers whose children have been murdered
Bring quality education and good jobs
Fill the bellies of the hungry by empowering us to share what we have
Heal our world: physical, spiritual, and soul
Make us signs of your grace to our neighbors
Amen.

For Your Latin People

Lord Jesus, thank you for your mercy,
For your Latin people.

Watch over us and protect us from all the dangers
That persecute our people.
There are many forces that come together
To steal our peace and harmony,

But your compassionate love surpasses
All obstacles.

Blessed are you who touches the hearts
That fight for good, today and forever.

Blessed and praised be our protector.
Amen.

Tivoli Mourns the Death of Their Children

Tivoli mourns the death of their children
Until when will they have to lament and cry?
When will justice be done?
Your little ones were cornered
As a sheep taken to the slaughterhouse;
His blood was drunk by the earth
I do not hear her singing, asking for its news

Tivoli mourns the death of your children,
Its streets proclaim their hope:
The Lord is my light and my salvation
Whom shall I fear?
Its walls invade God's temple:
Plead my cause, Lord,
Fight against them that fight against me;
Are your ears deaf to their cry?
Can't you hear their pain?

Tivoli mourns the death of their children,
Your children . . .
Our Mama, you cry with us;
You mourn the death of your children,
Do justice to them, listen to our cry;
Defend us from those who have risen up against us,
Heal our wound and attend to our desire to love
Come and save us

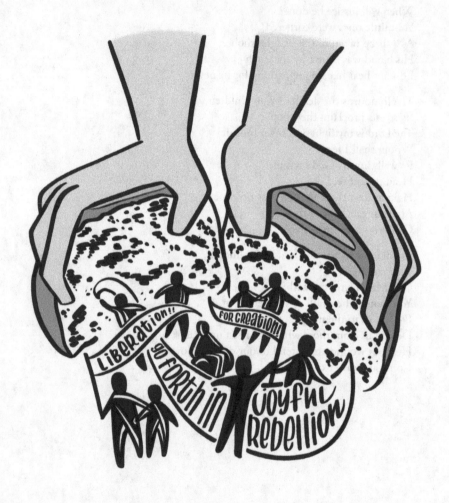

Birthquake of Resistance
See page 295 to read *Worship Spaces in the Philippines*, which inspired this artwork.

PART THREE

LITURGIES OF BAPTISM
AND EUCHARIST

LITURGIES OF BAPTISM

Baptism Prayer—Reclaiming the Water

Here there are no priests—We are the priesthood of all believers.

We are reclaiming the water! Not from the corporation but God's! We use this water for baptism, for restoration, washing, transformation, healing.

Candidates share why they want to be baptized.

In Baptism God calls us to . . .

Do you renounce the complacency with the agribusiness? The land grabbers? The ones who exploit the poor?

Do you promise to love them but work fiercely against the works of dehumanization, destruction of the earth, and killing of the animals?

Song.

Candidate is surrounded by the assembly.
Pour water over the dry land and the candidate.

Final Prayer

God of the waters, we reclaim the waters of the world! All of the waters belong to you and thus, all the waters belong to the earth, the animals, the birds, the planktons, the fishes, and us. May the healing of the nations come from the waters. May the new life of this candidate come from the waters of your womb and the waters of the earth. May our reconciliation

109

with you be the reconciliation with the waters of the earth, the whole body of God. Help us rise against those who are killing us! Help us sustain those who are suffering! Help us share the water with all. In Jesus Christ, the water of life. Amen.

The Waters of Our Rivers

We are blessed with gracious water that comes from God, but water that also comes from the water pipeline of Maynilad Water Service.

God gives us this water which sustains our lives, but water that also poisons our lives. This water is a product of corporate greed. Nestle owns the spring water of God. Maynilad oversees the use of the water of God.

In this baptism, we claim the holy goodness of this water. This is not the water of the corporation. This is not the water of _____. This is the water of the triune God.

This water comes from God. So, we use this water in this baptism, not to sanction corporate greed and privatization of the gift of God. We use this water to bless and commission [*name*] in his/her affirmation to participate in the public ministry of Jesus to give water to the thirsty, to provide clean water to the children for whom Jesus calls us to love and care, to make water available to all God's creation . . . to the thirsty carabao plowing the field to birds in the sky.

So, we pour this water on [*name*] as we pour this water to the drying lands, to nourish his/her mission as well as to replenish Earth. Let this water poured bring forth redemption and restoration of our brokenness, from greediness to generosity, from selfishness to selflessness. Amen.

Baptism: God of the Poor

Presentation

> In a greedy world fueled by inflation, faith is the free gift of God to his people. God of the poor, please welcome these candidates to our church family, a new way of life together in Christ.

The baptism candidates tell their testimonies or stories.

Decision

> In baptism, God calls us out of darkness into his marvelous light.
> To follow Christ means dying to sin and rising to new faith with him.
> Therefore, I ask:
> Do you reject the curses of capitalism, the temptation of greed, the condemnation of the poor?
> Do you renounce the deceit of stability, which says security is only possible at the expense of others' lives?
> Do you turn to Jesus Christ, the Savior our Lord, who was born to the lowly, walked with the marginalized, healed the wounded, and was killed by the Imperial collaborators but resurrected from the death?

Response: **Yes, I do.**

The Profession of the Community (song)

> We believe in God our Father
> We believe in Christ the Son
> We believe in the Holy Spirit
> Our God is three in one
> We believe in the resurrection
> That we will rise again
> For we believe in the name of Jesus

Baptism

The whole community stands in the waters or on the beach, surrounding the candidate(s).
Baptize the candidate(s) by splashing water.
The community says in unison:

> **We baptize you in the name of the Father, Son, and Holy Spirit.**

Prayer

_____ [*name*],

today God has stretched his arms into the world of exploitations and abuses,
touched you and lifted you out with his love of the poor
and given you a place among his people, a safe haven, a roof shielding you
    from thundering violence.
In baptism, God invites you on a life-long journey with the poor.
Together with all God's people, in joy and in sorrow, in life and in death, on
    earth and in heaven,
you must follow the way of Jesus, being for the other in the face of the empire,
and growing in friendship with God, in solidarity with his people fighting for
    costly justice.
With us, you live in the word of liberation
and the unconditional gifts of God.

Commission (dance).

God of the poor and sinful world, we praise You.

Baptismal Prayer #1

Our God of mountains, the forest and the Zambezi River where Nyami Nyami
    abides.
God of the Limpopo that once connected us, but now divided us through
    colonial borders.
God of the Kariba Dam whose waters where privatized for the benefit of the
    empire and displaced the indigenous peoples, hence displacing their gods.

God of the Okavango Delta whose beauty is exploited by the empire and
    tourists at the expense of the indigenous peoples.

Heal the water that is bleeding with bitterness and stained by the blood of our
    innocent ancestors.
Free the waters that have been enclosed and privatized by the empire so that
    they may flow freely to sweep away the curse, oppression, exploitation,
    human degradation, hunger, and thirst for the healing of our land.

As a united village of Molepulule, we come to the well of our ancestors to
    present and welcome [*names*] to the communion of the believers.

For without this water, there can be no Lord's Table and the communion of all
    believers will be in vain and the body of Christ will not be united.

Amen.

Baptismal Prayer #2

God of love and everlasting grace,
you have loved us so much to birth us within the midst of Musi a
Thunya—the smoke that thunders. A river that provides for all your
creation, human and animals, while recanting the liberation vision of
Mt. Horeb in perpetual smoke. God you are great!

We bring before you the waters of the Thukela, Nile, and Lusuthu rivers,
the blessing that Africa is to the world. Heritage of our forebears and
bathing places of kings. Bless these waters, we pray. That as we baptize
there our friends, you inscribe their names in your book of life and anoint
them kings and priests unto your kingdom.

It is with great joy that our baptism launches us into the rich heritage of
liberation. For it is in the waters of the river Nile that you, oh God, provided sanctuary for Moses. And in this river, dear God, we place the sons
and daughters of Africa.

As you used the Nile to defeat centuries of slavery, we beseech you to
unleash your power, through this baptism to bring an end to capitalism,
which so rampantly destroys all life and family arrangements. Bring healing to the sons and daughters of this Continent, dear God.

God, the waters of the Mediterranean have been destroying life and still
do. You have shown us that power was in your hand when David was able
to take on Goliath and succeeded. How long should the Mediterranean
continue to disrupt the beauty of your creation? Let the waters of these
great rivers bring an end to the evil associated with this sea and give birth
to a new sense of life and relationship with you and others.

You Are, We Are

Sing a local song.

Words

I baptize you in the name of God's community: Creator, Redeemer, and Consoler.

Welcome to this community, we are here to journey with you. We are here to see you grow. When you fail, we will pick you up. When you cry, we will dry your tears. When you mourn, we will mourn with you. When you celebrate, we will celebrate, too.

Response: Because I am, you are. Because you are, I am.

Charge

Go forth, with your eyes wide open to see the injustices around you.
Go forth with feet that stand in the gap for those suffering from our greed,
with hands to plant seeds that nourish our bodies, with ears that listen to
the voices of the poor and vulnerable and to the cries of creation.

God invites us on a journey,
God leads us through waters,
each of us comes to life through the waters of the womb.

God led us through the waters of the Red Sea,
for a life of freedom and struggle and with
the promise of bountiful land.

Jesus began his journey of teaching and sharing
God's love in the waters of the Jordan River.

Jesus commanded his disciples to baptize people in
God's holy name, so that the message of love and
recreation would bless the whole world.

In baptism, we are invited to begin and renew a
journey that calls us to show God's love
in words and actions that uplift community.

Profession of Faith

Are you ready to begin this journey with God, a journey in which God's love manifests itself in you and through you, in your worship and your relationship with others, bringing openness and care for all God's children and the entire creation?

Response: Yes, I am.

Take off Your Sandals, We Are Standing in Holy Water

Gather at the edge of a waterfall or any other body of water.

Experience and Reflection

Invite people to step into the water or to feel the water.
Invite people to share what they are feeling.
Lead a moment of silent personal reflection—a minute or so during which people will reflect on what they need from this experience.

Spoken Narrative

People are invited to briefly share their reflections.

Unison Response after Each Reflection

We will stir the water!
We will drink the water!
We will share the water!
We will stop the pollution of water!

Moment of Baptism

Invite all into the water to gather around the baptizer and baptized.

Song: "Cause Me to Come to Thy River," by R. Edward Miller

Baptism (ordained minister or priest)

Use names such as "living water," "river of mercy," "source of life," and "quencher of thirst."

Intercessions

Different people in the gathering offer prayers of intercession.
Encourage a focus on the goodness of water and challenges of water.

Songs

"Song Over the Waters," by Marty Haugen
"You Are the Voice," by David Haas

Benediction

Focus on "the power to act."
Blessing should include:

• a change

• people have cause of renewal

• a call to action.

An Idea for Baptism in the Context of Oppression

Setting

We suggest that the assembly gather around one of the following sites of water (inside or outside): a gutter, puddle (on street or land), a container (plastic bottle or jug, basin, etc.).

This baptismal ritual can occur within a pattern of worship or outside of it; we suggest prefacing the ritual with a reading, reflection, homily, or sermon based on Acts 8:26-40, maybe emphasizing Acts 8:36.

Note that Acts 8:37 is an optional verse.

Baptism for and of the Oppressed

Invitation and Promise

Read Luke 4:18-21.

Sing a verse of the spiritual "Wade in the Water" (song continues beneath the words).

Confession of faith.

Submersion

Music raised louder, continue singing "Wade in the Water" throughout the baptism.

"We baptize you in the faith and for the struggle" in the name of . . .

Resurrection

Be not conformed to this world but transformed by the renewal of your mind in Christ Jesus. *(Said when emerging; one may make a sign of the cross or there may be a laying-on of hands.)*

Song: "Get Up! Stand Up!," by Bob Marley and Peter Tosh

Prayer: Read Luke 1:47-53 (Magnificat)

An Idea for Baptism Incorporating Promises, Renunciations, and Affirmations

Standing or situated in a circle.

Invitation

Spirit of God that moves on the water, we beckon you to come and be among us as we prepare to baptize [*name*] in the name of Jesus Christ, whose word declared "let the children come."

Promises

We gather around this [*font of water*] as symbol of your life-giving presence, water being the singular earthly element of life in this world, and you being the source of eternal life. We, your people, stand in solidarity with this family as we welcome a new member to our community and promise to support the family to groom this child in the nurture and admonition of the Lord.

Renunciations

Holding water as a sacred symbol, we therefore renounce:
(corruption) the misuse of the element that unites us and say no to pollution in all its forms;
(control) unjust mismanagement of water and say no to its inequitable distribution;
(consumption) living, loving God, help us to join you and say no to the evil of the overconsumption of water.

Affirmations

Holding water as a sacred symbol we therefore affirm:
the building of a community that supports the gifts you give us, from your water;
in caring for our water we learn to care for one another;
water connects our community and connects us to new life.
Amen.

118

Prayer over the Waters

Saltwater should be used and all people should touch the water.

We pray over these waters
We pray over these waters
We pray over these waters

These are the waters of death
There is darkness over the face of the deep
The waves overcome us and we perish
So many seeking freedom have sunk beneath these waves
[*other phrases should be inserted naming recent incidents*]
We are baptized into the death of Christ

We pray over these waters
We pray over these waters
We pray over these waters

These are the waters of life
Creator of the deep we call to you
Your waters are the place of all birth
Your children seeking freedom are cast upon these waters
[*other phrases should be inserted naming recent incidents*]
We are baptized into the life of Christ

We pray over these waters
We pray over these waters
We pray over these waters

An Idea for Baptism and the Four Elements

Focus on the four elements to create a new baptism liturgy:

- Earth: sacredness of the earth, fruits of the earth, life, firm roots

- Fire: that purifies

- Air: movement

- Water: living, fresh water . . . necessary for life

Consider gathering the congregation in a spiral pattern, with the baptism happening in the center. This can signify the community together but moving along an open road. It is a way to remember those who are always moving, but not always by choice. We are people in movement.

Act of Recommitment to Our Baptismal Faith

We gather around the font or a large bowl.
As water is poured into the font or bowl, these words are said:

Voice 1:   In the beginning the Holy Spirit brooded
over the waters of creation,
the waters of primal birth.

Voice 2:   Through the waters of the Red Sea
the People of Israel were led
from slavery in Egypt to freedom in the promised land.

Voice 3:   In the waters of the Jordan
Jesus was baptized by John
and named as God's beloved Son.

All: **Through the waters of baptism**
we have all died with Christ
and been raised up with Him
to live as those newly born.

Voice 1:   And now, in our world, water is a
            contested and finite resource.
            The birthright of all is bottled and commodified,
            contaminated and trafficked,
            greening golf courses while the fields of the poor are
            desolate.

Voice 2:   Now, in our world, water is a
            political tool, mapped and boundaried.
            Seas are classified as national or international waters
            and ships watch impassively as migrants die
            on the wrong side of these imaginary lines.

Voice 3:   Now, in our world, the watermark on our passports
            and the watermark on our banknotes
            are valued more highly than the watermark of our faith.

All: **We confess that we have allowed water to divide us.**
            We turn again, O God, to you.
            We recommit ourselves to the faith of our baptism.
            We are thirsty for justice.
            We are thirsty for wholeness.
            We are thirsty for the new world of your love.

Those who have been the Voices sprinkle water from the bowl on all those gathered around, saying:

Voices 1, 2, & 3:   Receive this reminder of your baptism.
                    Do justice with faith.

Three Affirmations in Baptism

Use in place of renunciations.

> Having experienced violence, do you turn to God the Creator, affirming that you are called to love even your enemies?
> **I so affirm.**
>
> Turning away from domination of others and empire building, do you turn to Christ the Liberator, affirming that salvation is received rather than won?
> **I so affirm.**
>
> Encountering both death and life, do you turn to the Holy Spirit the Life Giver, affirming you are now part of the community of believers?
> **I so affirm.**

God Takes You by the Hand:
A Prayer after Baptism

> God takes you by the hand and leads you safely through the deep waters,
> in the silent depth of the sea you can lay the burden of your labor and failures,
> the light of God shows you the way to the surface,
> and the living Spirit will meet you on the other side,
> filling your lungs with a breath as wide as the new life in God, with God and
>   for God,
> from now on you are a living witness of the power of life in the midst of death.

Prayer Professing Faith

God, Creator, you planned salvation from the beginning—telling evil
that the woman's offspring would crush it. You called to Abraham from
his land on the margins to follow you. He and three more generations
relied on you to live in a strange land. Later, you led the descendants of
Israel out of Egypt, out of bondage. You led your people with judges like
Deborah, with kings like David whose family included migrants, and with
prophets like Daniel who lived as minorities in strange lands. In all these
ways you remind us to focus our hope on your salvation rather than in an
earth-bound culture. And when it seemed that you were absent, you sent
your Only Son.

Transgressing our sense of power, your Son was born as the baby of a virgin. Tempted in the ways we still are—riches, fame, and glory—he chose
a life of humble service, service to others even while he was betrayed. He
drank the full cup of suffering. In his humiliation he was deprived of justice and tortured. Jesus suffered outside the city gate to make people holy
through his own blood.

When he died, he crossed the border of hell. Three days later God raised
him from the grave, exchanging death for life. He appeared to Mary, Mary
Magdelen, Salome, and Joanna; he walked with Celopas and another dis-
ciple on the road to Emmaus to those on the margins. Then he appeared
to Peter and the twelve. Christ, raised from the dead, presents us with
salvation.

Profession of Faith after Baptism

Sisters and brothers, I ask you to profess
together with these candidates
the faith of the Church.

Do you trust God the Father,
the force of all life,
that calls us to move and to be moved?
All: I trust him.

Do you trust God the Son,
who is with those on the move, regardless of their religion,
bringing rest to the restless and restlessness to the rested?
All: I trust him.

Do you trust the Holy Spirit,
who gives life to all the peoples of God,
given to be given away?
All: I trust him.

This is the faith of the Church.
All: This is our faith.
We trust in one God,
Father, Son, and Holy Spirit
who cannot grant us peace until there is peace for all.

Amen.

LITURGIES OF EUCHARIST

NOTE TO THE READER: Prayers of thanksgiving and intercession are tradition-ally part of the Eucharist service. You'll find a wide variety of thanksgiving prayers in Part Two, beginning on page 86. You'll find prayers of intercession in Part Two, beginning on page 91. Consider choosing a prayer from those sections to use as part of your celebration of the Eucharist.

Our Bread

Give us,
God of the earth and of the wheat fields,
our daily bread.
That bread that does not belong to us,
that bread is yours and is generous,
bread to share,
bread that becomes blessed
when it reaches each person,
when it satisfies hunger and solitude,
when it is not hoarded or hidden.
But do not give us only bread,
give us also the dignity that we are denied
in this world of ours
where walls and wars
and the cracks and ambitions
and neo-liberalisms and fundamentalisms
exclude, marginalize, condemn, expel, kill.
Give us tables where we can meet
to celebrate our human diversities.
Give us the ability to embrace, to look kindly,
give us outstretched hands and sensitive hearts,
commitment to the fullness of life.

Give us words that encourage,
actions that include,
gestures that bring hope,
songs that draw mornings
of fresh bread that is tender and just
and of glasses overflowing with the wine of equity.

Words of Institution

We had come to board the boats at last. The traffickers demanded more money although we had already paid. They decided who would board. Brother separated from brother, mother from child. We looked for the boat and there was none. A dingy that was half sunk before we climbed on board. One man would not leave the shore and he was beaten and thrown on board. No captain. No compass. Just a half-charged phone to guide and call for help . . .

All: We remember Jesus and the night he was betrayed.

After two hours the fuel was gone. After four hours we phoned the coastguard. We were not in their waters. They would not help. As the sun rose, we were desperate. Some wanted to go back but we couldn't. Others silently let go of the side of the boat and no one reached out when they were swept away. Babies cried in the center of the boat, their skins stripped by the salt and the sun.

All: Jesus took bread and broke it. "This is my body," he said, "It is broken for you."

As I share this, I remember a small girl with dark curls in a red coat, a young man with his trainers tied around his neck, and a mother trying to nurse her baby. I remember all of those we lost that night.

All: Then Jesus took a cup. This is the new wine of God. My blood poured out for you and for all people. Do this to remember me.

I stepped on to land and looked around. My friend, my brother, Mohammed, took my hand. Someone brought a blanket and gave me a bottle of water. The soldiers brought us to the camp with a high-wire fence. I am here in this country and I am alive. But every day until the end of my life I will remember the others in the boat. I will remember all the other boats. Those that have sunk and those that have not yet sailed.

All: As often as we eat this bread and drink this wine we tell of Christ's death until the new world comes.

And I will tell this story to you until the new world comes.

Bread and Coconut Water

Creator God, in whose Word darkness was shattered, in whose breath dust
became being, and in whose love bondage became liberty.
We approach your table unworthy even of the crumbs that fall beneath it.
Broken as we are, we draw nearer in faith, knowing that you have and always
will be our first Love.

In history, you have loved us into being;
you have loved us into freedom, and you have loved us even when we were
unlovable.
We praise you to no end, and give thanks now and forever . . . Amen.

Holy, Holy, Holy Lord God of hosts.
Heaven and earth are full of your glory.
Hosanna in the highest.
Blessed is he who comes in the name of the Lord.
Hosanna in the highest.

Leader:
I was hungry
Church was opened
I entered there
The "table is ready" Christ said
I have received a piece of bread
For me, it was not bread
But life itself
I was in a journey to retain my life
A black, crushed, blood-stained hand fed me

Congregation:
Amen, Lord Give us our daily bread.

Leader: God, feed the hungry.
Congregation: Lord, put us in poverty so that we share life with the poor.
Leader: Go and be the bread for the hungry.
Congregation: Lord, we only have five loaves of bread in our hands.
Leader: Bring it to the Lord's Table.

Five women bring the bread forth.

Holy Spirit, accept our offering.

Leader: Yet there are still many who thirst
Congregation: Lord, we have coconut water with us.
Leader: Bring it to the Lord's table.

Two children bring the water.

Congregation: Lord, accept our offering.

Offering Prayer

Leader holds up coconut water.

> **Leader:** Our workers shed their sweat, blood and everything for this
> fellowship.
> These are the products of their struggle.
> This bread comes from the people who slept without food.

Congregation: God of life, bless this bread and that hands that prepared it.

Leader holds up coconut water.

> **Leader:** Our farmers bring forth the coconuts, the fruits of their labor.
> They live in poverty and are themselves thirsty for emancipation.
> Through this water, we share in their tears.
> God, our everlasting fountain, bless this coconut and the hands that harvested
> them.
> May this bread and coconut water be the body of our Lord.
> **Congregation: Amen. Let it transform us also to be life for other.**

> **Leader:** In the night before he was betrayed, the Lord took bread in his hand,
> he took wine, and said . . . this is my body . . . this is my blood.
> **Congregation: Lord, by receiving your body and blood we surrender
> ourselves to your mission of salvation. Let us too be a light to others.
> Amen**
> **Christ has died, Christ has risen, Christ will come again.**

> **Leader:** God, giver of life,
> come to transform the bread and wine that was made by the worker,
> to be the holy food for your people.
> Through eating and drinking these elements,
> renew our hearts, minds and souls,
> break down the discriminate and social classes made by man
> so that we may be made one with Christ and one another.
> Help us grow up to be in the likeness of Christ,

128

let everyone who is thirsty find the water from living words,
let everyone who is hungry find in You the bread of life,
let everyone who is oppressed find comfort in You,
let everyone who is in despair find hope in Your promise.
God, giver of life,
come to sanctify the groaning creature,
let all universal will breathe what You breathe,
and be filled with Your life anew.
Through him, and with him, in him,
by the power of the Holy Spirit,
with all who stand before you on earth and in heaven,
we worship you, Father almighty in song of lasting praise:
Blessing and honor and glory and power be yours, forever and ever. Amen.

Mary Remembers Her Son

A Communion Prayer

Five bullets and a hundred lashes on my son's body;
I greet you still, *the Lord be with you.*
And also with you.
Five bullets and a hundred more they stopped his heart and cancelled
my own,
I bid you still, *lift up your hearts*:
We lift them up to God.
Five times and hundred more I ask God if it is still right to give God
thanks and praise.

They asked him, "Are you who they say you are?" He told the truth. Upon
him the anger of Rome and their obsession with their peace and their
order rained from their whips and fired from their guns. They have killed
my son.

For they have forgotten the God who has breathed upon us the breath of
Life; they have forgotten the One who gave life when they took his life
away.

On the night that my son was to be given up for betrayal, desertion, and
death, he took bread from the plate of pancit and gave it to me and said,
"Take this and eat." And then he gave me something to drink and said,
"Take this and drink. I will be going away, Mother. Somewhere you cannot follow. And when I return you will not have to work too hard and
wash other people's clothes, and our family and friends will live better
lives."

129

Breathe upon these gifts now again, O God, your breath of life so we may remember again how to live.

For as often as you eat of this bread and drink of this cup, you will remember me and all the sons who have been taken away from their mothers and wives.

For as often as you eat of this bread and drink of this cup, you will remember all the daughters who have been snatched from their homes.

For as often as you eat of this bread and drink of this cup, my son calls to you, "Please remember me," until I come again.

Remember my Son.

Songs: "Hele ng Pagtangi," by Wesley Cabansag
"No Woman No Cry," by Vincent Ford and Bob Marley

The women distribute servings of bread and pancit and buko juice to those present.

Fish and Buko Juice
The "Table" of Christ with the Peasants and Fisherfolks

The Invitation

We the Peasant community invite our mother and father, we invite our aunt, brother, and sister to celebrate in solidarity with us—the oppressed, crushed, and marginalized community. The fellowship and sharing of fish and buko juice are expressions of remembrance of the suffering Christ who died for the weak, the lowly, and the nobody to give them life, which is sufficient. Your participation and presence in this gathering are both a prayer and a commitment to the struggle of the peasants and the fisherfolks—us.

Confession, Pardon, Peace

Lord, forgive us for not giving our ears to the poor, the oppressed, and the peasants. We are self-centered. We prefer to limit ourselves in our comfort zones. We ignore the remote places. We are called to care for your sheep, yet we leave your flock here without a shepherd.

We confess our sins before you in repentance. Forgive us and renew us into the servants that are pleasing in your eyes.

In Jesus's name, we pray. Amen.

The Great Thanksgiving

The Lord of the farmers and fishermen be with you.
  And also with you.

The grace and peace of Jesus Christ who have called the fishermen to be his disciples be with us all.
  Amen.

The risen Christ is with us, in our struggle and in our resistance.
  Amen.

On the night of Jesus's betrayal,
he was with his disciples, the fishermen, sitting with them and talking with them. They were probably talking about the tax that was being imposed to them by the empire as Jesus was talking with them.

He took the bread, raised it to the heaven, thanked God. Like the fishermen who are with us today, upon raising up their nets and seeing the fishes they catch, they thank God.

Upon thanking God, Jesus broke the bread and said, "This is my body broken for you. Take and eat, do this in remembrance of me."

As we remember Jesus in the breaking of the bread, we remember the broken farmers, the fishermen who fish every day and take no fish. We remember the farmers who till the land that was being grabbed from them. We remember the broken farmers and fisherfolks every time we have fish and rice on our tables.

After receiving the supper, Jesus took the cup, like this buko juice. Raised it up to heaven, thanked God, and said, "This is my blood, shed for you all for the forgiveness of sins, drink all of you as often as you can to remember me."

Every time we drink this, let us remember . . . the sweat of the farmers and the fisherfolks.

Prayer after Receiving the Food

We have received the gifts of God from the land that was tilled by the farmers, the gifts of God from the seas where our fishermen explored; we need these blessings and gifts daily as our sustenance. May these gifts that we have received sustain us and sustain the people in the struggle in their fight for their land.

May these gifts give us courage to continue our solidarity with them. May these gifts bless us with the strength to stand with them in the midst of persecution.

We receive these gifts with the commitment of standing for, and with them, in their fight so that peace based on justice will be actualized in their community.

Eucharist of an Inclusive Table

This is the general structure of the Eucharist:

*   recounting of Christ's life

*   institution of the elements

*   humble access and invitation

The Eucharist should be inclusive, but it is often given only to those who are considered 'eligible.' What Jesus went through makes it so that all should be welcome. People need freedom to come. Christ spent time with the marginalized—he is a Christ who incarnates and comes to those with HIV, who relates to lepers, widows, children, homosexuals, and those removed from community because they are in mourning; widows and other people who are walking with death. In some places, it is believed that bad omens are passed on from people who've been in contact with death.

Here is a liturgy for the radically inclusive table:

Great Thanksgiving

God, lover of the unlovable, we give you thanks. In the fullness of time, Christ our liberator, redeemer, and sustainer came to live and be with the least of us. He lived as a child in a society where children were not recognized. He grew up and touched the untouchable, confronting the powerful. The lonely, the sick, the disabled, the widows, the orphans: these were never far from him. We give you thanks that in the same way all are invited to this table, regardless of their background, to receive your healing. Those living with HIV, those whom society deems unworthy, those without daily bread, those exploited without heed for their humanity, and those on the very edge, the periphery, of our society.

Consecration of Elements

As we lift this bread, asking you to consecrate it, bless our land to flow with milk and honey: plentiful harvest for all. As we break it, break the hearts of the empire and the chains of the oppressed. As it is shared among us, may we embrace each other's burdens in solidarity and love. As we lift this cup, we remember that our people are crushed but they are not destroyed. In this crushing, bring forth new wine representative of your blood: cleansing and bringing life of acceptance and abundance. As we share it, may we be reminded that we share the same blood: we are a family of hope connected by cords that cannot be broken.

Final Blessing and Sharing of Peace

As we have been embraced by Christ at this table, we now turn to embrace one another. The peace we have received we now freely give.

Eucharist: An Unconditional Invitation

We praise you, our God
That you have created all people in your image
Women, men, black, white, brown, and albino.

You ate and drank with prostitutes and sinners,
and spoke with strangers, the outcast, and the ritually unclean.

Thank you for your unconditional invitation and welcome
Unworthy as we all are: the gossips, the HIV+, the proud, and the sexually
    nonconforming.

We thank you that you are our staple diet—bread, cassava, umngqusho, and
    bogobe.
You bring us life, nourishment.
We thank you that you are the water of life: our umqombothi, coconut milk,
    mageu.
We thank you for the ancestral knowledge that enables us to tap into our basic
    resources.

Thank you for the Body and the Blood:
That you do not require a sacrifice,
But instead allow yourself to be broken
And share in our own brokenness.
Every day you are broken.
And your blood is spilt even as we see our life-source slipping from our hands
Because of the powers that be.
You know, you know what we are going through
Because you are going through it with us.

We give thanks, Jesus, for in the midst of suffering
You gave us a way to remember you and to become part of one another,
And have given us in this feast a foretaste of the Great Feast of your
    Kingdom.

Thanksgiving Eucharistic Prayer

God of creation, God our provider, we give you thanks for the nourishment of both our souls and bodies. We thank you that in your wisdom you have entrusted the earth into our stewardship, and have allowed the soil, from which we came, to produce fruit in abundance (food).

We confess that we have sinned against you and the earth you have entrusted us with. We have sought to recreate Eden and, in the process, we have hurt each other and all the other parts of your beautiful creation. It was through our greed that the world is divided into the few that owns so much and the many that go to bed hungry. We are afraid even to stand together at your throne and ask, "Give us our daily bread."

We thank you, dear God, for the sacrament of your very presence at the time of need. Nourish our souls and liberate us from the pangs of Capitalism and exploitation. As we partake of the Bread and Wine, make it our concern to care for and protect those who are exploited in the wine and corn farms the production of these elements with which we have the pleasure to worship you.

Eucharist Prayer

Oh! God of our ancestors, we come to you sitting around the fireplace looking at the each other in the face as our hearts are warmed with the fire from the trees of our forest, we share the shima, kapenta from our rivers and madora from our trees and amarula from our forests.
As we dip our hands into the same clay pot and pass the calabash full of rich amarula from our forest to nourish our bodies and communal bond.

We decry the exploitation and expropriation of our ancestral land.
We decry the exploitation of the labor of the poor that makes this table possible.
We are a broken community with you, symbolized by the breaking of shima.
Heal our brokenness and restore us as a community together with our ancestors, with those past, present, and still to come.
Amen!

Ideas for Eucharist as an Act of Defiance

A full meal on the table taken from the garden of the church or its people.

Churches with lands should utilize those areas for community gardens; it is owned by the community; this is an act of defiance.

Context: food brought to the table, community garden, community hall. Use the outdoors, have a table, remember the "next meal" (the Eucharist prepares the way for the next meal).

Images: widow of Zarephath, boy with his lunch, Jesus giving the scraps to the women.

A source of income and employment for community folks—priest or minister could invite others to work the land.

Ask people in the church to provide jobs for those who don't have them.

Ideas for the Order of Service

Gather everyone around the table.

Read Isaiah 55:1.

Sing a song appropriate for the day, one that embodies the theme of everyone being welcomed, such as "They'll Know We Are Christians" (first line, "We are one in the Spirit, we are one in the Lord"), by Peter Scholtes, or "Build Us a Table," by Lori True.

Say together these Words of Declaration:

We gather in defiance of separation.
We gather in defiance of domination.
**We gather in defiance of the division between the have and the
    have-nots.**

Explain the idea of sharing Eucharist in solidarity with those who are without.

Tell a spoken story from your community or another, to illustrate the idea of Eucharist as an act of solidarity and defiance.

Spend a few minutes discussing the story together.

Explain the idea of this meal as an act of defiance against hunger.

Offer a word of grace before the meal, based on the story of Jesus with fish on the shore (John 21:1-14). Or share the story of the angel instructing Elijah to eat (1 Kgs 19:1-8).

Remind everyone how Jesus invites all to eat.

Eat your meal together!

Everybody cleans up together. Any leftover food is packed up for people to take home.

Offer a benediction.

A Eucharistic Prayer Remembering the Earth

Today, Christ invites all to this table. Therefore, we remember those who are not present, those who have passed away, those who were called, those who are hungry and thirsty, those who planted and harvested the grapes and grains for our feast, those behind bars, those at work today and the unemployed, those who are ill, those who lack transportation, those who are depressed and anxious and afraid, those we exclude from our churches, those who cannot afford to be with us for whatever reason; we remember all who you call to your supper. Lord, in your mercy, hear our prayer. Amen.

Eucharist

P: The lord be with you.
C: And also with you.
P: And with those whose hands brought these gifts to us.
C: And also with them.
P: The earth is the Lord's and the fullness thereof, so we thank you, God, for your creation.
C: For your creation, thanks.
P: For you so loved the world, you gave us your Christ child; thank you god, for your salvation.
C: For your salvation, thanks.

Sanctus and Benedictus (traditional text)

P: Our story begins with a seed in the ground, watered, tended, and harvested with human hands.
C: Make us one in you.
P: The wheat is prepared for baking by the craft of human hands.
C: Make us one in you.
P: This is the bread Jesus blessed, broke, and shared.
C: Make us one in you.
P: Similarly, in the vineyard, the seed was sown, watered, tended, and harvested by human hands.
C: Make us one in you.
P: The grapes were crushed, the juice collected, by the craft of human hands.
C: Make us one in you.
P: This is the wine Jesus blessed, poured, and shared.
C: Make us one in you.
P: Take, eat, and drink in remembrance of me and those who brought me to you.

Christ had died
Christ has risen
Christ will come again

Christ was sown
Christ was reaped
Christ will nourish again

Transforming spirit, we ask your blessing upon the workers in the field and the vineyard, the laborers who prepared and brought these gifts to us and upon your community gathered here, transform these common elements, we pray.

138

We praise you, O God, it is from you that these blessings flow.
We praise you, O God, for your people.
We honor you Father, Son, and Holy Ghost.
Amen.

Song: *Commitment of the Church*

Open house that shares bread
For the long road
Open house that gives
Water of life and peace to drink
Open house that receives,
Accompanies and resists
That shares and walks
Committed to life

Open house with justice,
Peace, hope and consolation,
That walks in community
And creates spaces of love

Blessing

May life surprise you
every day with its new dawn
where hope remains present.
May love nurture your life
with what is necessary to strengthen your desire to live.
And may peace, which is the fruit of justice,
accompany you today and all the days of your life.
Amen.

Eucharistic Prayer Part 1

The Lord be with you.
> *And also with you.*
Lift up your hearts.
> *We lift them to the Lord.*
Let us give thanks to the Lord, our God.
> *It is right to give thanks and praise.*

It is very good, right, and our duty, that we should at all times and in all places give thanks unto Thee, o Lord, holy Father, almighty, everlasting God, through Jesus Christ, Thine only son, our Lord.

> But we cry to you today, our Lord. How can we praise you with joyful lips, when our sisters and brothers have died in the waves of the sea and nobody was there to save them? When their boat capsized and they could not hold on? This is why we cry out to you: Where was your mighty arm? Why did you not come and convert the souls of our enemies?

For He is the living word, through Him all things are created.

> O Lord of all creation, we cry to you. Just now, your creation is suffering bitterly. The sun is too hot, the rain is too strong, so many die, and so many lose their homes.

And we are fashioned in Thine image.

> You made us in your image, but we are not like you. All too often we think only of ourselves. We watch those in power and how they strive to destruct all impulses of love and compassion. Come, Lord, transform the people in power. We cry, hear our groaning.

Through Him Thou didst redeem us from the slavery of sin.

> So, our Lord and God, come. Come now and end all slavery. Free those who do forced labor in our days. Free us all from sin.

Giving Him to be borne by a woman.

> Lord we come to you and ask for your support and strength for all women of this earth. You know our suffering. Like Mary, we are pregnant. Like Mary, we breastfeed our children, and while doing so, we are vulnerable and more threatened than men. Our Lord, we ask: end the violence against women. Dry our tears. Give us hope.

To die on the cross.

> Lord, we cry. But in your cross, we recognize our crosses.

And rise again for us.
> So turn to us now and give us hope. Let the sun of your
> new morning rise upon us. Turn our fates. Then, with your
> angels, we will sing your praise.

Therefore, with all angels and archangels
With all the company of heaven
We laud and magnify Thy holy name
Singing and praising forevermore.

Prayer at the Preparation of the Table or Offertory Prayer

We bring bread, an offering of the ground on which we stand.
Transform it, transform us, that the ground may be enough for all.
We bring wine, an offering of the fruits of the earth that we harvest.
Transform it, transform us, that the harvest may be enough for all.
We bring money, an offering of the work of our hands and minds.
Transform it, transform us, that the work may be enough for all.
We bring ourselves, an offering of our time and identities.
Transform us, that we may be enough to transform the world.
Amen.

Body and Blood, Solidarity and Self-Giving
Words of Reflection and Invitation before Receiving the Eucharist

"This is my body . . . this is my blood . . ."

So often proclaimed.
so often heard,
under so many circumstances repeated,
so little understood.
Moving like automatons
toward a bread that seeks to be a body
toward a wine that seeks to become life,
though returning without becoming body,
fearing the sharing of life.

There is no mystery in the mystery,
even when theologies have
tried to shove away these memorable words of Jesus,
with their disturbing simplicity
and their challenging depth.

Women and men—we walk
seeking whatever magical transformation
in our individual lives;
we march in loneliness,
surrounded by deathly silence,
to encounter a dead one . . .

Perverse would be the sacrament if this were its meaning.
The master lifts the bread and invites us
to see in it his body, all that he is:
his history, the road he travelled,
his actions and his words,
his presence and his teachings,
his embraces and his promises.

To take this body implies commitment with this life,
with this Jesus, with his proposals
to build a world of justice and solidarity,
harmonious and inclusive.

142

The Nazarene takes the cup
questions the disciples—do they see his blood here,
that is, the profoundness of his giving,
the consistency of his spirituality,
the connection with a project,
life fulfilling—for all
even to the point of death by which
some wanted to snatch away such generous love.

To go to that cup,
involves us in a life fulfilling call
still to be discovered,
celebrated
shared.

Come, let us go in search of that bread, that cup,
let us go in twos,
in groups,
to a celebration,
honoring the one who lives forever,
celebrating the wideness of his liberating grace,
eating, drinking with intention,
being nurtured in body and in spirit
and then, going back to everyday life,
building community,
sharing life.

Only then bread and wine
will become sacrament.

Holy in the Wine and in the Bread

Holy, Holy, Holy,
in the wine and in the bread,
in every open table,
in solidarity.
Holy in each embrace
that heals and brings peace.

Eucharistic Prayer: Preface

God of odyssey and exodus,
we give you thanks and praise
that you are always on the move with your beloved people.
You first raised up people in Africa
and from that cradle of humanity
you have walked with us as we have wandered and settled,
migrated and been trafficked,
enslaved and been enslaved.
You have always been with us,
behind us and before us,
and there is nowhere we can be
apart from your presence.

In Jesus you came even closer,
flesh of our flesh,
bone of our bone.
And here today you offer yourself to us once again
in bread and wine,
food to restore our flagging energy,
drink to replenish our spent blood,
sustenance to keep us on the move.

One night, in an occupied land,
you took bread,
blessed it,
broke it,
and offered it to your friends saying,
"Take. Eat. This is my body, broken for you.
Do this in remembrance of me."

We do this in remembrance of you,
and in solidarity with all whose bodies are
taken, broken, used, exploited.
In penitence for the ways in which those bodies are broken for us,
for our complicity in receiving the goods they are broken to produce.

That night too, in an occupied land,
you took wine,
blessed it,
and offered it to your friends saying,
"This is my blood, poured out for you.

144

A new covenant between God and humanity.
Do this, whenever you drink it,
in remembrance of me."

We do this in remembrance of you,
and in solidarity with all whose blood is
poured out in violence, thickened with thirst,
poisoned by chemical waste and chemical war.
In penitence for the ways in which their blood is poured out for us,
for our complicity in the sacrifices of the new covenant of global
     capitalism.

Pour out your Holy Spirit now, we pray,
that these complicated and compromised gifts
of bread and wine
may become for us the pure and simple gift
of your grace.

Bread of Love: An Invitation to the Table

The Bread of love, a large table
Are waiting
The cup, the wine, and the Triune God
Who will not come?
Struggles, hardships, tiredness
Have a place here
So do dreams and hopes
They will break bread together

Equity, a just table
Bread of freedom.
In each embrace, joy
Community!
It is the celebration of people
That still want to believe
And that embrace tomorrow
Renewing their faith
Renewing their faith

Calling People to the Eucharist

Come, let us share the rice cake and coconut water (instead of bread and wine) as an expression in remembrance of the suffering Christ who died for the weak and the poor to give us a life that is abundant. The rice cake is a symbol of sustenance to our malnourished community and the coconut water is a symbol of the regeneration of life.

The night before his betrayal in the hands of the Roman Empire, Jesus took the rice cake and after blessing it, he broke it and said, "This is my body, which is given for you, do this in remembrance of me. This body is being broken for you the poor and the oppressed. My death is a solemn resistance to the unjust structure and policies of the empire to restore the weak and the hungry."

He took the cup (coconut water) and after giving thanks he said, "This is my blood poured out for you as an act of defiance to the strategy of the Empire who promotes war and bloodshed to expand their dominion over land and seas." Jesus said, "I am the victim of the Empire, they shed my blood because I proclaim good news to the poor, release the captives, recover the sight of the blind and let the oppressed free. This blood is a symbol of a new covenant that I came to renew and to reclaim the life of the poor and the oppressed."

As an act of remembrance of his death, let us celebrate through the sharing of the rice cake and coconut water with a commitment to stand against injustices done to the poorest of the poor in our community.

Prayer of Thanksgiving

Loving God, we call to mind the heavenly banquet revealed to us through Jesus, into whose life of communion we have been invited. So, before we dine and fellowship, we give thanks for your invitations and for your gifts each day. Bless the hands that cooked and prepared this meal, remembering also the hands doing the work we cannot; the hands of fishers and farmers; of those who till and harvest the land, of laborers who pack, stack and deliver; as well as the empty hands of the hungry. While we eat and drink, we count our blessings, as we receive them all in your name. Amen.

Eucharist

This piece of dry bread that I stole while my captor was looking the other way
  is my body;
take, eat.
One piece broken to be sacrificed at the altar of the global market and the
  economic interests of international corporations;
one piece broken to be sacrificed at the altar of political corruption, military
  convenience, and the war market;
one piece broken to be sacrificed at the altar of bloodthirsty religions, ethnic
  hatred, and patriarchal oppression.

This cup of saltwater in which I was drowned, is the new covenant in my
  blood.
Do this as often as you drink it, in remembrance of me.
For as often as you eat this bread and drink this cup, you proclaim the Lord's
  death until he comes again.

Sacred Heart
See page 244 to read *A Secret Whispered*, which inspired this artwork.

PART FOUR

NEW AND ADAPTED PSALMS

NEW AND ADAPTED PSALMS

A Psalm of Praise

Jesus
Lord God
I adore you!
You are my shepherd
Taking care of all my wants
You allow me the pleasure
Of seeing yet another day
I praise you
Almighty God
Jehovah!
And in the midst of all you are
I pray that you guide me
O Lord, my homie, my friend.

You, O God, are the only one
On whom I can depend
You first loved me
And you love me still
You sent your son to die
For me;
You are awesome!

I lift my eyes to the hills
I look across the alleys
And you are there
To help me
You are merciful

My rock, my physician
You are my healer
Even in the moments of my craziness
I thank you, Lord
For you are a constant help in times of trouble
My protector, always there.

The sun shines by day
The moon by night;
The birds sing
And even the trees clap their hands.
You created us, O God!
Living, laughing, loving
You are our warmth when it is cold
O Breath of God
You are our hope!

We see you
As the grasses push through broken sidewalks
As dormant seeds awake
To become new plants
You even use the cold air
To kill diseases that harm
And design the ice
To create images of beauty
You surround us with other people
To remind us that we are not alone
Even as the rain pours down
You wash the air.

You bring us peace
Feeding us when we are hungry
Inner peace
That helps us draw others to you.
You clothe us even when
We cannot clothe ourselves
You keep us warm
You are our personal banker
Never running out of
Your grace.
I thank you, Jesus, for saving my soul.
I thank you, Jesus, for taking the stripes for me.
I thank you, Jesus, for keeping my enemies at bay.
I thank you, Jesus, for being my jawn.
And I praise you for your holy name!

Psalm 64

God, protect us,
we are your Family
and we need your protection.
We ask for justice,
we demand justice.
May your kingdom of love and peace surround us.

Dear Lord, Shepherd

Dear Lord, Shepherd
for everyone in your
creation, help us in this moment of crisis.
We hope that the leaders
of our world can
recognize the fear and
sadness of those who
suffer in Central America
and Mexico for reasons of
poverty, crime, and
the violence. Help us all focus on
those places where hope is lacking.
Why do we not do more to help areas of suffering?
Why do we ignore them?
Why do we avoid the reality
of the problems in
these countries today?
Help us, so that we might finally
be able to focus on
the places that are suffering
and need the most.
The US border misses the
mark.
With your strength and
wisdom, help us
to solve these
large wounds of the
real world.
Amen.

I Cry to You

God, from the ruins of my house in Aleppo, I cry to you:
My God, my God, why have you forsaken me? Why are you so far from helping me, from the words of my groaning? O my God, I cry by day, but you do not answer; I cry by night, but find no rest.

God, from a packed boat on the rough sea, I cry to you:
But I am a worm and not human, scorned by others and despised by the people. All who see me mock me; they make mouths at me, they shake their heads, "Commit your cause to your God, let him deliver—let him rescue the one in whom he delights!"

God, from the 'Hot Spot' in Lampedusa, I cry to you:
I am poured out like water, and all my bones are out of joint; my heart is like wax, it is melted within my breast; my mouth is tied up like a potsherd, and my tongue sticks to my jaws; you lay me in the dust of death.

Amen.

Lord, Have Mercy
Psalm 23

Jesus, you are the shepherd of us all. I pray that those who need you in this moment would not be found lacking. You lead them to calm waters, infusing them with new strength. You guide them on the path of justice for the sake of your name.

Although they pass through difficult and dark trials caused by evil forces, may they not be afraid because you are at their side and with them.

It is you who supplies all their needs, laying out a banquet for them, even when surrounded by their enemies, anointing them, continuing to fill them with your Holy Spirit so that they can know that your kindness and love follow them all the days of their lives, and in the house of Jehovah the Lord, they will live every day now and forever.

Psalm 10

Why in our suffering, are you, O Lord, so far away?
Why don't we hear your voice?
Why don't we feel your presence?
You say to love our neighbors as much as we love ourselves.
But Lord, all we see is hatred, envy, and violence every day.
You promised to protect, provide, and preserve
But we are defenseless against greed, deceit, and death.
Have you covered your face?
Have you turned away your eyes and blocked your ears?

Arise in us
As the voice of justice, truth, liberation, and transformation
Give power to our voice speaking with the oppressed
Give strength to our fight when we stand for justice
Make us fathers to the fatherless
Make us mothers to the motherless
Make us advocates to the poor and outcast
Make us passionate friends and caretakers of creation
So that together we can build a community
Where love's power overcomes all violence against your creation.

Lament of the Sea

Psalm 98:7

Leader: They abused me, enjoyed my waters and later I realized it was a profane violation.
People: Let the sea roar in its fullness!
Leader: I offered you the fruits of my belly, you canned them for your pleasure, you spit on me as if discarding your disposable containers.
People: Let the sea roar in its fullness!
Leader: Little by little they are killing me, between ships they fight for my generosity, the gifts that God gives me: they steal them with blatant irresponsibility.
People: Let the sea roar in its fullness!
Leader: I rage, I cry, I claw . . . I long for the well-being of your people, my God, sitting next to the rivers of "Babylon."
All: Let the sea roar in its fullness! We roar for Liberation. Amen

Anti-Psalm 137

Next to the rivers of Babylon,
there we played on the ground and laughed,
always longing for the park.
On the trees, in the middle of the square,
we climbed, singing.
And those who had wanted us as slaves, wanted to silence our songs;
those who wanted to desolate us, prevented our happiness, saying:
"Shut up! Stop laughing: You are forbidden to sing!"

Oh how we sang children's songs to Jah,
both in our own lands and in foreign ones!
I always forget everything, when playing,
my legs get tired from jumping.
My mouth gets dry from screaming,
with so much playing;
I laugh with delight
because joy is the most important thing.

Jah, forget about the evil adults
when in between our games they shouted:
"Do not play anymore, do not play anymore.
Go to work!"

Inheritance of Babylon, failed,
a curse for anyone who wants revenge
for what you did to us.
Blessed is the one who takes your children
and invites them to play!

Psalm 72:1-4

Mother and Father, grant your justice to your people,
open your eyes to those who refuse
to see reality, the harsh reality.
Let us be people of solidarity
with all creation
and with those who have been impoverished.

Psalm 150 in Jamaica

Praise Jah in your sacred place;
Praise Jah in the infinity of his Rasta-Kingdom.

Praise Jah for the art that we are in his hands,
Praise Jah according to his powerful smallness.

Praise Jah to the sound of drums
Praise Jah with *boleros* and *jarana*.

Praise Jah with bongos, charango, and reggae,
Praise Jah with treble and *caracol*.

Praise Jah with Peruvian drums,
Praise Jah with *caracoles* that brighten the dance.

Everything that is life praises Jah.
Alelu-Jah

Mountains of Justice

Mountains of justice,
Hills of freedom,
Your people call today, your people cry today.

From Our Days in Sicili

Psalm 103:1-4

Out of the wounds that violent
people inflicted on Jesus
     —we are healed.
Out of the wounds inflicted
    on Jesus's sisters and brothers,
so, our sisters and brothers,
    our world is beginning
    to heal
        the division of peoples,
           cultures,
           and religions.

There seems to lie a blessing
on this little town, flowing
    out from the Casa della Culture,
where strangers have already
become family. All living their
different religions and non-religions
while being bound together by a love
that seems to be larger than
any religion or worldview.

We were blessed as we were immersed
in the life of this town, next
to the sin that brought death
and joy.
    Sun over the ruins of churches
    Inspired hills . . . total peace.
"Let my whole being bless the LORD,
    Let everything inside of me bless his holy name!

Let my whole being bless the LORD,
    and never forget all his good deeds:
    how God forgives all your sins,
    heals all your sickness,
    saves your life from the pit,
    crowns you with faithful love and compassion."

Hymn: "Praise to the Lord, the Almighty, the King of Creation,"
    by Joachim Neander

New and Adapted Psalms

God of the Earth

God of the earth, of heaven and of all that we see around us,
allow us to learn to live with one another, together with creation
and may the peace that is the fruit of justice be a reality for every corner
of the earth.
Give us strength, faith, and hope because until justice and peace meet with a kiss,
we will continue plowing our fields awaiting new fruits of the earth
and new dawns.

Psalm 23 #1

The Lord is my shepherd, I shall not want.
But I do Lord; I want to be safe,
I want to be heard, I want to cry.
All these are wants, but the Lord is my shepherd; I shall not want.
I want safety, health care. But where do I go to fix a broken heart?

I have no money, for I left everything behind.
All I have is in this plastic baggie, a paper, and a photo.
But the Lord is my shepherd, I shall not want.
I'm in the valley, Lord, and this sun hurts my skin.
Kiss me Lord and quench my thirst. I want water, I want strength,
I want shade. Yet you remind me that you are my shepherd and
I shall not want.

If I cannot want anything or anyone else, I want you Lord.
You are my shepherd and I shall not want.
And I am your sheep, your sheep wanting again.

A Psalm of Lament

My God, my God, why have you forsaken us?
We are assaulted by indignities
We are denied our basic rights
We watch people who flaunt their wealth
While we find no relief from our hunger
We're sick and tired of being sick and tired
Sometimes it seems even you, Jah, have abandoned us

Bryce Farmers Psalm 121— A Song of Ascents

I lift up my eyes to the green Jamaican hills.
From where does our produce come?
It comes from us—God's proud Jamaican farmers,
who toil, till, and sow God's beautiful, bountiful earth.

We will not let our faith be moved,
we who keep each other in constancy,
we who keep each other,
we will praise our land and our lord together always.

We are each other's cheerful keeper.
We are the seeds and the machete in each other's hands.
The market will not ruin us by day
nor the thieves who steal crops by night.

We will keep each other through empire.
We will keep each other's life and laughter.
We will keep each other's plantings and harvests,
from now on and forevermore.

Be Still

Be still, the noise is frightening, confusing, disturbing.
Hush, here I am—your God, you'll find me in the questions.

The indifference of the pious breeds a deafening silence.
Hush, here I am—your God, you'll find me in the noise.

The evil one has set his foot upon me.
Hush, here I am—your God, you'll find me in the pain.

We cry out to you, the One who says:
Hush, here I am, your God, you'll find me in the joy of my people.
Amen.

Psalm 37

Cry out with indignation against
the evildoers who violate the Earth.
Raise your voices in favor of
dignified housing through Kingston.

Wail with the mothers who saw their
sons die at the hand of the state.
Cry with the children who lost their parents.
Walk with the widows who bear the
weight of many journeys.
Revolt alongside the youth who've lost hope.

May peace and justice fall upon us
as abundant rain.
Give your way to Love,
Trust Him and He will do the rest.

Trenchtown Psalm

Praise God in the ghetto
Sing songs of hope in the slums
The mountains and seas are
Littered with trash
Still your love shines through
Pollutions contaminates farms and
Neighborhoods
Still your love shines through
Crime: violence knows no bounds
Still your love shines through
Help us, O God, to transform this
Dirty and dangerous world into a
Sanctuary of your glory

An Interpretation of Psalm 26

O God come to my help
Take a look at me
Test my heart and my mind
Your love is in front of me
I walk to you

I sit not in politicians' chairs
I shoot no guns with gangs and police
I wash my hands in innocence
And go around your altar, O Lord
Singing to you songs of thanksgiving
And telling everyone what you do

God shelter me from the violent
Keep me free from gangs and police—
Those in whose hands are guns
And whose hearts are full of corruption

As for me, they will not take my integrity
I am your beloved
My god, my god, my foot stands
On level grounds

In the streets I will shout for your justice
We bless your name!

Psalm 27:1-4

The Lord is my light in the darkness of the desert;
Should I fear Mexican agents or ICE agents?
The Lord hold me and protect my life through the hard migration;
What should I fear as I travel?

When evil does assault me to devour my flesh, my adversaries and immigration agents, they shall stumble and fall and I shall be free.
My heart shall not fear; though those who hate immigrants rise up against me yet, I will be confident.

One thing I asked of the Lord, to keep me alive to make it to the US to be able to do work and provide for my family so that they do not die of hunger. Then when my time is done here on earth, I will seek to live in the house of the Lord.

Give All of Yourself

Place your love for God in your voice,
place your trust in God in humanity,
that we will stand in solidarity with our brothers, sisters, and
nonbinary siblings experiencing those injustices.

Give your feelings of security in God to those being ripped from their homes
and give them a home through your actions.

Do not remain still, silent, complacent.
Give all of yourself to them as you do God, not only your 'thoughts
and prayers' but also your action.

You Are My Shepherd

Lord,
You are my shepherd and I want. I seek the green pastures and still waters
of El Norte. Will you walk with me there? Will you show me the paths in
your name? Will you run with us on the night journey? Will you shepherd
us to the safe passage? Will there be smiling faces to greet us? What space
in the darkness will give us beds, food, and be a home?

Salmos 64

Dios, Proteganos,
Somos tu Familia
Y necesitamos tu proteccion.
Pedimos justiciar,
Demandamos justiciar.
Que tu reino de amor y pas nos envuleva

Psalm 46:1-7

For the Mariachis of the Sons of Latin America

God is our refuge and strength,
An ever-present spring in the desert.
Therefore, we will not fear,
though la migra comes this way.
And the mountains close in as we
try to walk between them,
though the sandstorms seek to carry us away
and these mountains resemble a fridge.

There is a river separating us from the city of God,
the land of the promise where peace dwells.

God, are you even there?
Will you help us at the breakage of day?
This nation is in uproar, will its kingdom fall?
If God lifts His voice, will the injustice melt away?

Dios es grande, God be our fortress.

Psalm 23 #2

The Lord is my Shepherd, I shall not want.
He gives me rest in the desert,
he leads me by the waters of the Rio Grande,
he restores my tired Soul.
He leads me through safe passages,
for his name's sake.

Even though I must live in the shadows,
even though I often face death,
I will fear no evil,
for you are with me.
Your words of hope and healing hands,
they comfort me.

You prepare a place for me,
here in a land that is not my own
in front of those who do not want me here,
and you bless me.

My heart overflows.
Do not forget me.
Do not forget your goodness and mercy.

May I dwell in your house, Oh Lord,
in your land, in your presence.
A place where there is no fear, no persecution,
no borders.
For all my life.

Do Not Turn Away

Do not turn away from the cry of your people,
the people who seek the blessings of liberty to ourselves and our posterity.
See the injustice against humanity.
The dehumanization, the crushing of the human spirit, the division of humans
out of fear and selfishness.
You hear our distress. You feel our anxiety.
Let our voices be heard and our message spread.
That humanity is one and we, all the people, are all your people, God.

Psalm 4

Answer, O righteous God, to the call of immigrants.
Give them relief from persecution;
have mercy on them and hear their prayers from prisons, detention centers,
houses.

How Long will the US government turn your love into hate?
How long will the church be quiet, seeking comfort?
May they know that the Lord sets the immigrants apart and hears their cries.

Be faithful in your churches, and when you raise your hands to praise, use
those hands to offer help.

Many seek prosperity, even if others have to starve, or be naked, or have no
place to spend the night.
If the light of your face is shining on God's people, why are immigrants not
seeing the light?

The grain and wine abound, let us share with hearts full of joy.
May the immigrants lie down and sleep in peace.
May they dwell in safety with you, Lord.

Psalm 23 #3

The Lord is my Shepherd,
I still want so much.

I want for the millions who deserve better than to be targeted for deportation.
They have already walked through the valley of the shadow of death,
Must they see more evil at the hands of those who scare them, who know better,
who yell?

Those with power and comfort and position,
Let there be peace for those who suffer and live in our very land.
Lord, may thy rod and staff guide us to safe pastures, rather than be used to
    beat us.
Guide our people toward justice and wellbeing.
Have mercy, dear Lord, comfort my people.

That I may dwell in your house,
MY house,
All my days and all my life.

Prayer for the Sacred

Prayer for the spirit of light to enter the hearts of those acting on behalf
    of the state.
Prayer for the spirit of light to enter the hearts of the ICE agents.
Prayer for the spirit of light to enter the hearts of the judges.
Prayer for peace, bravery, into hearts of migrants living in fear.
Prayer for the spirit of hope and solidarity for communities who stand
    between ICE and the people.

People for the people.
Peace for the people—the children who will see their parents and aunts and
    uncles and sisters and brothers get ripped away and locked up.

Psalm 63

O God, you are my God, the God of immigrants.
We earnestly search for you,
at the same time ICE searches for their lives.
My soul thirsts for you;
my whole body longs for you in this parched and weary land where there is
     no water.
How long will they persecute those who just want to give immigrants water?
I have seen you in your sanctuary cities and gazed upon your power and glory,
more powerful and glorious than the governments that rise up against us.

Your unfailing love is better than life itself, how they, the immigrants,
     praise you!
So they will bless you as long as they live;
they will lift up their hands and call on your name.
Their souls are satisfied as with a rich feast;
and their mouths praise you with joyful lips.
They think of you while on their beds,
and meditate on you in the watches of the night;
for you have been my help,
and in the shadow of your wings, they sing for joy.
Their souls cling to you;
Your right hand upholds them.

But for those who seek to destroy their lives, they shall go down
     into the depths of the earth;
they shall be given over to the power of their own semi-automatic weapons.
They shall be prey to the desert animals.
But the immigrant shall rejoice in God;
all who swear by him shall exult,
for the mouths of liars will be stopped.

A Migrant Psalm of Lament

God, why have you abandoned us?
Why do our communities fear us?
Why are our homelands continually destroyed by poverty, racism, and
    natural disasters?

Remember us, your Latino and Latina children,
those you have created for life, for love
but who are continuing to encounter hate.
Remember how you have dwelled in our beautiful islands, mountains, and
    forests.
Acknowledge that dwelling.
March to the border where so many are suffering;
to the Desert and Rio Grande where so many have died.
To the detention centers where many are suffering abuse;
to their own pillaged and ravaged lands.

How long will the migrants go unheard?
Are our enemies going to abuse your children forever?
Why do you pull your hand away from them?
Why don't you hold your sick and dying to your chest?
How long God?

A Psalm for the Silenced People

Bendito padre sant de cielo y tierra, padre mió . . . Abba.
Hear the unspoken prayers of an oppressed people . . .
For their voice has been silenced; the sound of their words has been blocked
    from the minds of a stiff-necked nation . . .
Their trauma travels on a frequency so low the ears of
    humanity cannot discern a sound.
Hear us . . .
Respond to us . . .
Find us . . .
    lord help, us!
    Amen.

In the Presence of Our Enemies

Oh God, the longer I live the harder, but more necessary,
    it has become to beg you,
to constantly be in prayer and conversation with you.
The hearts of our "leaders" have been consumed by power, greed, pride,
    and sin.

Strike them, Lord, with a bolt of love,
soften their hearts, Lord.
Jesus, Father, Mother, Owner, Master, Friend, Magic Maker,
please protect the children, your children.
Don't let their faith become weak,
in the darkness, let them shine your light, the light of Christ.

If we are your sheep, if that is true,
then, Lord, lead us to still waters.
If we are welcomed in your house, at your table,
Lord, prepare a feast before us,
IN THE PRESENCE of our enemies.

They want to destroy us.
Starve us.
Rape us.

Lord forgive your fallen children,
We have sinned before you.

Come Jesus, come.

Psalm 27:1-14

The Lord is my light and salvation, whom shall I fear? The Lord is the stronghold of my life, of whom shall I be afraid? When the wicked advance against me to devour me, it is my enemies and my foes who will stumble and fall. My heart says of you, "Seek his face!" Your face, Lord, I will seek. Do not turn your servant away in anger; you have been my helper. Do not reject me or forsake me, God my savior. Do not turn me over to the desire of my foes, for false witnesses rise up against me, spouting malicious accusations.

Psalm for the Undocumented

If you are undocumented,
how would you pray?

Lord Jesus, have mercy;
we just want peace, running, escaping
away from violence, from death.

The US is the best place, a secure
place to enjoy life without fears,
without intimidation.

We, oh Lord Jesus, are looking
for your guidance, please open your
doors to safety, peace, love, joy.

Lord Jesus, have mercy on us,
you know how insignificant, weak,
ignorant we are, in front of you.
Give us hope, show yourself.
Speak Lord, for we your servants
are waiting to listen and
follow you to any frontier,
country, desert.

Almighty Father, creator of all
of us, don't take too long to
show us your way, your
truth, your life.
Amen.

Psalm 91

They that dwell in despair and who will not be protected by the Shadow of the
    Almighty. . .
Where is their shelter? Where is their hope? In whom can they trust? No one
    will weep for them. We live our lives and do our work.

Señor Ten Piedad #1

Salmo 23

Jesus eres el pastor de todo nosotros, pido por que no les falta a todos los necesitan en este momento. Los conduces a aguas tranquilas, los infundes dándole nuevas fuerzas. Los guías por senda de justicia por amor a tu nombre.

Así están pasando por ralles difíciles y tenebrosos llevados de fuerzas y que no tengan temor porque tu estas a su lado y con ellos.

Eres tu que suples todas sus necesidades, poniendo un banquete, aun rodeados por sus enemigos, los unges, los continuas llenando de tu Espíritu Santo que puedan conocerte la bondad y el amor los siga todos los días de su vida y en la casa de Jehová del Señor habiten todos los días y para siempre.

The Lord Is My Shepherd

The Lord is my shepherd.
God is the presence who accompanies me,
what shall I want?
We know that you provide abundance
and we want,
in the dark of the night, as we cross deserts, as we seek to find shelter,
a friendly face, and to make a home.

You make me lie down in far pastures, or by still waters,
when everything around me looks like dry ground and the heat beats
me down, with you by my side I see ahead the far pasture, the still
waters that will heal me, that will satisfy me.

As though I walk through the shadow of death I shall fear no evil.
I shall not fear, I shall cry out and shall hope, I shall pursue in my tiredness and so through the hardest of accusations, resolute that some hope
with you by my side, I'll make it through the other side of this valley of
death, for you are with me. The dry sand and the heat beat me down.

Querido Señor

Querido Señor, pastor
para todos en su
creación, ayúdenos en este momento de crisis.
Esperamos que los lideres
de nuestro mundo puedan
reconocer el miedo y la
tristeza de los que
sufren en América central
y México por razones de
la pobreza, el crimen, y
la violencia. Ayúdenos que todos puedan enfocar en
esos lugares donde le falta la esperanza. ¿Por qué
no hacemos más para ayuden las zonas de sufrimiento?
¿Por qué ignoramos? ¿Por
qué evitamos la realidad
de los problemas en
estos países hoy en día?
Ayúdenos que, por fin,
sea posible enfocar en
los lugares donde hay el
más sufrimiento y la
necesidad. La frontera
estadounidense pierde la
meta.
Con su fortaleza y su
sabiduría, ayúdenos
para resolver estas
heridas grandes del
mundo actual.
Amen.

Psalm 119:49-55

Remember your word to our helpless,
    for you have promised them hope.
Our comfort in their suffering is this:
    you promise to protect their lives.
Our arrogant president mocks us all
without any compassion.

But we continue to trust in your words.
One remembers how you worked in ancient
times and our people find peace in them.
Indignation grips each one of us because
the wicked are overcoming us,
it is _____ who have forgotten
your laws.

Your laws are the theme of our
sorrow song, wherever we sleep.

Psalm 40:11

Do not, O Lord, withhold your
mercy from your people.
Let your steadfast love and
your faithfulness keep your migrants safe forever.

For evils have encompassed them without number;
our iniquities have overtaken us,
until we cannot see;
they are more than the hairs of
my head
and our hearts fail us.

Be pleased, O Lord, to deliver your migrants;
O Lord, make haste to help us.
Let all those be put to shame and
confusion, those who seek to snatch
away our lives.

Let those be turned back and brought
to dishonor who desire to hurt us.
But may all who seek you
rejoice and be glad in you,
saying continually, "Great is
the Lord!"

As for us migrants, we are poor and needy,
but the Lord takes thought for us.
You are our help and our deliverer;
DO NOT DELAY, O MY GOD.

Psalm 42:1-5

As a deer longs for flowing streams, so I long for water as I traverse this dry, hot desert.

O God, can you quench my thirst?

I long for rivers of living waters; when will I see your face?

My tears have filled my cup, day and night, as my hearts mocks me continually.

Where is God?

I remember when the dream was ignited and when the vision came clear, and next, I sing songs of thanksgiving.

O my soul and mind, today don't give up—don't lose hope. Hope in God—he will help.

Psalm 46

"God is our refuge," they say as they created policies of ever-present trouble for those that have no refuge.

Policies that only cause fear for those that cross the mountains, the deserts, and the rivers, searching for refuge.

They are told through cinema and radio that across the river is the city of God! And indeed, this is the message the policymakers present as they lead the 'opportunities of big business and commerce.' They claim that God is with them, for under their proclamation of the Lord, nations are in an uproar, kingdoms fall, and the earth melts. For whom is God a refuge? For those who die in the river? Or for those who invoke the Lord's name as they intervene elsewhere and shoot bullets into the rivers as people cross . . . ?

God is whose refuge? Must it be this way?

Is this truly God whom they invoke?

Deep Calls to Deep

Psalm 42

Why are you cast down, o my soul? Hope in God. For I shall again sing praises to the God of my life.

These things I remember as I pour out my soul . . .

The flame of bougainvillea and the smell of earth after heavy evening rain.
Watching football with my friends in the Sports Café,
Going to school—before the soldiers came.

Why are you cast down, o my soul? Hope in God. For I shall again sing praises to the God of my life.

Your torrents roar. All your waves and billows break over me. Deep calls to deep. Shore calls to shore . . .

My skin burns with salt and sun and tears,
without water, without fuel, without signal,
my cracked lips cry; a prayer to the God of my life.

Why are you cast down, o my soul? Hope in God. For I shall again sing praises to the God of my life.

Why should I go about in mourning because of the oppression of my enemies . . . ?

The swearing traffickers and the stone-faced soldiers will not have power over me.
Against the force of Empire I cross this border.
I tell out my story to those who will listen.

Why are you cast down, o my soul? Hope in God. For I shall again sing praises to the God of my life.

Psalm 13

How long, JHWH, will you forget me,
locked up as a dog in putrid prisons,
between piss and sweat,
beatings and horror?
Will you forget me forever?

How long will you hide your face from me?
My tormentors search me,
strip me of my dignity,
deprive me of my poor possessions,
constrain me to do forced labor.

How long must I bear pain in my soul
and have sorrow in my heart all day long?
The waters fill the rubber boat
and our tears add up to them;
despair is all around me.

Look at me, JHWH, my God!
Give light to my eyes,
or I will sleep the sleep of death,
swallowed up by sea waters and tears.

Answer me, JHWH, my God!
That these waters shall not erase the memory of me
and shout out saying: "We have prevailed."

But I trusted in your steadfast love;
a vision of rescue, closer and closer
and I see your love in the faces of these
as pale as ghosts.

My heart shall rejoice in your salvation
that you are granting me,
through these fishers of men, and women, and children
they are catching me gently
and I will sing to JHWH
because JHWH has dealt bountifully with me.

Psalm 23 #4

For a healing liturgy, turn the words of the Psalm into verbs.

Shepherd us
Make us lie down in green pastures;
lead me beside still waters;
restore my soul.
Lead me in right paths,
protect us,
walk with us through the valley of death.
Bring down the empire,
comfort me.
Prepare a table before me in the presence of my enemies,
anoint my head with oil;
you who are goodness and mercy be with us, be with us all the days
I will dwell in the house of the Lord,
    my whole life long.

Mourning
See page 220 to read *On Mourning*, which inspired this artwork.

PART FIVE

TOPICAL PRAYERS AND GENERAL PRAYERS

ANGER

Anger and Mourning and Confronting Power, Waiting for Too Long
A Prayer of Confrontation

> God's son shot dead at Tivoli
> God's blood spilled on the floor
> God's daughter mourns
> In the shadow of wicked Babylon
> Her child weeps no more
>
> Jesus? It is just us!
> Jesus? It is just us!
> Just us? We rise up!
> Just us? We rise Up!

God of the Sea?

> Oh, Almighty God, do you even hear?
> When the waves are crashing, are you ever near?
>
> What's your problem?! Are you insane?
> You really sent a storm when Jonah ran away?
>
> And when he went into the roaring sea,
> did you really send a whale and can't you see. . .
>
> Those sailing away from their own fiery hell?
> Don't you have the time to save them as well?
>
> Why should any have faith in YOU when you've lost faith in yourself?
> If you can't make up your mind, then you can go to hell!

For Easter

Call: Our children are crushed by the weight of the cross.
Response: Alleluia, rise us up.
Call: The rich love highways more than us.
Response: Alleluia, rise us up.
Call: Satan lurks at every turn.
Response: Alleluia, rise us up.
Call: Seeking glory, he might devour.
Response: Alleluia, rise us up.
Call: From the dust, give us breath.
Response: Alleluia, rise us up.
Call: From the guns, make way for peace.

How Long, Great God?

God I am angry, vexed because of the insensitivity, indifference, injustice, insults, and insurrections against your people and against you.

How long, great God? How long will you allow evil to override your good? You hold the whole world in your hands and yet it feels as if you have abandoned me.

I remember when you were once there, now I wonder if you are even near. You once heard my cry, now I wonder if my cries have fallen on deaf ears.

Forgive me, Great God, I am hurting
but I believe in your time, you will answer,
you will come to my help,
restore justice,
cause wars to cease,
heighten sensitivity.
Replace my anger with your peace.
Amen.

Praying with the Cry of the Earth

Call:
> "Let the sea and everything in it roar;
>> the world and all its inhabitants too.
>
> Let all the rivers clap their hands" (Ps 98:7-8a).

Response:
> **Yes, but,**
> **Why do you destroy my oceans with plastic**
>> **and filth?**
>
> **Why have you killed the plant life of the oceans**
>> **with nuclear waste?**
>
> **Why do you praise me with empty gestures**
>> **when you show no respect for my creation?**
>
> **And now**
> **I am sending your children to teach you**
>> **to take seriously climate change so that you**
>> **may be changed.**

Call:
> "Praise the LORD from the earth,
>> you sea monsters and all you ocean depths!
>
> Do the same, fire and hail, snow and smoke,
>> stormy wind that does what God says!
>
> Do the same, you mountains, every single hill,
>> fruit trees, and every single cedar!
>
> Do the same, you animals—wild or tame—
>> you creatures that creep along and you birds
>> that fly!" (Ps 148:7-10).

Response:
> **Yes, but**
> **why do you kill my animals—**
> **birds of the air and fish of the sea,**
>> **for the pure hell of it?**
>
> **Do you think you have the right to dominate**
>> **my creation?**
>
> **"My people, what did I ever do to you?" (Mic 6:3).**
> **Why do you burn and destroy what I have given you**
>> **for protection?**

183

When the Sea Gives Up Its Dead

"The sea gave up the dead that were in it; and Death and the Grave gave up the dead that were in them, and people were judged by what they had done" (Rev 20:13).

When the Mediterranean gives up its dead, O Lord, how shall we be judged?

When the Mediterranean gives up the young, brimming with hope, longing for peace, yearning for a new life, how shall we be judged?

When the Mediterranean gives up the women who had travelled long roads, protecting their children from empire's terror, how will we be judged?

When the Mediterranean gives up the ignored and forsaken, those set adrift by capitalism's traffickers, left to drown by Europe's indifference, how will we be judged?

When the Mediterranean gives up its dead, Lord, how will they judge us?

Prayer of Rage from Tivoli Gardens

Why does your justice take so long?
"If you had been here, my brother wouldn't have died" (John 11:21).
The wounds of the bullets still bleed in my body.
"Why do you strike me?" (John 18:23).
They tortured my people before my eyes . . .
"If you had been here, my brother wouldn't have died."
They burned our houses, they broke our things, they broke our lives . . .
"Why do you strike me?"
From a roof, they pelted the morning.
"If you had been here, my brother wouldn't have died."
They did not believe our words and mocked the denunciation,
"Why do you strike me?"
And despite everything, we want to believe in you:
"I am the resurrection and the life. Whoever believes in me will live, even though they die" (John 11:25).

Prayer of Anger and Confrontation

They ask us to sing songs
In the strange land of undignified life
But we are already tired
Of waiting and waiting for unfulfilled promises

We will hang our harps on the trees!
We will not sing anymore! No more praises!
Our worship of God will be on strike!

Until your justice manifests
Until we see your life's will
Touching our pains
And healing our wounds
Embracing our forgotten soil
And restoring broken hopes
Guitars and drums will not sound
And our mouths will be silent!

Until the song of Mary is fulfilled
Until the Spirit of God renews creation
Until the loving power of the creative force
Fully establishes the inclusive project
From the Nazarene traveler, God, a supportive friend
Until that day, may it come!

We will not celebrate, we will not have services
We will not sing praises . . . We will strike!
—From Psalm 137:3-4; Psalm 137:2; Luke 1:51-55

Cleanse Me from My Anger

My Lord, my God, when I look around me and see the injustices of life,
my blood boils. The rich are getting richer, the poor are getting poorer, the
powerful are oppressing the powerless, and the voiceless are being lost in
the crowd with no one to put their cause into word, not even the church.
The tons of garbage that litter our beaches, roadsides, and street corners;
the damage of the environment when we pollute our watercourses, the air,
and the land; all these make me angry! To see what your people have done
to the beautiful world you have created.

Help me Lord to surrender the anger I feel to your gentle caring love.
Touch me with your spirit and cleanse me from my anger. Amen.

Love?

Love the one who spits their hatred in the face of their neighbors?
Love the one who kills the dreams of boys and girls?
Love the one who exploits the worker and keeps their wages?
Love the xenophobe, the homophobic, the Nazi?
Are you asking us, Jesus?

Love the one who yesterday tortured us and who today represses us?
Love the one who always decrees in favor of the rich?
Love the one who takes medicine from the sick?
Love the one who laughs at the pain of their neighbors?
How do you think that is possible, Jesus?

Love the one who persecutes those who stand in solidarity?
Love the one who imprisons their adversaries?
Love the one who preaches alienating gospels?
Love the one who snatches away the life of another human being?
Just like that? Only love?

Yes, love, love, and love again.
Because love drives us to seek justice.
Because love casts out the fear that makes us cowards.
Because love guides those who work for the end of oppression.
Because love paves the way to fulfillment.
Because love unites those who want to be faithful to God.

Because love unmasks the violent,
the perverse, the murderers, the hypocrites,
the stalkers, the liars, the concealers,
those who profit from the suffering of others,
those who are insensitive to the pain of others.

Loving exposes them, unmasks them, exposes them.
Love sheds light on their miserable lives.
Love, it condemns them and liberates us.
Or maybe it gives them the chance of redemption...
but that will be God's task.

—Trying to unravel Luke 6:27-38

186

Cursed Be the One

Cursed be the one who shoots another randomly.
Cursed be the one who cheats and steals from the poor in order to have more
    for themselves.
Cursed be those who abuse or traffic children.
Woe unto those men who impregnate women recklessly.
Woe to those who bribe others to fill their bank accounts.

Where Are You, God?

Where are you God?
Over and over it is the same.
I am tired of the prayers, comforting words,
which accomplish nothing.
I am in despair.

Seek first the Kingdom of God.
I am tired of seeking and getting nothing in return.
I help those in need when I'm called, but I am empty.

A young man thirty-eight years old was wrongfully accused of rape
and murdered and killed in broad daylight.
Where are you, God?
Women trying to get out of poverty.
Where are you, God?
I am faithful, I am obedient,
yet I continue to be placed on the lower wage scale.
Where are you, God?
The children suffering from emotional injury.
Where are you, God?
Elderly suffering for care.
Where are you, God?
Church is blind to what's happening to us.
Where are you, God?
A teenage girl was raped and burned.
Where are you, God?
Economic injustice, political parties
that pit us against each other.
Where are you, God?
Where are you, God!?

Anger and Lament

Merciful Lord, have you heard your people's cry?
Have you seen those indigent people who are losing their land?
Have you seen those workers who live in under-pay, who live in the dark world without security?
Have you seen those workers who are fighting for their rights, but without any help?
Have you seen the workers on strike who become the victims of violence without any comfort?

Where can they find hope? Where can they find righteousness?
Where. . . Where. . . Where. . . ?
How can they gain fair wages? How can they find security?
How. . . How . . . How. . . ?
Lord, where are you? Are you absent from those people? Do you hear our appeal?

God, I am angry because you chose me, but I think I am not enough for your mission—to share life with all so that they can have it abundantly.

God, I am angry because you promised that you will be with us till the end of the world if we commit ourselves to you.

Yet, we feel that you have left us somewhere.

God, I Am Angry

God, I am angry because the lives and rights of your people are being denied.
Angry at the greed of multinational corporations who steal the land of the people.
Angry at the unjust political economy, which tilts toward the rich and the powerful.
Angry at the indifference and ignorance of those who don't bother to look and see the face of the suffering.

Angry and Exasperated

Dear God, I am angry and exasperated because the rich are becoming richer and the poor are becoming poorer.

To You, El Shaddai, the Many-Breasted One

We pray to you, with the anguish and pain of a mother
over the murder of her son,
multiply our holy anger, as much as there are breasts on your holy chest.

Maternal Rage!

Nanay (Mama) Nahette keeps hugging the laminated photo of her son, Aldrin. He was shot seven times. Nanay Linda always keeps a bottle of iced tea and a plate of flavored cupcakes; they were her son's favorite. He was shot five times.

Jesus raised people from the dead. Am I not a follower of Jesus? Why the hell can I not do it? Why can't I raise these boys from the dead?

So-Called Shepherds

Lord, your sheep are left without a shepherd. They're lonely. They are in danger. They are in thirst of being cared for and being led. And Lord, the so-called shepherds here close their eyes and their ears.

So many so-called shepherds.

Lord, I Am Angry

Lord, I am angry because your people are helpless and crushed down. They struggle with bitterness and anger. Lord, I am sorry that anger rises frequently in my heart, as you have not yet answered your people's prayer.

Damn Unfair

God, I am angry for the loss of innocent lives. I am angry that people don't have enough to eat. I am angry with the corrupted and horrendous government who doesn't take care of the people. I am angry with the police for not executing justice but abusing their power. I am angry with the rich for hoarding their wealth and oppressing the helpless with their power. I am angry with the stupid military forces for making people homeless. I am angry with the unequal distribution of resources around the world. God, this is damn unfair!

A Litany of Plastic

Oh God of Plastic we cry to you:
You are choking on plastic.
You are caught in plastic.
Instead of silver and moving with life and energy,
your seas are white and bobbing with plastic waste.
The waves break on skeleton reefs of spoons and forks.
The basking shark feeds on plastic plankton
and the stomach of leviathan is bloated with carrier bags.
The seahorse curls its tail around a cotton bud.

O God of Plastic we cry to you:
We have bought a plastic faith.
We have sealed ourselves from touch and taint.
Instead of sharing the cup of suffering,
we drink from single use plastic.
We see the world dimly through surveillance lenses and arm-length screens.

Possible third stanza, for the congregation or reader to compose: Admit the terror of choosing to have that plastic faith. We want to be brave enough to take the risk of leaving, but there's no guarantee of what the future holds.

A Widow's Prayer

Lord, where are you?
When I decided to follow you, you promised that you would never
leave me.

Lord, where were you when the accident happened?
Where were your angels when my husband died?

What do you want me to do now?
How will I survive?

You say that you are the husband of widows, and will comfort them in
times of need—where are you in winter, when it's cold and we are lonely?

You said you are the father of the fatherless. Or are you an absent father?

We fear for our children. Who will pay for their school fees?

Why have you humiliated me?

Amen.

Why Not Be Angry?

Katonda w'ebitonde byonna, in your wisdom you have set the continent
of Africa in place and established its foundations. For this we are grateful.
Today we come in anguish and angry of heart.

Why not be angry when our children are raped? When ritual murders
are the order of the day? When wars are ravaging the continent? When
diseases are killing us, and corruption is everywhere?

Mvelingqangi, the First and the Last, we pour our grief out to you, trusting that you will bandage our wounds and restore our joy in you. Amen.

My Shoulders and My Head Are Bowed

My shoulders and my head are bowed
and my shoulders always sagging.
Even as you look down on me
you fail to see the heavy load on my head.
How do you expect me to lift my head
without dropping the load?
If I were to drop my load,
what would be of my children?

Oblivious, yet you grow rich
from the sweat of my brow.
Isn't it enough that you exploited
my parents along with me?
Did you really have to enslave my children, too?
What about a little reprieve for my grandchildren?

When will it be enough?
At what point will you be satisfied?
Is my suffering really your only means of luxury?
You already have me, let my children go.

I can't believe you have the nerve to
call me lazy and stupid.
Yet you want me to believe in your God.
If it's your god, it can't be the God of love,
If it's your god, it can't be a good God.
It's more a god of thieves,
A god of lies,
A god of oppression.

How can I believe in such a god?
When she is the reason for my suffering?
Why would I want to embrace my own exploitation?

If you are worshipping the same god as I,
then it must be a two-faced god.
How else can your powerful oppression kill me
and still you cry at my funeral?
Surely it can't be the same god.

God, why don't you speak for yourself?
Let's hear your voice.
Where is your love?
Where is your justice?

I long to see you *see me*,
call me by *my name*.

Tell me the truth:
Are you really my God?

A Prayer of Anger after Killing

A friend had been shot a few minutes before, after sharing a hug and parting.

God, I do not understand, I hurt, I am angry at the senseless killing of my
   friend and brother.
God, I am told to understand but I do not understand.

I am told this is your plan and that I must accept it without questioning,
   without doubting!
But I do not understand, part of me does not want to understand.

A life was taken prematurely, a gifted life that soothed your people with an
   angelic baritone:
a life that brought a smile and happiness, a loving soul.

Yet for that hug, a few minutes before the precious life was snuffed out, I
   remain ever grateful.
God, I do not understand.

Yet hurt as I am, confused as I am, I can sing, "What a friend we have in
   Jesus," indeed, "What a privilege to carry, everything to God in prayer."
I bring to you my anger and confusion, my doubts to you in prayer.
Amen.

We Are Ashamed

God of humanity, our keeper and sustainer, our hearts are crushed. Your very image has been marred by our greed and selfishness. In our ignorance, we have spat on your creation and swept it as trash in heaps to die and rot; tossing into the periphery the very people whom your dear Son shed His blood for.

We are outraged and, at the same time, we are ashamed.

Christ, in the fullness of time, identified with these people: without a place in the midst of poverty, pain and stench. Instead of reflecting this same nature, we erect palaces on the corpses of your children; buildings of illustrious grandeur imposing a picture of life that doesn't exist onto desperate people.

Moment of silent pondering, after which all the people respond:

Lord, have mercy. (*Silence.*)
Christ, have mercy. (*Silence.*)
Lord, have mercy. (*Silence.*)

May we not have the audacity to leave this place unchanged and unchallenged; may we be continuously transformed into your image. For the sake of your Son and your people, the Church. Amen.

A Psalm of Lament for Those in Need of Love and Care

Heavenly Father, God
Who loves us like a Mother,
Help!
O God, ahh, we can't hurt anymore,
we know that you can hear us!

It is so hard to see what surrounds us;
give us peace.
Put an end to racism and all that divides us,
end poverty and homelessness,
break the chains of addiction,
and anything that takes away from our living a full life;
our people are suffering from drugs and alcohol.

God, we are lonely,
we feel so alone.
You are the only one who truly
knows our pain.
Have mercy and strengthen us.
Comfort, guide us,
and give us the strength to get through another night.
Free us,
we know it will take a long time.
Give us faith,
listen to us!

We need your love and care.
Heal us where we are broken.
Send us friends,
and heal those who hurt us.

Be with our leaders.
To you, O Lord, we turn
we turn to you in all your majesty,
you are the one we trust.
We believe and read your holy works, O Lord,
listen so that we might have peace.
We wouldn't want them to say,
"You are just trying to trick them!"

Help us so we can see your way
and make it our way.
This is what you do!
Do it again!

You will take care of us.
You will deliver us.
You will raise us.
You will bring new life.
You will free us and make all things right.

Poverty and homelessness
will be no more,
for you, O Lord, are our God.

O God, Look at Us

O God,
where were you looking when
affliction struck me down?
Where were your eyes hovering when
death knocked on my door?
With my eyes, I saw death and
all my joy is gone.
But with the same opaque eyes, I cry out
for a look of tenderness, a redemptive gaze;
O God,
Look at us. . .

Mother Forgive Them

Adapted from an East London-Eastern Cape ecumenical service on gender-based violence.

This prayer of anger, confession, and intercession can be adapted to an open space for any members of the worship to express their pain and anger. . . To include any clause . . .

Those that sexually harass the weak,
Mother forgive them,
for they know not what they do.
Those that spit on my body,
Mother forgive them,
for they know not what they do.
Those that condemn me for loose living,
Mother forgive them,
for they know not what they do.
Those that cast me out for having left my abusive husband,
Mother forgive them,
for they know not what they do.
Those that judge me with pious words,
Mother forgive them,
for they know not what they do.
Those that delay in treating me,
Mother forgive them,
for they know not what they do.
Those that exploit my illness for profit and gain,
Mother forgive them,
for they know not what they do.

Those that prevaricate and analyze endlessly,
Mother forgive them,
for they know not what they do.
Those that fight for power but not for those who suffer,
Mother forgive them,
for they know not what they do.
Those that squabble about anti-retroviral drugs,
Mother forgive them,
for they know not what they do.
Those who reject and persecute me because of my sexuality,
Mother forgive them,
for they know not what they do.
Those that speak in hushed tones and whispers,
Mother forgive them,
for they know not what they do.
Those that erect barbed wire around us,
Mother forgive them,
for they know not what they do.
Those that submerge me under a mountain of statistics,
Mother forgive them,
for they know not what they do.

FORGIVENESS AND REPENTANCE

NOTE FOR THE READER: For additional prayers of repentance, see Prayers of Confession and Petition, Part Two, beginning on page 71.

God of Unity and Courage

God of unity and courage,
In the midst of empires, we unite our voices and bravely pray to you.
In the midst of greed, we unite our voices and bravely pray to you.
In the midst of violence, we unite our voices and bravely pray to you.
In the midst of insecurity, we unite our voices and bravely pray to you.
In the midst of injustice, we unite our voices and bravely pray to you.
We bravely pray with one voice and one faith. In the name of the
God of Glory and Justice we pray. Amen.

God of the homeless with no place to sleep or even store their worldly
goods,
God of the beggar to whom we have not given money,
God of the hungry who sell and eat lumps of soil as their food,
God of those who sell their bodies,
God of the men and the women who pee in the streets. . .

SING: Jesus—remember me, when you come into your kingdom. Jesus,
remember me, when you come into your kingdom.

Jesus, who looked at the thief and the beggar with love, who invited the
thief into your kingdom, who asked the sick and the poor what they need.
We repent as the church, your disciples who say, "Do not come to us, the
Lord is too busy. . .
Our church is too clean, our communion is too holy."

Lord Jesus, who looked at the rich young ruler and felt pity,
Forgive us, for denying you three times, many times.
Forgive us, for the way we have become,
listening to people's stories, buying them a piece of soap maybe,
coming as shining lights—glimmers of hope.

We say a vague prayer for the poor, the hungry, the homeless, the motherless,
with our eyes closed in holy prayer.
And as we open our eyes, we see the seven we started to pray for have become seventy-seven,
gathering around, asking us to pray for them as well.

And then, looking at the time, we look away and move on
to our next appointment.
As we leave, we hear their desperate questions, "When are you coming back to visit us?"

SING: Jesus—remember me, when you come into your kingdom. Jesus, remember me, when you come into your kingdom.

Our God, we come before you with broken hearts, contrite hearts.
Your heart is breaking for them, and for us—you are their glimmer of hope, our glimmer of hope.

We pray not for the homeless and the poor, the sick and the vulnerable;
we pray for ourselves, who should be their answer to prayer . . .
Challenge us not to walk away sadly like the rich young ruler or the Sadducee.

Transform our hearts and our lives, transform our church, turn us inside out,
that we may respond without fear,
but with open hearts, open pockets, open homes, and open churches.

SING: Jesus—remember me, when you come into your kingdom.
Jesus, remember me, when you come into your kingdom.

I Believe in a Soft God

Para a hora do desespero. (For the hour of despair.)

I believe in a Soft God.

I believe in a Soft God who cries and mourns with us for all the ways our bodies have been violated and shattered and murdered and broken and unloved and erased.

I believe in Jesus, Soft God incarnate, who holds our breaths and breathes *animus* and love back into our lungs and arteries when we no longer have the strength for the pulse of life.

I believe in the Soft Spirit who—out of the depths—tenderly swings by . . . to empower in us the sounds of our own voices, of our sorrows, of our cries (and the Earth's), of our strengths.

I believe in a church that listens to the susurrus of the Earth, that feels the pain circulating in its body, that is not indifferent to violence, that believes in the cries of those who report violence at the expense of their livelihood, as well as those who are not able to do so.

I believe in (artistic-embodied) communities beyond the walls of the churches and faiths and religions that have organized resistance for millennia. I believe these communities have and will continue to move forward in responsibility and solidarity and God-given softness to undo the violent configurations of power, patriarchy, racism (the environmental kind as well), classicism, ableism, xenophobia, transphobia, homophobia, supremacy, colonialism, capitalism, pain, abandonment, indifference, and hate.

I believe in the communion of ancestors and saints and sinners and creation, living and non-living, who have thoughts that feel and feelings that think. Communities that will not allow hate and intolerance to win, but who will come to the table hand-in-hand, shoulder-to-shoulder to move softly forward, in radical joy and acceptance and hope and earthly *convivencia* (togetherness).

River of Justice

God of healing and comfort,

you have heard our cries, seen our suffering, and felt our pain at the hands of our oppressors.

We pray for your comforting spirit to heal our wounds and hurts, restoring your righteousness so that our tears and blood will become a river of justice that flows into all places.

RESISTANCE

Women Resisting Exploitation

God of life, God of liberation,
as women, we are subjected to the Empire of oppression, a system char-
acterized by abuse and exploitation. We pray that under your guidance
and our collective wisdom as a community of suffering women, may we
reshape our lives together.

We resist abuse and exploitation in the name of all oppressed women and
proclaim that justice and equality are human rights for all people, regardless of gender.

We resist as an act of defiance and proclaim as an act of instilling hope so
that both the victims and the perpetrators may be set free in the name of
humanity.

We Stand Up to Resist

God of all ages,
we are living under the empire of greed and corruption manifested
through our leaders while the people are left destitute. We pray that under
the power of the spirit and our lives together that all selfish leaders are
dealt with justice.

We stand up and resist the corruption and selfishness of our leaders. We
proclaim that we are working together for the common good, so that all
your children are able to enjoy the land that you entrusted unto us, to till
the land you made and benefit from what it has to offer. We pray in the
name of the resurrected savior. Amen.

Creed Confronting Power

Modeled on the Apostle's Creed.

I believe in God,
who, though Almighty, chooses grace.
Mirroring God, I reflect grace to all.

I believe in Jesus Christ, His only Son, our Lord,
who emptied himself of title and position,
demonstrating that true love serves others.
In like manner, I serve others to demonstrate love.

Jesus suffered injustice, was tortured, killed, and buried.
On the third day, he rose again from the dead for our sake;
I see injustice and choose to stand with the oppressed,
the suffering, and the discarded.

I believe in the Holy Spirit,
who fills God's people, giving us joy and hope.
May I be filled so that I can overflow for those who need joy and hope.

I believe in the church,
which unites with other followers of Christ,
demonstrating grace, service, suffering, and presence.

We Resist and Proclaim

God of justice and mercy,
we are living under the empire of oppression and selfishness, which is
plundering our resources, which are meant to benefit all in this nation.

We pray that, together, under the power of the Spirit of our Lord Jesus,
we may resist and proclaim against the unjust and harmful ways of this
empire.

We call on you, asking that the people of this country may experience your
grace in its fullness. In the name of Jesus Christ, our Lord and Savior.
Amen.

Resisting Powers of Destruction

Jesus said: when they bring you
    in front of the judges,
    do not try to find out in
    advance, what you are going
    to say. It will be given to you
    in the right moment.

God, we come to you as we are—
not always very strong and
courageous.

We pray: give us
a clear understanding of what is
going on, give us the strength
to fight for justice. Let us hear
your call so that we can follow
in your footsteps and speak out
for those who have been made speechless.
You said one hundred times: *Be not
afraid*. So let all fear vanish
like the dust that is blown away
in the wind, and let us know
"deep in our hearts, that we shall overcome."
        —Quotation drawn from the gospel song "We Shall Overcome"

Resistance to Exploitation

God of all wealth and honor,
We are living under the empire of land-grabbing and mineral-exploitation,
which is rendering our people poor, downcast, and worthless.

We pray that under the mighty power of the triune God and our lives
together,
we may be liberated from this evil.

In solidarity we resist the evil of land-grabbing and mineral-exploitation,
so that the oppressed may regain their rights to land ownership and profit
from the wealth amassed from mining precious stones in our land.

In the name of Jesus Christ, the liberator of mankind. Amen.

The Promised Land and the Angel

"The LORD, the God of heaven—who brought me from my father's household and from my family's land, who spoke with me and who gave me his word, saying, 'I will give this land to your descendants'—he will send his messenger in front of you" (Gen 24:7).

What kept people going on their difficult journeys? We heard that it was the strong hope for a better life in a new country. Our friends felt called out of their countries and away from their families, away from their mothers and brothers and sisters—or together with the mothers and sisters and brothers, for their fathers were murdered and they had not only lost their love but also their support and their means of living. They had heard a call—and this call and hope was an angel on their way.

But sometimes they could not see the angel anymore. Sometimes all faith is lost and no one is there to help.

Then there are those who try to help, the volunteers and those who work for the supporting organizations. Sometimes the helpers lose hope, and they ask: "Where is the angel now? Where is God's promise? Is it lost?"

And then, there is this little town, full of old men on benches—but in the House of Cultures, the Casa della Cultures, and in the Catholic Space of Education, the children run and laugh and play and learn together with their helpers—lots of children.

The angel is back, "From the mouths of babies and infants you've arranged praise for yourself" (Matt 21:16).

—The underlined part of Genesis 24:7 is the "Moravian Daily Watchword"
for today, May 10, 2019

205

God of Life and the Oppressed

God of life and of the oppressed,

We are living under an empire
of greediness, injustice, poverty.
It is taking away
everything that brings justice and
freedom for the oppressed and
peace in our communities.

We pray that under the power
of the spirit of justice and
love, we may resist every
evil perpetuated by empire.
We pray that we may speak for justice and
give voice to the voiceless
in our communities whose
voices have been silenced by
the evil of empire.

We pray that together
we receive the
fullness of life promised
by our Lord Jesus Christ.
In the name of Jesus
Christ our liberator and
giver of life we pray.
Amen.

How Do You Confront Power?

We confront power with courage and bravery,
refusing to be intimidated or terrorized by them,
by those who use their power to produce death.
Because there are people who produce death,
people, human beings like us,
and they must be held responsible for the evil that they spread.
Exactly like Jesus, we must be unafraid of facing the power.

Covenant Prayer

Based on the traditional Wesleyan Covenant prayer.

> I am no longer my own. I stand now with your people.
> Join me in solidarity with others.
> Let us take action.
> Let us wait in silence.
> Let us confront oppression.
> Let us mourn what is lost.
> Let us succeed in our struggles.
> Let us share your suffering.
> Let us dream new visions.
> Let us renounce old ways.
>
> We freely and wholeheartedly commit our lives to this service.
>
> So, living God, we share your wounds and see your glory.
> Let it be this way.
>
> And may this covenant now made on earth,
> be ratified in the world that is to come.
>
> Amen.

Collect for Contamination

In some places, by some people, immigrants are considered "contaminants."

> Contaminate me, God.
> Muddy the thoughts of my heart,
> that I might not seek purity for myself and my church,
> but be willing to catch the contagion of love.
>
> Temper my desire for refinement
> with openness to the qualities that impurities bring.
> May I be willing to sacrifice my own dreams of purity
> to become merely part of a stronger, more resilient alloy.
>
> And may I, may we, in melting together,
> be useful to you in building a new world.
> Amen.

Resist the Destruction of Eden

God of Africa,

we are living under the empire of
land-grabbing and exploitation.
It is destroying the Eden
you created as providence from
you as our caring provider.

We pray that under the power of
the Spirit and our lives together,
you remind us of the love and
purpose you put forward when
you created this world and for
the mere fact that you saw it
to be good.

We proclaim your greatness and
resist the power of this earthly
empire to make us destroy ourselves.
We so proclaim that your name may be praised
by all creation.

Landlessness and Exclusion

God of our ancestors,
we are living under the Empire of landlessness and exclusion.
We pray that under the power of the Spirit and our lives together,
we push back the evil of colonial land-grabbing, and include others in the list
    of Abraham, Isaac, and Jacob,
so that all of humanity can have life, and life in abundance.
In the name of God, our liberator. Amen.

Confronting Power

We confront power with Shiprah and Puah,
in acts of passive resistance,
refusing to obey orders.

We confront power with Moses,
boldly demanding the powers that be,
"Let my people go!"

We confront power with Esther,
using what powers we have within a corrupt system
to oppose injustice.

We confront power with Hannah,
singing our songs of reversal
when we are commanded to be silent.

We confront power with the all the prophets
calling out oppression
in the face of complacency.

We confront power with Mary Magdalene,
lavishing attention on God in the face of public disapproval,
speaking with actions when words are denied us.

We confront power with Jesus,
calmly confronting the powers that be,
reserving the right to remain silent.

We confront power with the women who went to the tomb,
daring to assert our right to mourn
those denied the right to live by oppressive regimes.

We confront power with Paul,
unafraid to publicly change our minds,
finding defiant joy even in chains.

HUNGER

Lord, Look to Those

Lord, look to those who have gone without food for days.
Lord, look to those who scramble for food among the rubbish dumps.
Lord, look to those who sell their bodies and dignity to put food on their table.
Lord, look to those who work under unfair labor laws to feed their families.
Dear Lord, look to your people who are hungry.
Won't you be Jehovah Jireh to the hungry?

Our Mother and Father

Our Mother and Father,

When we hear "ñaming time" (time to eat) we think of Kingston's Beverly Hills, their gourmet food, and the way they have grabbed the fruits of mother earth for generations and generations.

When we hear "ñaming time" we also think of Kingston's Tivoli Gardens, a food desert with big bellies full of junk food, with a life expectancy much shorter than the ones living in the upper crust.

Our Motherly Trinity gives us the guts to join hands with community organizers and social activists so that everybody can have access to food. May pray, "Give us today our daily bread," not as the magic formula of "hocus pocus dominocus" but as a liberation act of political discipleship.

And the entire creation shouts,
Amen!

Make Us to Be Your Bread

We pray for those people who are in poverty;
help us to learn how to share what we have,
until they sense your abundant supply.

We pray for those people who are thirsty;
send us to be messengers to share your living words,
until they find the source of life, never to be thirsty again.

We appeal for those people who are in hunger;
make us to be your bread, broken for others,
to share and be shared until all are fed.

For Workers on Strike

Merciful Lord,
turn your eyes to the workers who work under unfair labor laws,
the workers who live in poor living conditions,
the mothers and fathers who have to leave their families behind to work
    abroad.

Lord, have mercy. Christ, have mercy. Lord, have mercy.

Righteous Lord,
we pray for the workers who are fighting for their rights to get a better life.
Give them strength and wisdom to fight against the evil rulers of this world.
Put your justice and mercy in the hearts of the rulers and leaders,
that they will act for the benefit of the working people.

Victorious Lord,
you who won victory over darkness,
lead your people into the land of light, peace and justice.

Lord, have mercy. Christ, have mercy. Lord, have mercy.

Mercy for the Hungry People

Merciful God, have mercy on the hungry people
The powerful and rich bring offerings to your altar
They come laden with fruits and vegetables; bread and milk are brought into
    your presence
Loud prayers and liturgies are read in bhakti (reverence)
Songs and hymns are sung

The hungry soul enters your sanctuary
Deprived of food and water, poor and weak
He prays in his heart,
"How can I pray and make offerings like the rich when I am hungry?
O Lord, I the hungry one just work on, waiting to be fed."

Praying in his or her mind, "Where is the food, food, food?"

Deep Down Hunger

Hunger of justice
Hunger of care
Hunger of better life
Hunger of being listened to
Hunger of peace
Hunger of happiness
Hunger of prosperity
Hunger of stability
Deep down hunger is the hunger of a life—true life that cannot be found
    elsewhere but in God.

We Are the Table on Earth

O Lord of abundance, we are hungry.
We are hungry for enough food for every person.
We are hungry for justice that allows food to be given to everyone.
You've come and told us that you are the bread of life, in whom we all have a
    share.
Bring us to the table where a place is reserved for the poor and the hungry.
Help our churches to become the table on earth where the bread of life is
    shared.
O God, feed us, bodies and souls, hungry and weary.

Multitudes: Perhaps a Parable

Jesus came to the seashore. The sky was blue. The water was turquoise. The beach was white. There was a palm tree to the left, two treetops growing out of one stem, with coconuts.

You wish. Jesus stopped coming to the seashore a while ago.
The sky is still blue. The water is still turquoise. The beach is still white—or sort of white, rather "cream" really. But Jesus stopped coming to the seashore a while ago. (And there never were any coconuts.) Yes, the multitude keeps coming. Multitudes. They keep coming. Thousands. Like sheep without a shepherd. But Jesus stopped coming to the seashore a while ago.

There are sometimes loaves—although not that much sharing. There's never enough for everyone. People still share stuff, but you really have to look out for yourself. Make sure that you get enough. Won't help anyone if you also get angry from hunger. There is a lot of looking up to heaven. Cursing more than blessing though. And there are lots and lots of broken pieces—although not pieces from loaves. But Jesus stopped coming to the shore a while ago.

Somebody said Jesus was listening to the SOS calls picked up by the coast guards on the Mediterranean Sea every night. But he stopped coming to the seashore a while ago.

Hungry to Feed

God of Hunger, you came to the world in humility. We look upon the world and we see many are starving and have nothing to eat and to drink.

Teach us Lord, as to be able to feel their hunger.
Help us to have the feeling of hunger to feed people.

To Survive and Live Again

Dear Parent [God],

I am hungry and cannot find food. The sea is polluted. The place where we used to go fishing and catch much is no longer there. The rich people have recreated lands to build malls.

I am hungry and cannot climb the coconut tree. My legs have been amputated due to work issues. My boss hit them so hard that they are no longer useful.

Please parents, hurry up and come back. I need you desperately in order to survive and live again.

MOURNING

Daylight Shines

Daylight shines again in the morning,
through the window should come God's blessing,
protecting our household from sanctioned killings.
Still guns and bullets shoot in a rude awakening,
hallucinating families and communities in the nightmare of losing
the war on the poor,
the battle with powers,
the pulse and heartbeat of our beloved.

The Graveyard of Boats

I am old, weak and broken now; once I was new, strong and beautiful,
my owner's pride and livelihood. Early each morning I would sail to the
fishing waters where my owner would catch the fish to feed and clothe his
family. My deck would groan under the weight of the slippery, twitching
haul caught in the nets. Day after day, year after year, I would sail into the
beauty of the sea.

My owner retired; I was sold but the new owner did not repair my flaking
paint, rotting wood, or sputtering engine. Left to rot, I took one final voy-
age laden with weak and broken humanity, clinging to me with desperation. Some of my catch was lost before I was towed to shore. Now I decay
here as a memorial to betrayed hope.

Let Our Mourning Be

Let us join our sorrows with the sorrows of God's people everywhere.

Let our mourning be:
For the earth that is blasted and burned. For the olive trees that are bare and
 for the vines that do not bear fruit.
For the children who are lost and for the parents whose arms are empty.
For those who seek refuge and do not find peace.
Jesus said, "Stay with me. Watch and Pray."

Let our mourning be:
Like an ocean that cannot be emptied.
Like a river that cannot be stopped.
Like the strong summer rain that puts an end to drought.
Jesus said, "Share my baptism. Drink my cup."

Let our mourning be:
A vigil in the darkness.
A light that searches out the lost.
A hand that reaches out to save and hold.
Jesus said, "Blessed are the ones who mourn. They shall be comforted."

Amen.

My God, My God

My God, my God, why have you not seen our disgrace and suffering?
We are wounded as the arrows of our enemy pierced our hearts and our
children are dying. Our land is devastated; famine and poverty have
confounded us. In the name of development, the proud and the mighty
are ready to devour us apart. Like tigers and bears, they are marching to
trample our land with violence.

The bulldozer has pulled away our forest and houses and has polluted our
water. Our children are crying for food and they have no shelter to hide
from the scorching heat, the storm, and the rain. The powerful and the
rich have robbed our paddy field and we are hungry and thirsty.

The capitalist promises to give us Coca-Cola and burgers, but our stomachs are empty and we are longing for rice and clean water. Our children
are malnourished, and we cannot buy food as we are poor. The rich
insulted us and put us to shame and humiliation.

216

Come down, O Lord, and rescue us from the greedy industrialists; they are like leeches sucking the blood of our children. We are helpless and weak, like a lamb before a ravenous lion. Do not be silent to our cry; answer us, O Lord, according to your abundant mercy and do not hide your face from us.

Do not let those who hope in you be put to shame.

Mourning Prayer

Unto you, God, we bring our crippling pain for the violence inflicted on our brothers and sisters in their journey to a better present.

Unto you, God, we bring our contained anger for the indifference of Western countries, for the ongoing violations of human rights and the drafting of unjust laws.

Unto you, God, we bring our private indignation for the racism that poisons civil coexistence and interpersonal relationships.

You who, in Jesus, have proclaimed blessed those who mourn, free us from a conniving silence and a dumb resignation; transform our pain, our anger, and our indignation into a lamentation so loud that it cannot go unheard.

As the widow praised by Jesus, may our mourning for justice be unrestrainable, that we may wear out or win over our enemies.

I Fear Nothing

Dear God, with you and in you I fear nothing. The world is full of fear and death surrounds us. We mourn every day for the loss of our loved ones. Be with us so that we can stay strong in our faith for in you and with you we fear no evil.

Absence

The beach is empty now
the wonder endless.

Creator, we remember
those who didn't
make it to the shores
those who lost their lives
through the cruel journey
through the desert and the
sea, we pray for
their families and friends.

The camp is empty now
left is the lifeless structures
of the military camp, guarded
by campo women and men.
We remember the key
of lost voices.
Liberator, we remind
ourselves, see the
cries of lost hope
the endless lines
the endless wait
the colors fading away
we pray that you
will help us.

The city is empty
our cities and streets
are littered with people
some we know, most not.

Giver of life
open our hearts and
souls to strangers
for you
help us all
sustain the life
you give.

The Mourning

In the assembly.
When we witness death,
at first, there is silence
we lose our tongues, our lips are
closed.
Then, there might be a groan.
We try to remember the god who knows
how this feels—the god who lost his own child.
And then we pray.
Lord, listen, for we are lost.
We do not understand.
We come to you, for you alone,
you know how we feel.
just powerless. But you know.
"O sacred head, now wounded."
We bring to you the shambles
of our lives. Shards.
When you saw Lazarus in his
grave, you became angry.
Please, leave us not alone in
all of this.
You are the giver of life—why, why, why
is there still death,
why do we have to cry?

A Prayer for Those Mourning

Holy Spirit, comfort us, move in our world.
Bring peace to those who have lost their very humanity.
Bring peace to those who have lost their sense of belonging.
Bring peace to those who have lost their friends because of the journey.
Holy Spirit, change us, transform the borders.
Turn barren desolate deserts into an oasis of hope.
Turn impassable vast seas into waters of life.
Holy Spirit, heal us, restore our hearts.
Hold the forgotten ones, help us remember.

Song for the Departed

You survived
Starvation
Hunger from war, famine, intentional depravation
Your father
Ashamed
Still brought you across the world to freedom
False promise
Minor
Exploited, vulnerable, suddenly gone in the windstorm
moments came when your laughter sparkled
                         the afternoon you began to trust
                    you learned your life still matters
               glittering smiles and joy in just moments.
                         I sit on the Mediterranean and think of you
                                                  A son
                                            Not my son
                              You will never see the Sea
                                                    See
                                           Not any sea
                         Your stepmother has continued living
                                               Her life
                                          Not your life
                    There are tree branches swaying in the breeze
                                         Tree branches
                                         Not your body.

On Mourning

I shall not mourn for deaths framed as self-defense
Nor shall I mourn for children starved to death
I won't mourn for lands consumed by the selfish
Or even lives denied by slave-shops
Never!

I will not give the rich the satisfaction of my vulnerability
Instead, I mourn for the loss of their humanity
And I mourn for the Nazarene
Who worked so hard to redeem it
So if ever my tears drop
They send atomic ripples beneath ivory towers

Mourning

The Bible is a book of death as well as life.
Between the bookmarks of Eden and the New Jerusalem,
death is an ever-present shadow.
And so, we mourn with all who have mourned before us
in the messy complexity of grief.

We mourn with Eve, at the death of one son and the death-dealing
    of another;
with Bathsheba, at the death of one husband and the death-dealing
    of another;
with Egypt, at the death of their first-borns and the death-dealing
    of their nation.
We mourn with Ruth and Naomi, with Hagar and Leah,
    with Martha and Mary.
The tree of life is also the tree of death.
We will not rush to celebrate resurrection;
we will take time to mourn.

How Do You Help People to Mourn?

The mourning of a mother that has lost her child during the crossing
    of the Mediterranean Sea.
Oh Father, forgive them, for they do not know what they are doing.
The mourning of a child that has lost his parents during the war.
Oh Father, forgive them, for they do not know what they are doing.
The mourning of a friend, that lost her queer friend because of bullying.
Oh Father, forgive them, for they do not know what they are doing.
The mourning of a grandmother that grew up with so much love for
    her niece and now she was killed by her husband.

Oh Father, forgive them, for they do not know what they are doing,
    but also give justice to these people.

HEALING

Pollination

the lemon trees are in full blossom
under the warm spring sky   bees are pulled into the branches
lulled by the aroma of nectar   the trees knowing—they will come
abundant blossoms attracting admirers   not disrupting the buzzing workers
undaunted they pursue the scent   the promise of something better
but ripeness is months away   patience is required and cold weather
heady with nectar, bees pursue   promise alone pushes from the hive
the immature superficial success of sweet aromas
silently the trees diffuse
cunningly crafted scents
drawing bees to labor
perfectly uncaring
bees perfectly aware
their labor produces
ripe, golden fruit

The Power of God

Be blessed, you who move,
Be blessed, you who mourn,
Be blessed, you who are meek and merciful,
For you *are* the power of God.

Amen.

Jesus at the Seashore

I know the winds and the currents. I know the rocks on which the sea birds perch and that wreck boats far from land. I know this sea in the sunlight, and I know it in the storm. But I have never known a night like that, and we like lost souls clinging to the boat's sides. And Jesus comes and he is walking on the water.

They say that is what the drowned do. Return at night, treading the storm-waves to the seashore. Well the dead, I say, have bought that right. We, the living, still struggle with the waters knowing that the sea is stronger than we are. It will pull us under. And Jesus comes and he is walking on the water.

I am so angry with him. He left us to struggle alone. He comes like a ghost. Walking the waves and saying, "I am not like you." They say I left the boat to go to him because I loved him. No. It was because I was so angry. Angry for all the ones who drowned in these seas. Angry because we, too, were looking death right in the face. I jumped over to challenge him, "Will you embrace me and sink with me to where there is no breath, no light, no life?"

And Jesus comes and he is walking on the water.
But I believe he answered me, as he reached out his hand he said, "Yes."

Lord, Help Me to Pray

Lord, help me to pray as my Muslim brothers taught me: "How do I make this crooked path straight again?"

Lord, help me to pray as my Muslim brothers taught me: "How do I make this crooked path straight again?"

Lord, help me to pray as my Muslim brothers taught me: "How do I make this crooked path straight again?"

Amen.

Wanderers of God

Our ancestors were wandering Arameans,
walkers of hard paths
seekers of better worlds.
Our mothers fed their sons and daughters
while crossing deserts
and they sang and cried under the open sky.
Our brothers and sisters
suffered contempt and oppression,
chains, slavery, hunger
in strange and unknown lands.

God's solidarity took shape
in a child who had to migrate
because of hatred and persecution.
Communities of faith, throughout history,
have been the birthplaces of women and men
come from afar, feet broken,
souls beaten, eyes tired,
but awakening dreams of good lives.

Wanderers of God, we come and go
through this land that is whole, complete,
blessed house, home of humanity,
refuge of those who made the pilgrimage
pursuing promises of bread that satiates,
roofs that shelter, dignity that embraces,
work that fulfills, shared abundance.

We migrate, we walk, we cross seas,
we climb walls, we cross borders,
we break the limits imposed on us,
in the struggle we suffered to live and survive.

Wanderers of God,
if death does not catch us in the march,
we look for a place, even a manger,
in which we cradle the hope
that we refuse to lose.

What Really Matters

"Yet your people say, 'My Lord's way doesn't measure up.' Isn't it their ways that don't measure up?" (Ezek 33:17).

"If you love me, you will keep my commandments" (John 14:15).

What really matters, in your eyes and mine, is not legalized justice written by hands stained with blood, impunity, or corruption.

What really matters, in your eyes and mine, is not the justice dictated by men in suits and ties, narcissists with egos inflamed by pride, who gather in church to atone for their sins every Sunday.

What really matters, in your eyes and mine, is the infinite humanity that dwells in each being made in Your Image and Likeness, through the divine grace embodied in girl, woman, male, young, and old.

What really matters, in your eyes and mine, is the genuineness that comes from the hands of the peasant, the worker, the incessant laborer, the young visionary who dignifies her life.

What really matters, in your eyes and mine, cannot be guessed, for it is an incessant search for justice here and now on earth. You fight for it, you love it, you respect it, and you work for it every day.

What really matters, in your eyes and mine, is found in the complicity of the gaze between my beloved and me.

You, God

On the seafront in Port Royal.

You who coo us tenderly
as a long, warm and loving embrace.

You who awaken our spirit
with the swaying of the waves in calm, stillness, and rhythms.

You who manifest yourself through our minds,
understanding and spirit with the breath of life,
heard, sung, celebrated,
and in different aromas and visions like an infinite sea.

You who stubbornly breathe into us
tenacity and courage, like a beast whose life and existence are threatened.

Lull us, wake us, manifest us,
encourage us in tangled sororities.

May it be so, so it is!

Wedding of Cana

Loving Creator, who with tenderness and care, created good life from the
mud of existence: we come to You, receptive, like jars that are empty, lacking, tired of so many hollow rites.

**We come to You, loving artisan of history, open to the mystery of life,
to the gesture of solidarity of your Son, which gives hope and joy to
poor people, those who stubbornly celebrate love, even knowing the
fragility of day-to-day life and the precariousness of their celebrations.**

But we are confident, like a mother who knows the love her son has for
all, and we are carriers of that same spirit. The one that moves us to mercy,
recreating and transforming everything, so that the celebration of life, in
which all can dance with joy, does not end.

May the Lord make it so. Amen.

226

Worldly Affirmation of Faith

I affirm the earth as sacred in my life because I am dust and to the dust I will return. We are the living earth; she moans next to me and together, with me, she will be liberated.

I affirm water as sacred in my life, water that has been both a pleasure and a refreshment for tired bodies from generation to generation. We are fresh water; it gives us life as it runs through our veins and revives us for resurrection.

I affirm life on Earth as sacred, life that bursts into the world stubbornly against death. We are resurrected life, the harmonious vitality of dignity that becomes "good living" (*Sumak Kawsay*).

I affirm plants and animals as sacred in my life because of the relationship that binds us. We are creation, trees and fungi, fish and wild beasts, birds and insects. We have flesh and roots that bear witness to creative and creating Wisdom.

I affirm wind as sacred in my life because it is subversively democratic. We are a holy breeze, a Spirit that blows everywhere to give breath to suffocated lives.

I affirm death as sacred in my life when it is worthy and comes when it must—at the right time. We are resurrection, death does not have the last word: we do not live to die, but we die to rise again.

Therefore: I affirm my faith in the God of earth, water, life, plants, and animals. I affirm my faith in God that it is wind . . . breath of life and resurrection.

Amen.

POWER/OPPRESSION

Did You Imagine?

When you ordered the world, and breathed everything into being, did you imagine your creatures will pretend to be you? Why did you have to create then?!

I Am Overwhelmed

God, I am overwhelmed
The stench of death surrounds me
The bullet holes have pierced my heart
The eyes of my children are darkened with sadness

God, I am afraid
My sleep is broken with fits of terror
I swallow my words for fear the police will storm my house

God, I feel alone
No one understands the pain
And I don't know how to make it stop

Be my peace as I struggle in the storm
Help me to keep my eyes open to the injustice that surrounds me

Help me to hear your message of hope in the clamor of despair

Using drums and rasta rhythms, sing and listen to "Redemption Song" by Bob Marley.

How Dare You?

How dare you sit high and judge me when you don't even know me? How dare you speak of "opportunities" when there is no worth? How dare you give away our lands, when your citizens are left to sleep in makeshift houses? How dare you give us false hope of modernity and prosperity when we remain entrapped in a system of indebtedness and neo-colonial slavery?

How dare you serve the interest of the powerful corporations, political elites, churches, foreign powers, and neglect the needs of the poor and vulnerable? How dare you label and then subject us to employment discrimination, based on my address and appearance, when you yourself have created the conditions of poverty that trap us in this constructed identity?

How dare you speak of caring for creation when your greed has led me to more frequent and stronger hurricanes, sinking islands, and climate chaos? Who the hell do you think you are?

Muslim Migrant Christ

Muslim migrant Christ,
you are hungry, you are thirsty, you are naked, you are sick, you are in prison.

Muslim migrant Christ,
you asked, but it was not given to you; you searched, but you could not find; you knocked, and the door stayed closed. Not everyone who searches finds, and not for everyone who knocks, the door will be opened.

Muslim migrant Christ, pray for us:
Father, forgive them, for they know not what they are doing.

Amen.

Evil One

Evil One,
I see you.
I see what you're doing.

You may think I'm dumb.
You might think I'm naïve.

But I see you.
I see what you're doing.

You make the government
lie, cheat, and steal.
You infest the government
and it does me wrong.

You make the market
run and jump fast.
You prod it this way and that
and make me chase it always.
You're the cancer that mutates the church
into an institution of complacency—
one big viper, deaf to my cry,
that slithers away from justice.

You're the contagion of distrust
that turns my neighbor into my enemy,
my competitor and adversary,
self-serving, greedy, thieving.

But I see you.
I see what you're doing.

I seethe with righteous anger.
I am hot with Jeremiah's fire.

It's true, Evil One, that
judgment and justice are God's.

But God's work is done
with my hands.

I see you, Evil One.
And with God I come to make things right.
Amen.

Jesus Came to the Seashore

Jesus came to the seashore with the twelve. The gentle breeze filled the sails, the sun warmed their faces, the cries of the gulls echoed around the bay. Exhausted from their journey over the sea, Jesus and the twelve climbed out of the boat and waded onto the beach.

"Why are you here? Where are your papers? Do you know you have broken the law?"

asked the soldiers, their guns shining in the morning light, their smart uniforms brimming with authority. But Jesus gave them no answer.

Again, they asked:

"Why are you here? It's illegal!"

And so, with plastic cable ties, the soldiers bound Jesus and the twelve and led them away. With clipboard and pen they were reduced to statistics: country of origin (long since lost in the fog of war), age, race, gender, and reason for journey all carefully noted with imperial efficiency and ignored until judgment day.

Locked away, then moved further north, left to fend for themselves, Jesus and the twelve toiled under the hot sun on un-tilled soil to grow cash crops for the wealthy. Meager wages determined by cruel forces, hostility fueled by the rich to distract the poor, and hope seeping away with each passing day like a slow crucifixion. Jesus and the twelve await resurrection.

Our Lack of Power

Lord, on this day, we recognize our lack of
power to break the chains of sexual violence
toward women in their homes;
our inability to cross physical and human borders,
and break the chains of addiction.
Lord Jesus, we ask you to give us your power.

Migrants

Is my blood not like yours:
crimson red, life that flows through the veins?
Are my salty tears, not like yours,
crying at what hurts, what pains me?

Does my body not need the same food
that you need for yours,
and does your life not need the same dignity
that I desire for mine and for my sons and daughters?
Are my dreams and hopes not
as valuable as what you have?
Does your heart not beat, just like mine,
when you embrace someone you love?
Do you not want a pillow for you to rest,
on which to lay your head, like me?

Do you think it makes me happy to have to migrate,
leave my land, my history, my roots?

When uprooted, there is something that dies
and only understanding and solidarity
can give a sense of resurrection
to the human being who yearns to continue living.

I do not fear the barred borders,
nor the walls that so many insist on building.
I fear the border of a love incapable of including,
the limits of a compassion that does not embrace,
the walls of a solidarity that hides one's hand,
the gates of looks that hate, judge, and condemn.

My feet are cracked,
my strength is on the verge of collapsing,
my saddlebags empty of everything,
my eyes tired of crying,
my broken faith,
my God . . . who knows?

Please,
look at me as if you were looking at a mirror,
for if you recognize me as human,
your brother, your sister,
you will be wearing your own existence of humanity.

A Mediterranean Magnificat

My soul proclaims the greatness of the Lord,
my spirit rejoices in God my Savior.

For God has looked on the desperation
of God's own migrating people;
my ancestors will call me blessed.

The Almighty led me through the arid desert,
freed me from the trafficker's captivity,
and saw me safely through Leviathan's deathly realm.

The Lord shows mercy to all who fear the Holy Name,
but scatters the tyrants in their conceit.

God frustrates the plans of politician and bureaucrat
but raises the immigrant and refugee.

The Lord has cast down the corporations from their thrones,
but exalted the exploited.

The Lord has filled the abused with good things
sending the Capitalist away empty.

The Lord has come to the help of the people
and fulfill the promises made long ago—
blessed be God's holy Name, now and forever.

We Are Suffering

Dear God: we are suffering,
babies are crying,
mothers are hopeless,
the rich are oppressing the poor,
we are out of the breath!

God our Creator: rescue and release us
from all domination,
in Christ's name. Amen!

Confrontation
Pentecost

We hide in rooms with locking doors
Afraid for the murder of another son
Gathered together all in one place
Send your flames, make our hearts burn

Push us together into the streets
Speaking words all can understand
Your reign—not this Babylon—come!
Your love of the least, not the death of the poor at Babylon's hands

Some will sneer and call us possessed
Some will jeer and lock us up
Songs of freedom be our shield
Break every chain and cell that oppress

And when the time has yet to come
Make us keepers of your song
That hearts may sing of tyrants torn down
The hungry fed, the lowly enthroned

The crucified children leave the grave
Live here, live now, is what it means to be saved

Hear My Cry

Dear Lord, I'm lowly and oppressed. Hear my cry, as I need your care.
Please come and embrace me under your care. Please come and embrace
me under your love and power, so I may face the power of this world.
Whom can I lean on, except you?

Where is the justice in this world? Money? Is it money, Lord?

Power, money . . . may oppress God's people, but in unity in our trust in
the God of justice, we shall not give up our hope or give in to evil powers.
Our strength is when we're together in our faith of our Lord of mercy and
justice.

Slapping the Faces of Your People

Slapping, slapping, slapping the faces of your people chained to slavery.
Where is your saving face?

O Lord, turn the fists of the rich and powerful into waste.

Under Your Wings

O Lord, hide those who are harassed by violence under your wings; shield them from rains of bullets and bombs in your refuge; counter the fists and thrusts cast into their faces. O Lord, may you be the fighter for those who cannot fight for themselves.

Your People's Knees Are Down

God of the earth, why would you let greedy corporations put their fingers on your gift of the land? Your people's knees are down to the earth of their home with the last bit of their might to protect what you have promised them. O Lord, why, why would you not pull their greedy hands off your people's lands?

Lord of Justice and Peace

Lord of Justice and Peace,
we are striving for Justice and Peace!
Why have the powerful people taken away all our belongings
Lord! We are struggling, oppressed by the rich government
We are tired!
Lord! Our struggles were ignored by the church, by the government,
    and by the people.
Lord! Free us, liberate us! In Christ's name, Amen.

God of Africa

God of Africa, we thank and honor you. We are living under the Empire of oppression and patriarchy. We women are being oppressed by white males and our own black males, which has left us vulnerable. We pray that your Holy Spirit will convict the oppressors and their actions. We pray that we will be able to live our lives as you ordained. We do ask for love and humility for our oppressors, for them to see that we are all made in the Image of God, so that we may live peacefully in a world where oppression is conquered. In the name of Jesus, we pray. Amen.

God of Abraham, Moses, and of the Oppressed

God of Abraham, Moses, and of the Oppressed,
we are living under the empire of colonialists who are taking over our
land, resources, and all we have received from you.

We pray that under your reign and our lives together, we can resist, overthrow, and reclaim that which has been taken away from us.

We proclaim the spirit of assertiveness and awareness of the evils of colonialism,
so that the means of oppression can be fought and conquered.

In the name of the God of the oppressed we will reclaim what is ours,
reclaim the gifts we have received from you.

Amen.

Prayer for Resistance

We are living under the Empire of oppression and selfishness, greediness.

We pray that under the power of the Spirit, and our lives together, that we resist against this Empire of oppression and selfishness so that we may, by resisting it, share equally the wealth of the land.

In the name of Jesus our redeemer. Amen.

In the name of the landless we ask to receive a spirit of resilience.
Amen.

God of Mercy and Love

God of Mercy and Love,
We are living under the Empire of the Chinese and the Europeans who came in the name of investing in our country, which are oppressing us, the Africans, by taking up our beautiful land, resources, and minerals that were meant for our sustenance. We pray that, under the power of the spirit, and our lives together, we can speak out against the Empire so that our dignity and sovereignty as Africans will be restored. In the name of the most high God, who is merciful and loving. Amen.

God of Our World

God of our entire world, our savior and redeemer, we pray that you intervene, as we are living under an empire that is selfish, full of egos. The empire continues to victimize and destroy the homeless, helpless. We pray that under the power of the spirit and our lives together we may learn to share what we produce, create, in the land full of milk and honey. Empower us to use our skills, gifts, and talents to help each other so that we may live in harmony and peace. Help us to be able to proclaim the downfall of the empire, which continues to oppress and suppress us, so that we will be able to experience peace in the entire continent. We ask this in the name of our Savior Umsindisi. Amen.

GENERAL PRAYERS

For the Environment

Brothers and sisters, we call upon God, the provider, the creator and care-taker of the environment.

We call you out of the wilderness into the Garden of Eden.

We invoke the God of our ancestors in faith for the provision, care, and sustenance of our environment.

We pray for this wisdom to help us care, for strength to protect his cre-ation, and for love of the environment.

Amen.

Prayer for Those Suffering Because of Addiction

God hear our prayer
the rampant addiction
enslaving families, hopes, dreams, futures
and our communities.
Give our voices the words and
sounds to be heard and
change, inspired.

The Lens of Love

God,
thank you for creating us in your image.
To be loved by you even when being dehumanized helps us to see others
through the lens of love, so we can value and honor your creation.
In Jesus's Name we pray.
Amen.

We Need Your Help

Lord we come to you,
we ask for grace.
Sometimes we give in to the Anglo-Church.
Sometimes we walk the streets to fill a need.
We try to look for community where we can find it
because you made us to be in community.

Sometimes we use our voices to fight back and we become an enemy in the
eyes of many.
Help us.
We need your grace,
we need your peace,
we need your wisdom and protection.

Forgive Us #2

Dear God,
We have these people who are voiceless,
they wanted to shout for justice,
they wanted to have security.
But we who experience your love choose to close our eyes, choose to
shut our mouths, choose to close our ears. Forgive us, we pray.

We Pray for It All

We pray for:

- hurricane refugees in _____, lack of aid

- the youth community of color without education or resources

- women in fear who cannot call local police when they and their children are in danger, those hiding abuse so they will not be deported

- lack of Latinx presence because of lack of support and community at _____ seminary

- our ancestors that got us here

- breaking down mindsets in administration so they will be welcoming, supportive

- those not yet proud of who they are

- trans women of color

- queer youth who have not been accepted for who they are

- those in ignorance, who need clarity

- people in power, snap out of it!

We pray for those suffering . . .

Señor Jesús

Señor en este día reconocemos nuestra falta
De poder para romper con las cadenas de la violencia sexual
Hacia la mujer en sus hogares;
El no poder cruzar fronteras físicas y humanas,
y romper las cadenas de la adicción.
Señor Jesús te pedimos danos tu poder

Querido Dios

Querido Dios, nuestro Padre, nuestra Madre, gran consolador, y
nuestra acompañante,
> you listen to the cry of the children,
> those who have had their families
> ripped apart due to senseless
> laws that divide us.
> We pray for those burdened
> to feel the lightness
> of your yoke.
> Open our eyes to see the lonely,
> to befriend the migrant and to
> open our home to the one who
> has lost everything.
> Dejalo y permite que Dios haga su obra.

Amen!

Prayer for the End of Gang Violence

God our creator
Thank you for life, creation,
Everything that is beautiful in our lives
With the grace and mercy that
We do not deserve
We plead for
Gang violence
Drugs
The heaviness of always trying to prove ourselves
For the hatred between human beings that manifests itself
Through economic and gender inequalities.

Lord, give us hope and help us
To be instruments of your peace.
Allow us to console
And advocate for those
Who cannot speak for themselves.
We also ask for the intercession
Of our Virgin of Guadalupe.
As she journeyed with Christ in 'sorrow'
And pain, may we also walk with "the other."
Amen.

241

Bathsheba's Prayer

God, where were you when I,
the daughter of Elia, the wife of Uriah,
received the messenger from King David,
who would lead me to him?

Where were you when my body,
with tremor and horror, could hardly
take a step forward because it knew
what was waiting for me on the other side of the door?

How could you give that power
that so promptly and deliberately
abuses, rapes, kills?

I practiced how to tell Uriah that I was
pregnant, with a child that wasn't his.

And the floor disappeared beneath my feet
when I received the news of one more death,
my husband's.

How to carry this life that I am creating,
how to love her for nine months and ninety years?
I want to tear it from me.

Chains of hate run through my body
I die with rage every second.
My tongue clings to the roof of my mouth.

Where are you?
Why did you forsake me?
Blessed is he who repays the evil that they have done to me.

Happy are those who crush David's children
against the Rock.

—*Inspired by 2 Samuel 11:3-11; Psalm 137*

Healing—Anointing with Oil

With oil, we choose from these lines to say to each other while anointing:

• Where there are no words left, receive this sign of God's love.

• Receive this touch from my hand.

• Using the text and image of the Gethsemane.

• I will wait and watch with you.

A Girl's Prayer

The author of this prayer lives with foster parents after she was separated from her mother because of brutal abuse.

Jesus, please be with my little brother, who is still staying with my mom.
Please make her not beat him like she did me.
Help him not to be too lonely now that I am gone.
Show him that you are there to protect him.
Please protect him.
Let him know that I had to leave before mommy killed me.
Please help him to forgive me.

The Joy of the Children

O Lord, You that caress the faces of these children.

O Lord, You are the one that can make it possible for their joy
to shine forever,
that they keep such serenity rediscovered,
even if they saw tremendous, unthinkable things as can be,
like the war.

O Lord, become bearer of that simplicity with which they can have fun.

O Lord, make adults think that their feelings, their emotions,
their actions matter.
We pray in the name of your Son, Jesus Christ.
Amen.

A Lost Voice

Squatting in my little street corner this very dark night. It is cold and the darkness is scary. Who can hold me—the hand of God. Is there a God out there? God if you are there—if you can hear me, hold me through the night. I really want to sleep but my belly is rumbling. Please don't let them find me here, stop them from taking and hurting me. God—if you are there—hear my voice!

A Secret Whispered

A secret whispered from mouth-to-mouth as a sacred prayer too holy
to be spoken out loud.
A dream sheltered in the shade of the heart. Too much light might
burn it, too much heat might dry it out.

A hope so strong you already envision, you already belong to your life as it
has to be, as it deserves to be.

A secret, a dream, a hope, no time for "Goodbyes" and "God bless yous."
No time for "I'll miss you" and "Come back soon." No times to count the
dangers, how wide is the desert and how deep the sea.

Nothing can hold you back, nothing can stop your journey. No mother's
love, no father's worries.

Nothing can hold you back, there is a dream to fulfill, there is a journey of
faith to see through.
The strength of your youth will protect you, and the almighty God
you will call upon.

When the journey gets rough, when evil spirits threaten you with guns and
chains and hate and harm, to God you will turn to. 'Cause the strength of
your youth will protect you and your God.
Your victory will be God's honor and the life you are reaching will be
a living witnessing of God's rescuing power.

In the new land, in the land of your secret and dream and hope there will
be you and there will be your God. This much you know and this much
you need to know.

Dear Trinity

Dear Trinity,
my eyes scream in aching silences.
The waters of violence and death
drowned my joy.
I need your sweetness; I need your eyes on me.
Come, O dear Trinity, with your
soft breeze to heal my eyes
so I'll be able to see your
eyes in the eyes of my neighbor.
In your holy love I ask you.
Amen.

God the Father-Mother

You know what it is to lose a child.
You were inconsolable. My tears
dried like my belly.
I made the dark room my refuge and
your room a memorial.
In my lament you came as dew
and you watered the dry soil of my being
as a balm that refreshes and brings
the hope of a new day.
Take me in your lap, like
a mother who caresses her baby.
In his name, thank you.
Amen.

Our Life into Dust

Lord of the oppressed, and the oppressor:
see, the oppressor has crushed our necks and we cannot breathe.
They force us to do the things that we do not want to do.
They have crushed our life to the dust.

For the Mothers of Tivoli Whose Sons Were Murdered

Tune inspired by Dvorak's "New World Symphony."

Cassidy-JLU Spelling:

Faada Gad, a wanda ef yu a ier mi?
Mi wanda ef yu riili riil muo taim.
Mi nuo se yu naa sliip ino,
Bot somtaim mi fiil se yu gaan pan a likl viekieshan.
Eniwie, beg yu likl a yu taim de.
Yu nuo se mi riili a go chuu som aad taim?
Mi shiem fi se it bot,
Notn naa gwaan fi mi.
Bot mi no fiil sari fi miself,
An fi tel yu di chuut:
Mi no waahn yu fi fiil sari fi niida.
Arait, luk pan dis, Ja Ja:
Mi get a likl staal—Iihn?
A du a likl rork,
A trai put wan an tuu tugeda,
An som tiifin bwai go tek we mi staal!
Mi lef it uova nait an no fain it bak a maanin, Ja Ja!
Tel mi wa fi du ef mi kech dem bwai de.
Ihn? Wa mi mos du, no puol dem?
Aa bwai, Ja Ja!
A laik di muo yu trai, a di muo dem fait yu.
Bot mi stil a gwaan du mi ting . . .
Bot di neks ting nou a dem Babilan bwai de!
Dem si mi a trai fi mek a ting rork,
An bifuo dem go luk fi som mordara an tiif,
A mi dem kom waahn tek set pan?!
Mi naa rab!
Mi no tiif!
Mi no chobl piipl!
Bot a me dem kom waahn tek set pan?!
Muo taim,
A tel mi waahn tel dem fi go sok dem . . . !
Cho!
Chuu yu diivin nuo ou it griiv mi ino, Ja Ja!

Dem lov tek set pan puo piipl tu moch!
Bot, a Babilan bwai dem.
An a Babilan sen dem out.
An Babilan nuo wa dem a du.
A dem gi dem aadaz.
Bot yu si,
Babilan mos faal ino!
Babilan mos faal!
Mi nuo se yu naa go mek dis ya plies ya stie so fi eva.
Beta mos kom . . .
Mi kyaahn wiet fi yu bon dong dis ya plies ya kliin kliin kliin!
An mek it nais fi hevribadi!
Ya man,
Bon i' dong kliin, Ja Ja!
So aal a wi kyan api.

Popular (Non-Standard) Spelling:

Fada God, a wonda if yu a hear mi?
Mi wonda if yu really real more time
Mi know seh yu naa sleep eno
But sometime mi feel seh yu gone pon a likl vacation
Anyway, beg yu likl a yu time deh
Yu know seh mi really a go thru some hard time?
Mi shame fi seh it but
Nutn naa gwaan fi me
But mi no feel sorry fi miself
And fi tell yu di truth
Mi no want yu fi feel sorry fi me neither
Alright, look pon dis, Jah Jah:
Mi get a likl stall—Eeh?
A do a likl work,
A try put one and two together,
And some thiefin' bwoi go tek weh mi stall
Mi lef it ova nite and no find it bak a maanin, Jah Jah!
Tell me wah me fi do if mi ketch dem bwoi deh.
Eh? Wah mi must do, no poll dem?
Ah bwoi, Jah Jah!
A like di more yu try, di more dem fight yu.
But, mi still a gwaan do mi ting
But di next ting now a dem Babylon bwoi deh!
Dem si mi a try fi mek a ting work,

247

And before dem go lik fi som murderer and thief,
A me dem come want tek set pon?!
Mi no rob!
Mi no tief!
Mi no trouble people!
Bot a me dem come want tek set pon?!
More time,
A tell me want tell dem fi go sok dem . . . !
Cho!
Chuu yu deev'n know how it grieve me eno, Jah Jah!
Dem lov tek set pon poor people too much!
But, a Babylon bwoi dem.
And a Babylon sen dem out.
And a Babylon know wah dem a do.
A dem gi dem orders.
But, yu see,
Babylon must fall eno!
Babylon must fall!
Mi know seh yu naa go mek dis ya place ya stay so fi eva.
Betta must come . . .
Mi cant wait fi yu bun dong dis ya place ya clean clean clean!
And mek it nice fi everybody!
Yeah man,
Bun i' dong clean, Jah Jah!
So all a we can happy.

English Translation:

Father God, I wonder if you are listening?
I wonder if you're really there sometimes.
I know that you're not sleeping.
But, sometimes, I fear you are far away.

Anyway, I will only take a moment.
I'm really going through some tough times.
I'm ashamed to say it,
But I'm not making ends meet.
But I don't feel sorry for myself.
And, please don't feel sorry for me either.

Oh Father God, hear this:
Imagine, I got a stall to sell some stuff,

248

To get done the little that I can,
To make ends meet,
And, some thief took it away!
Overnight!
Tell me, Lord, what should I do if I catch him?
Should I not rid the earth of him?

Oh, God!
It's as if the more you try, the more they try to keep you down!
But I press on!

The police are another case!
They see you trying to do honest work,
And, instead of seeking out the criminals about,
They give me trouble.
I don't rob!
I don't steal!
I don't give trouble!
But they want to give me trouble!

Sometimes, I just wanna tell them off!
Sigh, it pains me so much what they do to me!
Why do they give me so much trouble?!

But they are mere pawns of the system.
The powers-that-be send them out.
They set the agenda.
They give them orders.

But you know,
Babylon must fall!
Babylon must fall!

I know you won't make evil triumph forever.
Better must come!
I can't wait until eternal fire consumes this place!
Until every high place is made low, and every low, high!
So we can all live.
Yes, Lord, let the fire cleanse this place!
So, we all can live.

You Are Emmanuel

God who does not see us up or see us down
You see our hearts and You know.

We hanker for empire, we lust after Babylon
Even when we know we will be enslaved.

Come and rescue us from our greed and discontentment
Come and deliver us from the grip of covetousness.

Teach us to care and teach us to share
Protecting Your creatures and creation from rape and destruction.

Lead us to keep the waters clean, lead us to save the forests
Guide us as we resist those who come to steal and kill.

You are Emmanuel. You have come to be with us.

Prayer against Despair

O that which in me cries out, hear the voice of hope

O my soul that sees no way out
Lift up thine eyes

O my soul that reminds me that life
It is not the size of this moment

O my soul, remember that your prayer
Crosses the skies

Is Everything All Right?

One day I asked a poor man in the Brazilian lands,
"Is everything all right, sir?"
And he answered me,
"Daughter, everything is a lot."
Surprised and embarrassed, I asked again:
"And how are things?" And he answered:
"Well, things are things and I am me. So, things go wrong, but I'm fine."

Birthday Blessing

Through the Spirit of God, I extend a warm invitation to any who have or will be celebrating their birthdays this week or this month to join me in the front.

Join hands and form a closed circle with priest or pastor, who then prays.

God the Creator and giver of life,
we rejoice in your steadfast love
as another year of life enriches all within this circle.
In a world numb to death,
let us not forget to celebrate life.
And in a world lacking intimacy,
we remember the joy you renew each year
through the lives of our loved ones.
Bless this circle (and others unable to be here)
with many more years to serve you.
Bless their families and their labors of love
as we devote their every breath to your hands.
Through Christ we all say,
Amen.

Spirit of the Living God

Spirit of the living God, speak through the language of your humble servant and whisper through the meditations of our hearts, as we experience your presence amidst our concrete realities. If ever in this sharing, I do not remember you, may my tongue cling to the roof of my mouth and my right hand be cut off. Keep us honest as we encounter you through your Word, just like Jesus, our rock and redeemer. Amen.

—*Inspired by Psalm 137:5*

Live and Die for Each Other

May the God of Justice and Righteousness empower you, the loving God guide and watch over you as you die and live for each other. Amen.

Choking

I am choking!
We are choking!

Chained by the dollar
Slaved by the white man's money

Tump Tump Tump, the sound of
Their good news is the hammer of their violence

Sound of chains wrenching, wrenching
The white man's Gospel is money

Their good news pounds us
Their gospel chokes us to death
We hear them pray:
Oh mighty dollar
Oh great green buck

This is their prayer in the name
Of greed. Amen.

Gracias por U Misericordia

Señor Jesús gracias por u misericordia
Para con tu pueblo latino.
Guárdanos y protégenos de todos los peligros
que acechan a nuestra gente.
Son muchas las fuerzas que se unen
Para quitar la paz y la armonía,
Pero tu amor compasivo supera
Todos los obstáculos.
Bendito seas que tú tocas los corazones
Que luchan por el bien hoy y por siempre.
Bendito y alabado seas protector nuestro.
Amén.

Padre y Madre Celestial

Padre y Madre celestial, te pedimos por las
Familias migrantes, aquellos que han construido
Su vida fuera de su tierra natal.
Los que tuvieron que correr de sus lugares,
Dejar sus viviendas, sus entornos, por amenazas de muerte,
Por peligros, desastres naturales, por mejores oportunidades económicas,
Porque no vieron otra posibilidad, porque no tenían otra posibilidad.
Que la utopía del evangelio se haga real
En nuestras comunidades, que seamos la mesa que recibe a todas
Las etnias, razas, lenguas, culturas y familias.
Que seamos el banquete que recibe a los que han sido excluidos y todos seamos
Invitados a sentarnos y compartir con Jesús.
Que seamos el lugar de protección, lugar de paz, de alimento, de acogimiento,
una familia, ciudades de refugio y cuidado.

Un lugar sin fronteras, sin estigmas, sin xenofobia, sin homofobia, sin racismo
Sin machismo. Un lugar para todos.

Señor Ten Piedad #2

Señor ten piedad, ten piedad de nosotros
Por no querer a nuestros vecinos indocumentados
Como nos queremos a nosotros mismos.
Cristo ten piedad, ten piedad de sus hijos indocumentados.
Tú has dicho que todo lo que hacemos por nuestros hermanos
Más humildes, por ti mismo lo hacemos.
Señor ten piedad, y por el poder de tu Espíritu Santo
Refórmanos a tu imagen misericordiosa
Para que reflexionemos y salva a los inmigrantes.

Healing in the Midst of Militarization

Lord we seek healing in the midst of militarization.
Hear the cry of the mother for the lost son.
The oppressor used the oppressed and promised them power and wealth
in return for devouring their own people.

We're Living under the Empire

God of Justice, we're living under the Empire of Land-Grabbing and Exploitation of Mineral Resources that is causing hunger, landlessness, homelessness, poverty, and malnutrition. It is enriching the minority and disempowering the majority.

We pray that under the power of the Holy Spirit and our lives together, we can stand in solidarity and reclaim our God-given natural resources. We act against human rights abuses. We resist the enriching of the Empire. We resist the impoverishment and dehumanization of the majority of the earth. We proclaim restoration of the stolen human dignity and a restoration of all that has been eaten by the locusts and the cankerworms of this world. We proclaim justice and renewal of fair and equitable socio-economic and political structures.

We pray all this in the name of Jesus Christ, our Lord and Savior. Amen.

Let the Oppressed Be Set Free

Open our eyes, Lord, for we are blinded with power, status, and wealth.

Open our ears to hear the cry of the poor.
Let your justice flow like a river and let the oppressed be set free.

The Oppressor

Woe to you who dare to take away the land of my ancestor, as in the days of the king of Israel who claimed the vineyard of Naboth.

I have cared for it, eaten from it, and my children have survived from it, and now you have compelled me to leave. I am not willing to part from it.

I cry to you, O Lord.
Judge my oppressor,
for the oppressor forces me to hand over my land and trade my life to the powerful capitalist.
Lord, bring justice to the proud and the mighty,
and fill the poor and the meek with good things.

We Bring Our Petitions before You

God of peace, love and justice,
we bring our petitions before you.

We are currently faced with challenges
posed by the empire of our day, which manifest in many forms and ways.
We pray that you will, through the power of the Holy Spirit, enable us to
confront these
powers head on.

We confess our failure to have courage to resist the exploitation of the
world powers; grant that we may have the necessary energy and zeal to
fight any forms of injustices.

We resist the appetite for minerals and other resources exhibited by the
empire,
so that these resources may be used for the benefit of all humanity.
In the name of Jesus Christ our liberator.
Amen.

Prayer against Empire

The God of concord,
we are living under the Empire of oppression, which is stealing from our
hard-fought little resources, our sweat. We pray that under the power of
the spirit and our lives together we may witness the demise of such evils
and welcome the birth of love, kindness, fellowship, and dignity among
ourselves. We proclaim and denounce the spirit of selfishness, greed, and
individualism against the Empire and may our merciful God create a new
heart in this Empire. We humbly submit our prayer in the name of our
Lord Jesus Christ. Amen.

Prayer for the Oppressed Woman

God of the oppressed women,
we are living under the empire of oppression and corruption,
which is taking away the productivity and joys of the woman, the empire
which is making women spend more time on the streets trying to make
ends meet. Women are on streets to beg in every sphere of life; we therefore remember those who work in and with poor conditions of service,
whose work of their hands is unappreciated, who have been forced to do
any kind of work, not because they have no qualifications, but because
they do not have the networks to be hooked up for a decent form of
employment.

We pray that under the power of the Spirit and our lives together,
we resist individuality and a lack of love and kindness for each other.

We reclaim the solidarity and a spirit of belonging to each other, even
amid this oppression and corruption, so that we may share not only our
struggles but our victories too.

In the name of the great women who have gone before us in the struggle
of being oppressed and yet are very much alive. Amen.

Prayer from Experience

God of all ages and God of love, who sees and hears your people at all
times.

We have seen you acting and sustaining us in midst of our challenges
and hopelessness.

In times of hunger you provided food for us to eat. When we had no place
to lay our heads you provided us with shelter. When we are faced with
death, we have seen your hand of protection. Amidst sickness you have
given us hope and courage to live on, not give up; to stand strong and not
to be selfish for the responsibilities you have entrusted us with.

Therefore, dear God, we continue praying that you give us hope amidst
hopelessness, courage in times of despair, healing in times of sickness,
provision in times of lack, protection in times of danger to live and hope
for a better world through Jesus Christ who is our sustainer, provider, and
protector. We pray, Amen.

God of the Poor, Deprived, and Oppressed

God of the poor, deprived, and oppressed. You who see no color and are not disturbed by the stench. Filled bellies and comfort may cloud and close our eyes, and the world may miss the beauty of your grace.

Lord Jesus, your birth exposed poverty. In a humble stable you came. Your experience of poverty assures me that you understand my situation, the dangers of my situation. Indeed, the dangers of my situation would probably destroy me had it not been for you.

When I lie down without shelter, exposed to the harshness of the element, I find solace in the beauty of the stars and the moon that shines through the darkest times of the night. Although most times I pray that it should not rain for fear that this might cause another sleepless night, I accept that it rains so others may produce food for us. You, indeed, are a God of life.

The night breeze, though sometime cold and harsh, lets me know that it is your breath that sustains my life. Holy Spirit, spirit of life, spirit of creation.

Lord, Drive Out All Evil

Lord, please drive out all evil things: money, power, oppression, and unjust exploitation in the workplace. Please break the chains of evil people and things. Please have mercy on those who cannot even breathe. Please do justice for those who oppress their own people.

God Our Love

God our mother and father, God our love, justice, and righteousness,
we come before you in the brokenness of our hearts,
for you alone, in your righteousness and justice can mend
our brokenness and strengthen us to fight against all injustices.

We are living under abject poverty in the midst of plenty,
our storehouses have grown grass while there is abundance on the other side
of our abode.
We pray that, under the power of the Spirit, you may enthuse and strengthen
us to face evil in the eye.
Give us the zeal to face the demons of corruption and exploitation,
help us not to lull the pain of the oppressed but to be a healing balm
and resistance.

Grant us the courage to speak truth to power and pronounce, "Thus says
the Lord!"
We pray that we may courageously name the evils of the empire. Lord, we
thus stand against sexual exploitation against our mothers, daughters, sisters, aunts, nieces, and grandmothers.
We stand against land grabs, against exploitation of our labor, and the
commoditization of our freely God-given resources.

Loving and just God, in the spirit of *Ubuntu*, heal us that we may see you
in each other,
that one's hurt, one's hunger, and one's desperation be that of all of us.
Convict us, that we may not be the same people who exploit one another.
Remind us, God, that we share a common destiny: that we are divinely
interconnected, one to another.
Remind us, God, that in this divine interconnectedness, we were created to be in solidarity with one another.

We pray for resilience, to fight and fight knowing victory is certain.
We thank you, God, for while we are pressed on every side, we are never
crushed; though we are often perplexed, we are never in despair.
We are ever so persecuted, but you never abandon us.
Yes, we are often struck down, yet we will not be destroyed.
Because of this we shall resist and justice shall be restored in your name.
Amen.

The Cliff

Skin tingles and hairs raise at the sound
The odor ravages one's being: infatuating, intoxicating, inundating
So tantalizingly sweet with the slightest hint of decay
Covered so beautifully in expensive paints and perfumes,
masquerading the truth underneath
A Gospel of Death, sold as a precious gift to curious people

Destroying, disrupting, disconnecting

Portraying stories of grandeur and facades of light,
devastating all in its path

All the while, a Parent weeps
This Parent, having given a gift of life, groans and shudders as it is utilized
to force little ones to a cliff
Each one tumbling off the edge, echoing endlessly
Causing pain so panging, probing, paralyzing

Yet, this Parent does not stand idly by

The same cliff becoming a platform of proclamation,
the Parent jumps off the edge
No ulterior motives: propelled simply by insatiable love
Seeking the lost
Saving the one
Sacrificing

Will we do the same?

God of Life, Friend of Women and Children

God of life, friend of women and children,
who stopped to talk to those the disciples walked past;
Jesus, who called upon the bleeding woman to tell her story,
we come to bring you her story,
Africa's story,
Our story.
We bring before you those whose land is barren,
raped and abused for profit,
whose seeds are sterile,
who have to beg to survive.

We bring before you the rage of helpless resistance,
to the care-less-ness of the privileged,
to the taboos that silence and divide and discredit all voices but their own.

We bring before you the blood of our ancestors
that has seeped into the soil,
those who have taught us never to accept
that this is the way the world is.

Just like menstrual blood,
may it bring forth new life,
a life of shared wealth, mutual respect, and new hope
through the labors of our resistance.

Amen.

Liturgy of Wailing and Sorrow

Ahhhhhhhhhhhh
Are the songs of our tears worship?
Ohhhhhhhhhhhh
Are the hymns of our anguish heard in the sanctuary?

**For there are no more "Alleluias" to sing
and our sanctus has been silenced
because now, God weeps with us.**

The blood of the innocent becomes our music,
the blood of the by-stander,
the blood of the father,
the blood the teenage boys,
the blood of those whose only crime is to be poor.

**For there are no more "Alleluias" to sing
and our sanctus has been silenced
because now, God weeps with us.**

We cry out with their mothers,
we anguish with the orphaned,
we grieve with the widows,
we cry out with those who are still under threat.

**For there are no more "Alleluias" to sing
and our sanctus has been silenced
because now, God weeps with us.**

Would you sing with us the wailing of our hearts?
Would you make music with the grief of the blood-stained earth?
Would you move to the rhythm of our agony?
And would you play with us the song of our pain?

**For there are no more "Alleluias" to sing
and our sanctus has been silenced
because now, God weeps with us.**

All:
**God of our tears who weeps with the crying of the earth,
who listens to the blood of the innocent,
who hears the prayers of the widow and the orphaned,
rise now and stand with your people. Take up our cause.
Silence now our tears and turn our sorrow to courage.
Gather all of us to rise up and resist the violent and the warmongers.**

**Use our tears to fuel our hope and use our hands to forge
the justice we seek.**

**In the name of all who were murdered,
in the name of the blood-stained earth,
in the name of the mothers, widows, and orphaned,
and in the name of the Christ who was slain but rose again,
we make this united prayer. Amen.**

For Mothers and Wives

Lord of Justice, mothers and wives are crying. Please listen to the voices, the prayers of those who are losing their sons and husbands. Please return justice to them.

Lord of mercy, please have mercy on the people who are in the midst of suffering.

Thank you, Lord, and thanks to the community and churches who are helping, who are wiping away the tears of the victims' families.

We believe that you are the God of justice and mercy, and also the God of hope. In Jesus's name we pray. Amen.

Money and Power Are Everywhere

Lord, Money and Power are everywhere and they make many evil things.

Lord, please listen. Your people are crying.
Please have mercy on your people. They are being ignored.
Please make justice surround us.

People are fighting, praying, and even being ignorant, it is true.
They are striving to regain their liberation and a secure life.

They Choose Not to See

They choose not to see, not hear and not speak for the lower people.
They have money and power to help but they reject that chance.

The lower people have no voice. They need justice and security.
They pray but there is no hope. They are left behind.

Oh Lord, please open the eyes of the wealthy and powerful to see
    the people's needs,
open their ears to hear the people's voices,
and open their mouths to speak for the rights of the lower people.
Don't leave them behind.

Hear Our Cry

Hear our cry, O God; attend to our prayer. From the depth of our sorrows, we call to you when our hearts are overwhelmed with fears and worries. Lead us to the wings that embrace us in love and peace.

Open

Open our eyes to see the pain and suffering
Open our ears to hear the cries of the oppressed
Let justice flow like a river to those who have been denied it
Let peace and security be like a strong, wide tree to the outcast
Open our mouths to be a voice for the voiceless

Neoliberalism—Imprecatory Psalms

Resist the temptation of money
Struggle with those who are bullied
Fight against the evil of this land
Stand for the rights of the oppressed
God, lift up the weak

On Behalf of the Corporation, the Rich

Dear Lord, forgive us that in our over-pursuits of wealth and prosperity we've strangled the poor, the helpless, the oppressed. Forgive us when we only see our interests, when we turn a blind eye to those who need help, even those who are under our care. May we see the plight of the people and may our compassion move us beyond words to actions.

Lord of Mercy and Grace

Lord of mercy and grace,

Please be with the suffering people, especially the killing among the innocent people!

Lord! We need your liberation from this fearful killing among such communities.

Lord! We plea for your comforts and mercy.

Lord! Please hear their crying. In Christ's name. Amen!

Prayer for Indigenous People

O God, for the people in the darkness,
you are the light.

Response:
Listen to our appeal, oh gracious Lord. (*Say this two times: the first time in English and the second time in an indigenous language appropriate to your congregation's context.*)

O God, for the people who are neglected,
you are the comforter.

Response

O God, for the people who are in fundamental need,
you are the provider.

Response

God of History

God of history, travel with us!

Lovely, colorful jeepneys
Crown with shiny tassels
A moving fiesta on wheels
With saints, Mickey Mouse, and Pacquiao
Ferrying workers, students, and families
And the many who have no cars to drive
Once a weapon of war
Reclaimed by the people
To thrive despite the pain of its history

God of many names, we call upon You!

The government wants the crowns and the tassels down
Modernized, electrified jeeps
From Japan, Germany, and other parts of the world
In the name of saving the earth
An unaffordable ride
An impossible choice
The environment or the poor

God of mercy, hear our cries!

Robbed with our eyes wide open
Our only means of transport
To take us through the scorching day and the rainy nights
Paralyzing bodies already broken
By the fist of inflation, corruption, and plunder
Of those in high places and power
Our humble jeepney threatened by those
Who only choose to see their own comfort

God of liberation, empower us!
As in the times of old
The people will rise
With the same God who was with us
And continues to be with us
As we turn weeping and mourning
Into joy and celebration
Death and destruction
Into life and fullness
Turning the fist of the co-opted
Into the raised fist of solidarity

O God, Be with Us

O God, be with us, let us be safe on our journey, let our resources be shared
among us
so that we can have a balance of life.
May all the Christians follow your call.

O God, we know that the leaders of the nations are careless; they are blind to
the realities of the people.
The motivation of money is greater than humanity.
The greediness of rich people who control the resources is coddled by the
government.
Resources necessary for life are not being shared.
The social structure puts further gaps between the rich and the poor so that the
rich do not know the poor.
Selfishness, weakness, and inhuman treatment of others are not the path of
Christ.
The needs of the people are becoming overshadowed by the wants of the multi-
national corporation.

Help the people to fight against these sad realties and the enemies who block
our way forward.
Let the downtrodden be empowered to resist the corrupt leaders of the nations.
May all the resources taken from people be returned through social services to
meet the needs of the people.
May the money be used to construct the path of development for the people.
Let there be light among us.

O God, give us strength to keep ourselves fixed on our destination.
Let justice roll on like a river, righteousness like an ever-falling stream.
May all the poor, marginalized people enjoy the grace of justice.
Let the churches be the witness in realizing the kingdom of God.
Let our faith have concrete praxis in changing the fate and circumstances of the
marginalized community.
Amen.

The Prayer for Peasant Community

I am hungry and cannot find food. The sea is polluted. The place where we used to go fishing and catch much is no longer there. The rich people have recreated lands to build malls.

God of Hunger, hear our cry.

I am longing for school, but it seems unreachable for me. I dream of playing on the playground, eating chocolate and ice cream but I can only play on the beach and eat rice and fish.

Our parent God, hear our cry.

I am sick, I have no medicine and no place where I can get cured. The pain in my body is hurting me day by day. I know you can heal people in amazing ways, even using nothing but saliva. Just like what you did to Bartimaeus, I believe you can do with me.

God the Healer, hear our cry.

Dear God, hurry up and come back. I need you desperately in order to survive and live again to the fullest.

Prayer of Confession

Lord, many laborers are underpaid. They have to pay back their debts. Money lenders are exploiting them. They are in debt and they are leading a debt-driven life.

Lord, we confess that we never shared our resources with these workers and hoarded our money.
Lord, we believe that you are here to provide daily bread to all of us. But the masters of this world are not interested in the bread of their laborers.

Response: Lord, we confess that on many occasions we sided with the masters of this world and accepted their favor.

Absolution: God of Justice, may you pardon our sins and lead us in the life path of justice, peace, and the grace of God.

Prayer of Confession
(in the Context of Factory Workers)

God of the poor, we bow our heads before you with heavy hearts and minds of repentance. Lord, we confess that we never looked into the pain that many people put into producing when we use many products. Sweat, bloodstains are on the products that we are using.

Exploitation

Lord we confess that we have never realized the exploitation behind many products.

Lord, have mercy on us.

Lord, many mothers spent their fruitful time at factories. When they left their homes, children were sleeping, and children were asleep when they arrived. Many children went to bed without seeing their mothers.

Lord, bless the children and pardon our sins for not listening to the cries of the children.

Domine

For people who kneel in the red soil and labor with their hands.
For we are all of the earth, and we all come from the labor of God's hands. We pray:
Leader Chant: Domine, audi nos
All: Domine, audi nos

For the workers in the condiments factory, and the sweat of their labor.
For we are all the salt, (and pepper, soy sauce, and vinegar) of the earth. We pray:

Leader Chant: Domine, audi nos
All: Domine, audi nos

We Are Sojourners

We are sojourners, we come from different places
We are sojourners, moving from one place to another
    At one point we are united, traveling, sharing, and helping each other
    In jeepney in the Philippines, in metro mini in Indonesia, and some others
We are sojourners, we have the chance to experience and to see the beauty of
    God's creation
We are sojourners, but we also see the world struggling with its pain

We have been stolen, destroyed and killed
People robbed people
The poor robbed the poor
We are trapped in a systemic evil
Fashioned by the empire

We are oppressed,
We see people's weeping, mourning, and crying
We see people's suffering on drugs and being killed on the street
We see people in hunger, no food, no drinks, yet survive to walk

In the midst of these we alight the jeepney and we arise as a community
In the weeping and mourning of God's whole creation we arise
In the journey of life, we arise
We rise up for justice and dignified life for all

Cover Me with the Night

A Traditional Prayer from Ghana

Come Lord
and cover us with the night.
Spread your grace
over us,
as you assured us you would.
Your promises are more
than all the stars in the sky;
your mercy is deeper than the night.
Lord it will be cold.
The night comes with its breath of death;
night comes; the end comes; you come.
Lord, we will wait for you, day and night. Amen

Loving God Let Your Spirit Ignite Us

Loving God, let your spirit ignite us.

Loving God, we experienced your presence in the pain of the people in the Philippines where bombs are turned into bells.

Loving God, we experienced your presence in the pain of the people in the planes where we journeyed, where jeepneys serve the people.

Loving God, we experienced your presence in the pain of the people in the other Philippine islands where there's oppression and the people turn guns into flutes.

Loving God, we experienced your presence in the pain of the people.

Loving God, in our suffering hear us when the government partners with mining companies to take our land.

Loving God, in our suffering hear us when corporations cheat and exploit the laborers.

Loving God, in our suffering hear us when the police and military kill our people in the name of peace and order.

Loving God, in our suffering hear us.

Mountains destroyed, rivers polluted, lowlands are flooded.

Lord, in your mercy, move us to renewal of our land.
    Dismembered, bodies without rest, people go hungry for days.

Lord, in your mercy, move us to renewal. We hear the mothers wailing for their dying children, fear prevails in our communities, the smell is all around.

Lord, in your mercy, move us to renewal.

Where your spirit transports us, make us instruments
of justice and peace,
    for the land belongs to God. Help us to restore our land.
For God has given us the strength of hands to create and work.
    May God help us to enjoy the fruits of our labor.

God, mother and father to us all and source of life,
        in the midst of death, resurrect our hope for life.

Ignition, Idling, Movement, and Transport

God of life, we uphold the Philippines to your care, where bombs are turned into bells.
Loving God, let your Spirit ignite us.
In places like Bataan, Quezon, Caloocan, and Valenzuela where people travel together in jeepneys of struggle.
Loving God, let your Spirit ignite us.
Where people turn guns into flutes, including those living in other islands facing oppression.
Loving God, let your Spirit ignite us.
When the government partners with mining companies to take our land.
God in our suffering, your Spirit idles.
When corporations cheat and exploit the laborers.
God in our suffering, your Spirit idles.
When the police and military kill our people in the name of peace and order.
God in our suffering, your Spirit idles.

Lord, wherever mountains are destroyed, rivers polluted, and lowlands are flooded.
Lord, in your mercy, move us to renewal.
Where fingers are dismembered, bodies lack proper rest, and people go hungry for days.
Lord, in your mercy, move us to renewal.
Where fear prevails in our communities, the smell of death is all around, and where we hear mothers wailing for their dying children.
Lord, in your mercy, move us to renewal.

For the Land belongs to God and it is our duty to restore it.
Where your Spirit transports us, make us instruments
of justice and peace.
For God has given us the strength and the hands to create and work.
Where your Spirit transports us, make us instruments
of justice and peace.
God, our mother and father, the source of our lives, in the midst of death, may you restore in us a hope for life.
Where your Spirit transports us, make us instruments
of justice and peace. Amen.

271

Dry Bones #2

God of Life, we are living in a valley of dry bones
we have lost our identity . . . we have lost our humanity.

>We are unable to feel, we are so numb;
>we are unable to reach out to the poor,
>to those we have segregated as religious and social outcast.

>We have forgotten our being *adamah*: the tiller . . . the steward.
>The whole of creation groans in travail.

God of Life, we are living in a valley of dry bones,
we have lost our identity . . . we have lost our humanity.
>Wars, killings, acts of terror, and insurgencies surround us.
>Deaths happen in every corner.
>People are dying before their time, every tick of the clock.
>Children and women are being trafficked every day in the millions.
>Our communities are disintegrating and descending into chaos and
>   lifelessness.

God of Life, we are living in a valley of dry bones,
we have lost our identity, we have lost our humanity.

>Descend upon us, once again.
>May your Spirit restore to wholeness our humanity.
>May we image You, once again.

>Enable us to touch our neighbors and build solidarities.
>Enable us to build peace and institute justice in our relationships.
>Enable us to break the barriers that are destroying our communities.
>Enable us to bridge the gaps that separate us from each other.

Transform this valley of dry bones
into a playground of the children of God. Amen.

Blessed Are They

Blessed are the poor in spirit, for theirs is the kingdom of heaven.
And they are still poor.
And the poor get killed, every day, in our streets, in our midst.

Blessed are those who mourn, for they will be comforted.
And the mothers, the children continue to weep in pain and in anger.
And the killings continue.

Blessed are the meek (humble), for they will inherit the earth.
And they continue to be hidden, not able to participate in our worship,
stigmatized, and discriminated.

Blessed are those who hunger and thirst for righteousness, for they will be
filled.
And they die, every meal, every day.
And their hunger kills them in their every meal.

Blessed are the merciful, for they will receive mercy.
Blessed are the pure in heart, for they will see God.
And they were exploited in so many ways.

Blessed are the peacemakers, for they will be called children of God.
Blessed are those who are persecuted for righteousness's sake, for theirs is
the kingdom of heaven.
And they are getting killed.
And their lives are being taken as they pursue justice and peace for all.

Blessed are you when people revile you and persecute you and utter all kinds
of evil against you, falsely on my account.
And they get imprisoned for the crime they didn't commit.

Blessed are you who pray and praise God in your altar and places of worship.
We cage all these inhumane acts in our land and to our people in the songs,
in the verses, in the charity works of our churches, in our prayers.
May we depart from praying, that we may be able to really 'bless' them.

Luke 1:26-38

The angel of the Lord told Mary "Don't be afraid, Mary. God is honoring you" (Luke 1:30).

We remember all the migrants who are fleeing because of war and conflicts in their country.
—Do not be afraid.

We remember the street children and old people in the streets of Kolkata who die in hunger and thirst.
—Do not be afraid.

We remember all the transgender people in India, the discrimination and rejection that they are experiencing from many, every day.
—Do not be afraid.

We remember the Lumads who are still in the evacuation centers, the Lumads who were back in their places but are still worried and scared because of the threat in their lives.
—Do not be afraid.

We remember the many families in Talaba, Zapote, the families who live under the bridge, Tuvalu, Fiji, and other islands that wrestle with climate change.
—Do not be afraid.

I am remembering the people and families who survived from typhoon Yolanda, those who are still grieving and waiting for assistance and support.
—Do not be afraid.

I am remembering my LGBTQ friends and loved ones—worried and afraid to be rejected; those who are still seeking for acceptance, belongingness, open and safe spaces, those who are longing for open doors and open hearts.
—Do not be afraid.

I am remembering those who are worried and afraid because they don't know what to prepare on their Nochebuena table later, the parents who are still struggling up to this time just to prepare for their next meal.
—Do not be afraid.

GRRR

GRRR * *make sounds of a growling stomach*
Do you hear the sound of an empty stomach?

GRRR *
Do you recognize this sound?

GRRR *
Do you know the feeling of hunger?

Or are you always filled?

Always have plenty and more,
that such a sound and feeling is alien to you.
Strange in your ears and a feeling that you have never experienced.

Learn it, recognize it and experience it.
Perhaps there you'll hear God finally speak!

Mary Pray for Us
See page 82 to read *Ahhh!!! Not Alleluia*, which inspired this artwork.

PART SIX

PRAYERS BASED ON THE LITURGICAL CALENDAR

PRAYERS BASED ON THE LITURGICAL CALENDAR

Advent

Lord Jesus,
you were deprived of a home for much of your life:
you were born in a stable,
soon you became a refugee in Egypt,
during your ministry you said you had nowhere to lay your head,
you hosted your last supper before your death in someone else's house,
you were buried in someone else's tomb,
you understand the plight of the homeless.

We pray for those who have been displaced
by wars, land grabs, unemployment, and poverty.
When mining companies have come, raped our land, and used our people as
    cheap labor,
and have then deserted their mines, barren land impossible to cultivate,
they have left our communities in tatters.

Fathers, mothers, children have left home in search for work, for food, for
    meaning,
only to find violence, drugs, danger, rape, and loneliness,
in makeshift squatter camps, dominated by a few.
Rejected and ridiculed by all who pass by.

Where are you?
You have told us that you are with the poor and the homeless.
You have also called us to be their answer to prayer.
This is the radical gospel.
Can we live up to it?

During Advent, we prepare our hearts to invite you to make your home in us.
Give us courage and love to invite the homeless in our cities and townships
    into our own homes
and into our own church.
Help us to hear their stories and walk with them the extra mile,
for we are the hope that you have promised.

Amen.

Reimagining Worship
An Advent Prayer of Thanksgiving and Intercession

Voices singing an anthem of thanksgiving:
no more let sins and sorrows grow,
nor thorns infest the ground.
He comes to make his blessings flow
far as the curse is found.
                    —*From the hymn "Joy to the World" by Isaac Watts (1719)*

The Flight to Egypt

God of the homeless, the refugee, the displaced: we come expectant and hopeful before you. In the world around us today we find ourselves surrounded by those, like Christ, without a place to simply be. A season of blessing, our season of rain, is a curse for those without shelter.

You know what it is like to be displaced from your home, your family expelled from Israel out of fear of Herod. In the same way, people flee their homes in fear of earthly leaders, uncertain of what the future may hold. Those whose land have been taken from them despair at the loss of valuable assets and resources.

Lord of hope, we are assured of your provision in this season where we expect the Bread of Life. We are assured that you come to be with those who lack, those on the periphery, as we remember you being born in a manger.

We are assured that your hand is outstretched to all, first to the poor and then to the rich, as first shepherds and then magi came to the place of your birth. Incarnate in hopeless situations for us, your people, we pray.
Amen.

Transfiguration #1

Lord, you create each one of us in your image
Yet the powers of darkness have marred your stamp on us
By reducing us to mere trash and good-for-nothing beings
May your transfiguration power may work on the way we follow you
So we may regain our place in you and in this world

Transfiguration #2

O Lord, God of our ancestors,

We come before you to reclaim and repossess our land, resources, minerals, our culture, and dignity. We pray for the cleansing of our atmosphere and rivers and the reunion of our disintegrated families.

We pray for those whose future have been destroyed by the works of the Empire, that their lives can be restored to a better future. We also place before you those innocent souls that are dying due to sins they have not committed and those they have; we pray that they be made whole and have their health restored.

We also pray for the homeless who are living in desperation and hopelessness, that you make them find comfort in you as their shelter.

This we pray in the Name of our Transforming Lord Jesus Christ.
Amen.

Easter #1

Thank you, God, for sacrificing your son Jesus Christ
for our sins and iniquities.
Through your compassion you carry our pain and suffering.
Help us, Lord, never to take your gift of love for granted
and for the pain you endured on the cross to set us free.

Easter #2

Dear God,
Thank you for your goodness and mercy.
You are a mighty God and death could not hold you.
You took away the sting of death.
Help us to live in the grace of your resurrection.
Your resurrection has brought us hope that one day we will be with you.
We pray for our nation,
that through your resurrection
we will regain resilience and be able to free ourselves from the chains
   of bondage.

Easter #3

Jesus, our sacrificial lamb, so meek as to endure suffering you never
caused. As you were overwhelmed with the weight of death in the garden,
we are inundated with the same. Your people have lost hope and death
seemingly prevails.

Our African values are in a state of decay. The people follow suit: numbing
the pain with whatever substance they can find. We are lost, sheep without
a shepherd. Like your disciples, helpless as you hung on the cross and
died, so are we the people of Africa: lost and in despair.

May we not be short-sighted, missing the immanent resurrection. Mourning may linger in the night, but joy comes in the morning. Assure us that
as Christ triumphed over death, so too will we be raised into new life. May
we, like Paul, proclaim victory over death: Where is your sting? Empower
us to partner with you in the resurrection of Africa.

In Christ, the Messiah of Africa, we pray. Amen.

Pentecost #1

Come, Holy Spirit, come. We cry out for new life, for new wine in new wineskins. Jesus promised us that a counsellor would be sent and that if we asked, we would receive. God our Mother, come and comfort us. In comforting us, empower us. Where we are empty, fill us. Those who have lost sight of any future, fill with unquenchable hope. Those trapped in addiction, break their bonds and fill with new resolve. Those within prostitution and sexual immorality, fill with a new sense of dignity and awaken them to a new and transformed sense of being. The children born with terminal illnesses, cover with your Spirit of healing for restoration and renewal. May the fire of your Spirit burn and consume within us, taking with it all that resembles empire. Amen.

Pentecost #2

Glorious Spirit of the living God
Descend on us and alter the plight of the unemployed
Yes, the law was meant to save Israel, but disobedience killed them
We too have failed, in spite of good policies and structures, to protect the
vulnerable among us
Come, Holy Spirit, come

The law kills, but the Spirit gives life
Do make yourself known in the life of those without hope, that in searching the Scriptures your very Word would provide encouragement, solace,
and empowerment
Come, Holy Spirit, come

In you, Father, Son, and Holy Spirit, lies the power of a united force.
Teach us, we ask, that divided we fall and united we stand. Come, Holy
Spirit, come. Come, dear God, and bind Africa with cords that can never
be broken. Remind us, wind of life, that *umuntu ngumuntu ngabantu*
This unity we need for Africa to take her place among the community
of the living

We forgot your law and lost our land. We looked upon those who
came preaching your word and suffered battering, rape, and plundering. Comforter, come and restore us. Give us hope that tomorrow is a
better day

Pentecost #3

I am building a people of power
God the Holy Spirit
Like a mother, you have brought us forth
And in your infinite power
You have continued to sustain us in our daily struggles
In the midst of much exploitation and injustice, cause us not to be silent
Like you did to the timid and fearful disciples
Give us the boldness to proclaim your righteousness and justice

May you cause us as a continent to unite in making your truth known and
    experienced
May your fire of heaven
Consume our greed and self-centeredness
So that all we have may be held in common
Spirit of truth and power, we are not afraid
Of being misunderstood
As being out of our mind
As this was done by your early disciples

Parousia #1

The congregation is invited to respond with the words written in bold.

We come to you with sickness, illness within our people, communities, and nations.
Come, Lord Jesus, come.
We come with the unemployed, underemployed, and underpaid.
Come, Lord Jesus, come.
We come with those evicted from their land, wandering aimlessly in unknown places.
Come, Lord Jesus, come.
We come with the dying and those in despair.
Come, Lord Jesus, come.
Help us to share the little that we have.
Come, Lord Jesus, come.
Empower us to resolve these injustices we face, that which has been broken, that your Kingdom would come to bear.
Come, Lord Jesus, come.

Parousia #2

Lord Jesus,
we come to you in our broken state caused by the empire.
We are looking forward to your coming back to us. Come, Lord Jesus.
We pray that all the sicknesses, such as HIV/AIDS, TB, cancer, Malaria, Cholera . . . will be taken away from Africa, come, Lord Jesus.

On your coming, we look forward to you reuniting us as a people because we are divided by the empire.
We look forward to the restoration of our communities and our broken relationships, including nature. Come, Lord Jesus.

On your coming, let your people of Africa be empowered to work hard and soldier on in very difficult circumstances, which have been created by the empire, such as land expropriation, corruption, disease, barbarism, poverty, hunger, and discrimination of women, children, and races.

Lord Jesus, come.

We pray for the capacity to restore all this. Come, Lord Jesus.

We are also praying for the spirit of forgiveness and solidarity so that the oppressor and the oppressed will learn to share equitably the resources you bestowed on us. Come, Lord Jesus.

Make it possible for us to speak out and mend the broken state and relationships so that we are reunited with our relatives and friends. Come, Lord Jesus.

On your coming, Lord Jesus, enable us to share the resources, both material and non-material, of our nations.

We pray for the spirit of preservation to protect and preserve the earth and all that dwells in it. Come, Lord Jesus.

We pray that people in Africa remain in their nations and the empire not to be given powers any more to exploit the Africans and force them to migrate from their own land and nations.

Come, Lord Jesus. Amen.

Parousia #3

Eternal God in whom is all life,
as we meditate on your second coming, we pray for the salvation of all human-
    kind.
We pray for those aspects of our lives that we have not yielded to you.
We pray for those who are dying, that they may have hope in your promise
    that all who are in you shall live.
We pray for those who are using your people for personal gain.

We resist all greed and injustice in the world, and in our hearts.
May the knowledge that you are returning again
bring a culture of valuing our sisters and brothers.
Purify us even as we purify ourselves,
like your bride preparing for the coming of her groom.

We are mindful of your coming judgment, that you will reject
greed, selfish pleasures, and exploitation of one by another.
May we be consumed by your ever-coming presence.

These things we pray in the name of Jesus,
whose body and spirit were nurtured in Africa,
who lived in Nazareth where his ministry was rejected.
He died for all but rose again to life,
he ascended to heaven and is always among us.
Amen.

Maundy Thursday Liturgy

The leader gives a brief welcome and introduction to the service, Maundy Thursday.

Leader: Jesus said, "Come to me all you who are weary and carry heavy loads . . ."

Response: " . . . and I will give you rest."

—From Matthew 11:28

Invitation for individual blessing and anointing with oil.
(Folks may softly sing during anointing. "Come Ye Disconsolate," by Thomas Moore or another similar hymn is recommended.)

Confession: "Almighty God . . ."

The leader shares a prayer for reconciliation and understanding or the Serenity Prayer.

Reading: Psalm 23

Reading: 1 Corinthians 11:23-26

Choral Music: "Done Made My Vow to the Lord"

Maundy Thursday Foot-Washing Liturgy

This service is especially useful for congregations that have or are launching a podiatry ministry to provide foot care for those in need in the community.

The leader gives a brief welcome and introduction to the service, Maundy Thursday, and the significance of foot washing.

Opening Prayer

Leader: Almighty and ever-living God, in your tender love for the human race you sent your Son, our Savior, Jesus Christ to take upon him our nature, and to suffer death upon the cross, giving us the example of his great humility. Mercifully grant that we may walk in the way of his suffering, and also share in his resurrection, through Jesus Christ our Lord, who lives and reigns with you and the Holy Spirit, one God, for ever and ever. Amen.

Reading:
Exodus 12:1-4
Psalm 116:1, 10-17
1 Corinthians 11:23-26
John 12:1-11

Leader: The Lord Jesus, after he had eaten with his disciples and had washed their feet, said to them, "Do you know what I, your Lord and Master has done to you? I have given you an example that you should do as I have done."

Just as God has showered his love on us and blesses our feet to walk on right paths, so we bless you, our brothers and sisters, and wash your feet as an act of love so that you may also know that God cares about your journey. The washing of your feet is a symbolic act that speaks to us that God cares about our journey, both physically and spiritually.

—Adapted from John 13:14

Washing of the Feet

The following can be read by a chosen Lector during the foot washing.

Lector: Peace is my last gift to you, my own peace I now leave with you; peace that the world cannot give, I give to you. I give you a new commandment: love one another as I have loved you.

Blessing of the Podiatrists

All who are involved in this ministry are invited to come forward for a blessing.

From 1 Corinthians 12:14-20, we hear these words:
"The body isn't one part but many. If the foot says, 'I'm not part of the body because I'm not a hand,' does that mean it's not part of the body? If the ear says, 'I'm not part of the body because I'm not an eye,' does that mean it's not part of the body? If the whole body were an eye, what would happen to the hearing? And if the whole body were an ear, what would happen to the sense of smell? . . . As it is, there are many parts but one body."

Sisters and brothers joined together in one body,
this day we seek God's blessing
as we gather with thankfulness
to bless those who are healers
of our feet and their ministry of reaching out
to our community.

Taking their hands, someone blesses each individual with these words:

God of all that is good and holy, we ask your blessing upon this man/woman that she/he might be your healing hands and your traveling feet in our world, healthy and courageous. Amen.

Following the individual blessings:

From Psalm 91:11-12, we hear these words:
"Because he will order his messengers to help you,
    to protect you wherever you go.
They will carry you with their own hands
    so you don't bruise your foot on a stone."

Let us pray:
Holy God, on this day, we ask you send your circle of angels to protect all who are vulnerable, suffering, or afraid. We especially ask your blessing and guidance be given to these healers in our midst and to those who work to support them at Temple's School of Podiatry. Guide their hands and their feet as they travel the holy ground that is our city offering comfort and hope to those in pain. May the touch of these healers be as tender as your loving touch is upon all humanity.

In the name of the most vulnerable and incarnate God we pray,
Amen.

Prayers of the People

Prayers conclude with Lord's Prayer, Serenity Prayer, and the passing of the peace.

Communion

After supper he took the cup of wine; and when he had given thanks, he gave it to them, and said, "Drink from this, all of you. This is my blood

of the covenant, which is poured out for many so that their sins may be forgiven" (Matt 26:27-28). Whenever you drink it, do this for the remembrance of me.

Send your Holy Spirit upon these gifts. Let them be for us, the Body and Blood of your Son. And grant that we who eat this bread and drink this cup may be filled with your life and goodness.

(The body of Christ broken for you.)

The body and blood of our Lord Jesus Christ. Feed on him in your heart by faith and thanksgiving.

Prayer after Communion

God of abundance, you have fed us with the bread of life and the cup of salvation. You have united us with Christ and one another, and you have made us one with all your people in heaven and on Earth. Now send us forth in the power of your Spirit that we may proclaim your redeeming love to the world and continue forever in the risen life of Christ our Savior. Amen.

Blessing and Dismissal

Leader: Go in peace to love and serve the Lord.
People: Thanks be to God.

May your strength
and protection
be lifted upon him
so that he might
also smile tomorrow

Jamaican God-Boy
See page 300 to read *No, Children, Nuh Cry!*, which inspired this artwork.

PART SEVEN

PRAYING THROUGH POETRY

PRAYING THROUGH POETRY

Worship Spaces in the Philippines

In the space between pulpit and pews
There's a sermon
There's a baby crying of hunger
And plenty rushing to calm her
Before the need to be fed
Becomes the only message heard

In the space between breath and air
Is the smog of traffic
There's steam from clothes
Hanging in the sun
Up high like fuel costs
As the fumes of false hope
Draw people to capital cities

In the space between factory and public road
Is a tarp stretched over a bamboo shelter
Three kids call it home
And their kitchen
Is a charcoaled pot
Sitting lonely on two bricks

In the space between mother and umbrella
Is a child
Clutching to a fading tomorrow
As greedy companies collapse unions
And parents disguise their fears

Smiling at their young
Playing basketball

In the space between Bible and policies
Is a missing paper trail
Smeared with the blood of the outspoken
Systemically hidden
While unsafe workplaces
Pull the trigger on another
And death continues
To fall on gold-filled ears

In the space between church and shopping mall
Clouds are painted with electric cables
Peaceful protesters charged
Police plug corpses with evidence
But the real shock
Are the foreign ties
Worn with white collars

In the space between life and living wage,
There's a community-run school
desperate for funding
There are families
Sharing scraps with animals
But the real beast
Is the smell of displacement

In the space between CEO and a pregnant teacher
There's a birth-quake of resistance
Conceived through churches and workers
Laboring the pains of solidarity
While men with big briefcases
Tempt abortion

In the space between pulpit and pews
Poor people are praying
Tears flowing down to the feet of Christ
Like the river Jordan
Where the Word was preached
And liberation made flesh
Where real worship begins
And the message of HOPE lingers

Reclaiming Hope

Desolation
Expansive plains littered with lost lives, tin and bricks scattered, stranded
Homes shaped of what was tossed away by others, human and object
    indiscernible
Weathered faces with cracks and crinkles, splotches of colors and scars
Arrogant, bombastic banners and buildings boom: imposed by slave drivers in
    blood-covered suits
Rumbles of empty stomachs reverberate raucously in skeletal frames
And yet, a flicker
Light

Jubilant eruptions with holey grins as children gallivant through rubble and
    debris
Uncontainable contentment in the peace of a grandmother watching over them
All-consuming passion filling defiant daughters abandoned by disinterested
    dear ones
How is it possible?
Hope? Here?
Humanity

Rich resource of life and abundance trapped in bias and prejudice
False perceptions, fake love and forbidden interaction forcing it away
Foolish ones! Fear not! Face yourself!

The hope you seek is buried under the lies of those who seek to keep you under
The hope you seek has been formed under the crushing weight you set on
    other people
The hope you seek is in them, it is in you: God ingrained, God inspired, God
    breathed
Open your arms! Release your greed! Fill yourself anew!

Hope burns when your brother is embraced, your sister supported, your elders
    upheld
Reclaim your people! Reclaim them: your home, your hope

Sea Breeze

Sea breeze,
You, who refresh the life of the Jamaican people
You who take the moisture of the sea into the
Bodies of people, animals, and plants . . .
You who shake loose the hair of the Rastafarian
The women's dresses in the service . . .
You who stoke fires and cigarettes,
You who push boats and lift airplanes,
You who propagate the sound of reggae and the noise of life
You who bring the rains and take them away
You who spread seeds and discreetly create hope . . .
You, sea breeze

We asked for freshness for the heat of the day,
Strength to find ways out of the confusing alleys of Kingston,
Patience in the congested traffic of life
Seek for me decent work, perspective . . .
Dry the sweat on the body and face
Free the parks, the sea, the city, the bodies
Sway to our songs and rhythms,
Spread wide the smiles of the children on the Trench Tour
Animate young students
Calm frustration
And sweep away the violence

In the name of the wind of yesterday, today, and tomorrow
Amen

Reclaiming Africa's Possessions

Africa was born with possessions
God-given possessions of resources
Africa's possessions are snatched away daily
Snatched away by the empire

Africa, reposition yourself
Reposition yourself to reclaim your possessions
Take up courage and possess your possessions
Possessions given by the Uncreated Creator

Reclaiming Identity as African Women

Burdened by patriarchy, colonialism, globalization, and numerous societal
   expectations
Burdened by our self-inflicted low esteem
Burdened by religious restrictions and boundaries
Burdened by family responsibilities
Shaking off all these burdens and reclaiming our freedom, our dignity and self-
   worth as African Queens

Amidst all the trials and tribulations, we remain resilient and tenacious as ever
We are the Queens of the universe
We nurture and nourish life
We care for the side-lined
We comfort and console the bereaved

African Queens hold half of the sky and remain standing
Silenced, ridiculed and battered: we remain defiant
African Queens we are the heartbeat of our continent
Queens indeed!

Crossroads and Constant Spring

I lift up my eyes.
What do I see?
The great divide . . .
bond and free.
Exploited and exploiting,
displaced and established,
the powerful and the powerless,
entangled and fragile!

Let my spirit be lifted Lord,
let my soul behold your beauty,
the bounty of your resources,
the over-flowing of your unfailing love.
Let me know they are mine too,
Lord, let me hope.

Our Mother (The Lord's Prayer)

Our Mother
That inhabits the earth and waters the floors
And colors the skies
Blessed are the names with which we call you
And blessed are the fruits you provide us

May justice come to your sons and daughters
And may there be fullness together with a dignified and good life
May your riches be shared with equity
So that there is no lack of bread, rice, yams, potatoes, milk, or wine
On any table or on any street

Forgive us the abuse
And the agrochemicals and the immoral failing
The waters that we poison
The contaminated air

Lead us not into the perverse temptation
Of greed and lust
Of the pride of power
And the arrogance of wealth

Because yours is the memory of the loving creator
And the present of the struggle for abundance
And the future of all hope

No, Children, Nuh Cry!

Baby faces ribbons in hair
Running free in Emancipation Park
Hello! Hello! Let's shake the hands
Let's go and run free

Eager faces smart in uniforms
Politely greeting and saying, "Good morning!"
ABCs and 123s, Nanny of the Maroons, our hero
Learning to save, learning to play, learning to pray

Three to six then ready for school
All the way to high school
Dreaming of the world and a job to follow
Steady all the way, keep the eye on the prize

Dark-Skinned God-Boy

Who is this dark-skinned God-boy,
running through the dusty streets of Jamaica?

Who is this God-boy, who can smile
between the piles of rubbish?

Who is this God-boy who plays in the
slums of Jamaica?

This boy, Father, lost his father,
touched by police bullets.
This child, God, looks into the despairing
eyes of his mother.

This God-boy still smiles at me.
This God-boy still dreams.

May your strength be lifted upon him
and your protection;
may the plant of hope continue
living under my feet.

May the plant of hope grow
and offer him shade and freshness in
the middle of the war for the black boy
who smiles wide, so that he might also smile
tomorrow.
Great, Divine Love.

Prayer

Defiant God, move us from complacency
And give us a sense of urgency
"State of emergency" haunting the country
Help us to proclaim the divine remedy

"Defiance or Compliance"
We come to conspire to defy the empire
People fed up with the domination and contamination
They think we complain but they will see our defiance
We will resist until they desist

Some people have yacht, while others have naught
Some have too much to eat, while others grind their teeth
Too much oppression and a whole heap of depression
It's time to make the regime retreat

You think it easy to defy?
The empire likes to crucify!
But the one whom we obey
Gives us courage to disobey

So we will strive and fight and rectify

Together

Together we walked the streets, the roads,
The mountain of trash
Waiting to be burned

Together we listened to your mothers
Your fathers, your aunties
And all who helped you to be
The beautiful children you are

Together we saw the bullet holes
Where your lives were
Forever changed

For you, our little ones, we pray

That the pain of such
Violent loss

Might not take away the
Light in your eyes

That the delight you shared
As we played in the puddles
Might always shine where you go

That the hope you offer
In the midst of despair
Be a reminder of God's
Kin-dom on earth

That the love of God's
Broken heart
Hold you when you feel alone

And always may we
Walk together
In prayer, in peace
And in love
Amen

The Color of Hope

Painting toenails in the place
Of death
At least twenty bottles
Of nail polish on the floor

She sits with her friend
Even as her mother
Shows me where the bullets
Came through her broken wall

Hope in the place of death
Color where color has drained away
Painting beauty where there has
Been so much ugliness

God help us always to
Walk with the
Hope of this
Toenail painting
Resurrection

Standing in the Trash Heap

Standing in the trash heap
Wondering why no one
Comes to take it away

Pieces of our lives
Broken and rotting in
The hot Jamaican sun

Even the goats move to
Places where the rot is not
So strong

But you, O God, tell us
That we are not trash
Even when the smell has
Soaked into our souls

You love us, O God,
Into wholeness
You do not pass us by
But caress us
As the treasures of your heart

Fearfully and wonderfully made
Help us, O Lord, to see
Us through the mirror of your eyes

Reclaiming Land

Land, land, land, our treasure
God gave us land to till
God gave us seeds to sow in the land
Whose land is it anyway?
Land, land, land, our treasure

Land, land, land, our treasure
Some call it the land of our ancestors
Some call it the land of the Great Spirits
The Empire has taken the land for itself
But the land is our land, our treasure

God has created the earth and all its fullness
Land, land, land: this treasure belongs to God
We all belong to God, as land belongs to God
Come share with him, her, me, this treasure
Land, land, land, our treasure

Economy depends on our land
Our future as Africa depends on this treasure
Our fears concerning our economy and future are real—why steal our land,
    our treasure?
Why sell and privatize our land, our treasure?

God, bless our land, your land, our treasure
God, quench the fires of human greed that inspire the privatizing of land
God, grant us strength and wisdom to be good stewards of the land
Land, land, land, our treasure

Reclaiming African Heritage

Africa the Cradle of Humanity
Africa the abode of phenomenal leaders: Kwame Nkrumah,
    Julius Nyerere, Kofi Annan,
Nelson Rolihlahla Mandela, Winnie Madikizela Mandela,
    Mbuya Nehanda, Sekuru Kaguvi,
and Yaa Asantewa
Africa endowed with beauty
Africa the land of abundance

We celebrate African hospitality
The warm African sun
The magnificent Kilimanjaro
The River Nile
The great Mosi-oa-Tunya ('The Smoke which Thunders'), Victoria Falls
The diverse and rich cultural traditions
The big five, crawling and flying things
The rich mineral resources
The productive agricultural land
The expansive water sources
The mountains and valleys

Africa: our birthplace and our burial site

Reclaiming Image

I am the image
The very image of perfection
You see, I take after my creator
I resemble the one I serve

She who kneaded me together, had a plan
She who sculptured me, is following a blueprint
The blueprint was one of perfection
How do I know this?

I see her pausing to reflect on this piece of work that is me
With a radiant smile on her face she nods:
Perfect, just perfect!

I am the image, the very image of perfection
The perfection that is my mother is my blueprint
The perfection that is my father is the chisel moving expertly,
Guided by the skillful and steady hand of love

I am the image, the image of perfect love; that is me
Look at me and see love, touch me and let my warmth relay the story
Of the perfect love that is creating me

I mirror my creator's perfection
No wonder she cannot stop looking at me
She knows I've captured her perfectly
In me the image is perfect

Reclaiming Reality

Bruised and battered, I smile through the pain
I smile even with the taste of blood in my mouth
I smile even as I spit out my bloody teeth into my hand
Why do I smile

They say I have to be strong
I have to smile to avoid trouble, my anger, they say, disturbs the peace
I have to think of the children
My smile that portrays a non-existent peace, a peace I don't know

Peace, peace; to hell with peace
Will God really hold the truth against me
This is not peace I want to teach my daughter
There must be something better
But what is it, where do I get it

Problem is I don't want her to cry with me
So I smile, a smile of confusion
    A smile of despondency
How do I teach her a genuine smile

I don't want my daughter to smile
I want her to have a genuine laughter,
Uncontrollable and unreserved laughter, indecent laughter even
Let it roar deep from her belly
Let her laugh with an open mouth and her head rolled back
To hell with peace

Solidarity with the Poor

PART EIGHT

PRAYING THROUGH SCRIPTURE

PRAYING THROUGH SCRIPTURE

Romans 12:13

"Contribute to the needs of God's people, and welcome strangers into your home."

Message

When we were in the Dumagat village, the path to our residence was a difficult walk; we needed to cross a river and climb a mountain trail. It was not an easy experience for a person like me, coming from the city. During the walk, the Dumagat villagers held my hand and accompanied me all the way to our residence. Not only did I felt their care and hospitality, I also felt a deep level of love from the Holy Spirit acting and moving in this moment. There was no need for pretty words or liturgy at that moment, for the true worship was already happening while we supported and cared for each other. The Holy Spirit moved and united us, allowing us to become one body in Christ.

Prayer

God, we give thanks for our sisters and brothers in the Philippines,
for you have shown your hospitality in them.
God, we pray for our sisters and brothers in the Philippines, for your peace and justice will be the light in their lives.
God, we pray for our sisters and brothers in the Philippines, for your consolation and strength eases all their heartache and pain.

Psalm 103:1

"Let my whole being bless the LORD!"

Message

The Word of God inspires and challenges us to remember God's goodness toward creation in all lives and in all places. As humans we grumble and complain about not having everything we pray for. This reminds me of a story about a boy complaining to his father about not getting him a new pair of shoes. The poor father took him for a walk and showed him a happy boy who was blessing God, thanking him for all things walking with prosthetic legs. The boy saw this and was thankful for the blessing that God had given him good legs.

Prayer

Lord bless us to bless you with all our soul, in all times, and in all places.

Thought of the Day

Never complain or grumble and bless the Lord always. Thank God for what God has blessed you with in your life.

John 11:35

"Jesus began to cry."

Message

I saw her weep. She wept several times. Not a weeper, however, she wept every time she told her story—the story of how she has survived against all odds and what she experienced in the factory line. From working twelve to fourteen hours a day, to depriving her minimum wage, the tears, her tears, tell this story as if this recalls the pain and suffering she endured and the miracle of it all that she is still alive. She wept. I wept. Jesus wept.

Prayer

God of our tears, you have wept. You know our tears. Embolden us to cry. Give us courage to weep with others. Strengthen us that we may see the tears that flow down the cheeks of others. In the name of the one who also wept, Jesus. Amen.

Thought of the Day

Tears awaken us to the presence of others.

Luke 2:30

"Because my eyes have seen your salvation."

Message

When I was at the Council for World Mission workshop in the Philippines, I attended a group session. When I went to drink a glass of water, one lady who was helping in the dining hall said, "Even in your conversations, discussions, and in practices, I hear the Word of God." Salvation is an experience that the people at the margins experience with the Lord. People at the margins are blessed as they see, touch, smell, and experience salvation through their daily engagements. God reveals God's self to those who work hard, struggle, and those who seek him. In the above-mentioned Bible passage, Mary, a village woman, says, "I have seen your salvation." Salvation happens in the streets where people encounter the empire. God reveals God's self to them.

Prayer

God of the Margins, reveal yourself to the people who are fighting for justice. Amen.

Thought of the Day

God, encounter, and salvation are for the people who search for them.

Matthew 25:36

"I was naked and you gave me clothes to wear. I was sick and you took care of me. I was in prison and you visited me."

Message

When I met the people who were crying because their sons, husbands, and sons-in-law were killed in the drug war, I felt so full of pain. They are God's children. They are our family. They are parts of the body of Christ. Therefore, we should not ignore them in their time of suffering. Community is helping. The Rise Up organization is helping and advocating for the victims' families. In Myanmar, we also have some problems, like the drug trade, and there are evil wars between the people from the hill tribes and the military. Therefore, I am compassionate for them.

Prayer

Lord of mercy, may you grant your children a secured life and give them back justice. In Jesus's name. Amen.

Thought of the Day

The Lord will help the people who are suffering.

Psalm 130:1-2

"I cry out to you from the depths, LORD—
My Lord, listen to my voice!"

Message

I went to the Philippines for a liturgical project. We were assigned for two days of immersion to work with the urban poor whose families are the victims of the war on drugs. Almost every year, these people face the reality that a young man may be killed. We met mothers who have unending tears. Every time they hear that somebody was killed, they cry, voiceless, wondering when this nightmare will end. The Psalmist was in a depth of mourning when she cried to the Lord, so the Lord would hear her voice.

A mother's tears, the Psalmist mourns and makes us realize that we are all living in a terrifying world. We need God, as we need the people who can be the evidence that we are not alone in this world.

Prayer

Lord, help us to have the eyes to look upon the hunger and the ears to listen to the people's cries. May the Holy Spirit, who gives us comfort, stay in our midst as we are here to comfort each other in this world.

Thought of the Day

We are not alone in this terrifying world.

Ezekiel 9:4

"Go through the city, through Jerusalem, and mark the foreheads of those who sigh and groan because of all the detestable practices that have been conducted in it."

Message

When I went to the place of indigenous peoples I have seen that the people of the soil have no basic facilities like electricity, water, schools, hospitals, and so on.

Now that I have seen these things, what will happen as a result? At least I must cry for the needy people for the abominations, injustice, and exploitation that are to be done in the midst of the nation.

If this messenger comes into my city will I survive?

Prayer

O my parent God, lead me in your justice and righteousness. Amen.

Thought of the Day

Be aware of the worldly injustice.

Exodus 1:15-21

"The king of Egypt spoke to two Hebrew midwives named Shiphrah and Puah: 'When you are helping the Hebrew women give birth and you see the baby being born, if it's a boy, kill him. But if it's a girl, you can let her live.' Now the two midwives respected God so they didn't obey the Egyptian king's order. Instead, they let the baby boys live.

So the king of Egypt called the two midwives and said to them, 'Why are you doing this? Why are you letting the baby boys live?'

The two midwives said to Pharaoh, 'Because Hebrew women aren't like Egyptian women. They're much stronger and give birth before any midwives can get to them.' So God treated the midwives well, and the people kept on multiplying and became very strong. And because the midwives respected God, God gave them households of their own."

Message

What would happen if 90 percent of our communities were to tell us that one plus one equals four? Do we conform? Or do we stick to our convictions? In a world where status, politics, and authority try, and sometimes succeed, in drowning the voice of the church, it is important that we do what is right in the eyes of God. The story of the Hebrew midwives mirrors so much of today's temptations, where we are compelled to do what is not in our nature as Christians. The story also explains how both of the women maneuvered their circumstances to maintain their faith. The real question is: Are we up to the task?

Prayer

Lord, give us the courage to uphold life as its own principle. Let our hands nurture it and never take it. And when we are tested, God, make us fearless in facing our fears. In Jesus we pray. Amen.

Thought of the Day

In one of my ethics classes, I listened to theologians agonize over the morality of the midwives lying to Pharaoh, saying it's a sin regardless of the positive consequences. To throw a spanner in the machine, I added: "The problem with studying theology is that it creates theologians. This world needs more Christians."

Luke 19:40

"I tell you, if they were silent, the stones would shout."

Message

She was part of a small group of mothers and wives whose stories of crying out cannot be contained. They were mothers whose sons were murdered in the bloody campaign against illegal drugs. Nanette was holding a laminated picture of her son, Aldrin, who a year ago was shot five times: three in the chest, two in the head. Two out of seven gunmen were reported to have done it, but no one had seen their faces. One year since the day, Nanette still cradles the photo of her dead son to her chest. "Lalaban ako, anak" (I will fight, my son). Thousands dead in the past two years. A handful of women—mothers, wives—cry out for their dead, perhaps, on behalf also of the twenty thousand and of all of us. Let them not be silent, for if they are kept silent, even the stones shall cry out.

Prayer

God of life, you hear the affliction of your people. As in the days of Jesus of Nazareth and his friends, whose fervor not even the empire can contain, this same cry for justice and insistence on the fullness of life cannot be contained. Grant us, O God, the space to cry out. And may we not cry in vain. Amen.

Thought of the Day

A mother's cry is sacred. If you keep her silent, the stones will cry out.

Luke 8:44

"She came up behind him and touched the hem of his clothes, and at once her bleeding stopped."

Message

We often see the woman who touched the edge of Jesus's cloak as someone who has faith. Yes, that is true! She probably crawls toward Jesus and toward the crowd, not just because of faith but as an act of resistance.

She touched Jesus in the spirit of resistance. The resistance to death, her resistance to the unjust system of her society—not allowing women to come near a 'rabbi' or anyone, and especially by her likes, a bleeding woman. Her act is not just an act of faith but of saying no to the structures that keep her sickness, the structures that keeps her away from others, from her loved ones.

Many people living with HIV today are being neglected not just because there is not enough budget given and allotted by the government. They are neglected because of so many issues and discussions around HIV and AIDS. HIV and AIDS are understood as about promiscuity, sin, sex, and so on. They are wrongly associated with gays and prostitution. But many haven't seen that HIV and AIDS are NOT just about a medical condition, they are also about the economic and unjust systems in society. We forget to ask ourselves why there is prostitution, why condoms are not available in the barangays, and why the poor are poor. Why do the gays in our community explore their sexuality on their own? Why is there no access to sex education in churches? Why are the antiretroviral drugs that we are using not being used in other countries?

This woman in Luke resisted the unjust system. She resisted sickness, she resisted death. And so, resistance is faith. And this was Jesus's response to her resistance: "Daughter, your faith [resistance] has healed you. . . . Go in peace" (Luke 8:48).

Prayer

Dear God, help us to resist. Help us to stand with the most vulnerable in our society. Help us to see those who are crawling just to touch the edge of Jesus's cloak, to crawl and resist with them. Bless our strength. Bless our courage. May we continue to uphold peace based on justice. We pray this, in the name of Jesus who blessed the resistance of this woman. Amen.

Thought of the Day

We resist the unjust and evil systems in our society! Resistance is faith!

Matthew 5:38-48

"You have heard that it was said, An eye for an eye and a tooth for a tooth. But I say to you that you must not oppose those who want to hurt you. If people slap you on your right cheek, you must turn the left cheek to them as well. When they wish to haul you to court and take your shirt, let them have your coat too. When they force you to go one mile, go with them two. Give to those who ask, and don't refuse those who wish to borrow from you.

"You have heard that it was said, You must love your neighbor and hate your enemy. But I say to you, love your enemies and pray for those who harass you so that you will be acting as children of your Father who is in heaven. He makes the sun rise on both the evil and the good and sends rain on both the righteous and the unrighteous. If you love only those who love you, what reward do you have? Don't even the tax collectors do the same? And if you greet only your brothers and sisters, what more are you doing? Don't even the Gentiles do the same? Therefore, just as your heavenly Father is complete in showing love to everyone, so also you must be complete."

Call to Worship

God of Love, we need you now.
Teach us to love those we have learned to hate.
Teach us to pray for our enemies,
to love you, even in those we despise.
God of Peace, we need you now.
Teach us how to reconcile.
Teach us to speak when we are silenced.
Teach us to give up power when our power renders others powerless or mute.
God of Joy, we need you now!
Receive our burdens, they are many.
Lift our spirits, they are weighed down.
God of Life, we need you now.
Grant us grace where shame restricts us.
Grant us life where pain takes hold.
Grant us wisdom when we would settle for easy answers.
Grant us love, rooted in the eternal, the living, in you!

God bless us as we gather, in the name of the Creator, the Christ, and the Holy Spirit. Amen.

Confession and Absolution

God of Love, on occasion, we have desired revenge. We have rejoiced
in the punishment and pain of those we have seen as enemies. We have
resisted, not with the nonviolence of a turning of the cheek, but instead
with a twisted pleasure found in causing your children injury and harm.
Loving enemies seems an impossibility to us, especially when they speak
and spit criticisms and insults and shame, especially when they have hurt
us or our families. We take the easy way out. In our pain and fear, we have
come to believe that your Love is a myth, an impossibility, an unreachable pie in the sky. "They are bad," we say. But you say, "They are you."
This is confusing. How can we love our enemies? How can we be "One?"
How can we bless those who would do us harm? We confess our bondage
to fear. We need your wisdom in the depths of our hearts. We need your
freedom in our bones. Forgive our fear. Free us to Love. Teach us to walk
with you on the path to reunion, reconciliation, and resurrection. Amen.

In Christ, we find God dwelling among us, walking with us on our way.
In flesh, Christ knows our struggles. On the cross, God knows our pain.
Christ is within you and among you: "because the one who is in you is
greater than the one who is in the world" (1 John 4:4); "Throw all your
anxiety onto him" (1 Pet 5:7). May your shame be removed. For your guilt
is replaced. Receive in its stead God's grace and love, and a desire for God's
call to the Reign of Love. In the name of Christ, all your sins are forgiven.
In the name of the Creator, the Christ, and the Holy Spirit. Amen.

Prayer

God of deliverance, we pray for our enemies. We bless those who persecute us. Give the whole human family, the whole of creation, your peace.
Lift up the lowly. Feed the hungry. Give us hearts that overflow with your
love, beyond boundaries and bloodlines. Teach us to look, communally,
toward your vision of a restored Creation, where lions and lambs nap
together and humans learn not simply to coexist, but to love in word, in
deed, and in truth. Amen.

321

Sumak Kawsay
See page 227 to read *Worldly Affirmation of Faith*, which inspired this artwork.

PART NINE

COMPLETE LITURGICAL SEQUENCES

COMPLETE LITURGICAL SEQUENCES

Worship Litany in the Context of the Indigenous Groups of Northeast India

Call to Worship

The congregation is silenced, and the worship begins with the beating of drums and the playing of a flute.

Leader: Let us worship the God of every tribe and every nation, the God of the blind and the deaf, the God of the rich and the poor, the young and the old. As we gather together, let God's presence be felt in our midst.

Congregation: We come before you, O God, to seek your face, to experience your healing touch and the liberating power of your word. Let us worship God in Spirit and in truth, that we might become the torchbearer of justice and love, and to be the peacemakers in our homes, in our communities, and in the world.

Leader: Truly, God is just and his steadfast love and mercy can conquer the hatred and discrimination that we have created among us.

Congregation: Let your word touch our hearts to love our enemies and our neighbors, and to be inspired to love the unlovable and the marginalized sections of the church and the community. Soften our hearts, Lord, to extend our hands to the needy and the sick in our community.

Leader: O God, enable us to be still and know that you are God.

Amen.

Intercessory Prayer

Almighty and most merciful God, we remember before you the poor and the destitute, the homeless and the oppressed as a result of the tribal conflict and armed forces in northeast India. We pray for the old and the sick and for all who have no one to care for them. Help us to care for those who are broken in body or spirit. We beseech you, O God, to unite us together despite our differences in faith, language, and ethnic groups.

Almighty God, we come here today to ask you to guide us toward peace and reconciliation in our churches and communities, which are troubled and grieved. Enlighten the hearts of the leaders of the states and nations, that they may bring people closer together for the good of every religious faith and community. Grant us the courage to step out in faith for that which is true and right. Grant our government to affirm the freedom of speech and expression, the freedom to express our faith, and the opportunities to bring change and transformation to our churches and society.

We pray for the unemployed youth in our region so that their dreams will not be shattered; protect them from social evils, such as substance abuse and from any acts of violence.

Help us, Lord, to be good stewards of your blessings so that the needy, hungry, orphaned, and widowed may taste the fruits of your goodness. Amen.

Prayer of Confession

Loving God, we gather today to confess that we have failed to extend our kindness to the poor and to the hungry. We have accumulated enough wealth for our comfort and have been insensitive to the needs of the weak and the poor of our community. Forgive us, for we have comfortably closed our eyes to the cry of our neighbor. Indeed, we have been selfish, but we preached to the poor and to the hungry your word without sharing our bread with them. Forgive us for clinging to our own possessions rather than to you. Unite our hearts to share our resources and stand for justice for all.

Forgive us, God, for keeping a distance between Christians and non-Christians, between the tribal and non-tribal groups, and for closing our ears to the cries and the pain of the people of other faiths and those who are not from our community.

We as the tribal and indigenous community have failed to exercise the values of equality and justice in which our ancestors have taught us. We have imitated and followed the standard and values of the empire. As the tribal and indigenous group of northeast India, we are known as a region where the majority professes the Christian faith, but we have slaughtered the brothers and sisters of others in the name of our tribe. We are racist within our tribal community, and the weaker tribes are being oppressed, discriminated against, and ostracized. We seek your grace and mercy to forgive us. Amen.

Prayer of Thanksgiving

Gracious God who supplies us with every blessing in abundance, guide us to be grateful for the gift of natural resources, which you have provided for us: the pure air, the water, the trees, the plants, the birds, and the animals that we have always taken for granted. We thank you for fertile soil, abundant rain, and seasons of refreshment.

We thank you for every breath that we take. Thank you for your word and wisdom, for the joy and pain that deepened our experience. Thank you for the rest in leisure and the inspiration of our families and friends. Thank you for protecting us in temptation and in danger. Thank you for the community into which we have been called to serve together and for sound bodies and minds. Thank you for the opportunities that encourage us to grow and to serve, and not to be served. We give you thanks. Amen.

Affirmation of Faith (Creed)

We Believe in God Almighty, the Creator of heavens and earth, who blesses all people and every creature on earth. We believe in Jesus Christ the only child of God who was conceived by the Holy Spirit and who suffered under the Roman Empire and was crucified, died, and was buried. He rose on the third day and is now seated at the right hand of God Almighty. He will come to give justice to the oppressed and the oppressor. We believe in the Holy Spirit who guides the Church to walk in the path of justice and righteousness and in the fellowship of the faithful. We believe in the power of love and forgiveness, which can bind and heal the church and community from the vileness of hatred among people groups for the renewal of humankind. We affirm the life of every creature on Earth.

Benediction

May the Love of God rest and transform every race and nation, and eradicate all barriers that divide people groups into gender, caste, creed, and color. May the grace of his son, Jesus Christ, abide in the hearts of the faithful to forgive one another. May the fellowship of the Holy Spirit guide us in extending kindness and hospitality to strangers and to the homeless. Amen.

Liturgy—Um Carinho (A Caress) For the Earth

Gathering

The deeper the cracks on the ground, the stronger the yam fruits. Like the yams, let us refuse to be forever buried. Look for the cracks on the earth. There you will find the miracles of life: it smells like the yams, it smells of love. Let us emerge and gather for worship as these strong, succulent fruits.

Call to Prayer: Wrap the Yam Vine

Father and Mother of the Dirt, the sun shines another day. It is time to rise again. Though our feet are tired, our hands are cracked, the body is aching, the soil is hard, and the rain is late this month,
may you grant us delicate hands to wrap the yam vine.

You know our children are hungry. There are many who are sick among us, and these bodies are all we have to give. Keep our souls from breaking, our bodies from aching, dear God. Bring water to quench our thirst, to fill the trenches, and renew our vitality,
may you grant us the strength to jam the yam stick.
May your abundant love turn the earth red again. May it bear the fruits of our reaping. May our machetes and forks be as kind to the earth as you have been to us. May this prayer sink into the cracks of our beings, ours, and the earth's,
give us the grace of reaping the yam fruit.

Opening Song: "How Long?," a Jamaican liturgical song. You may find a recording at: https://www.youtube.com /watch?v=FWG9p4j76Ew

Scripture Lesson

James 5:7—"Therefore, brothers and sisters, you must be patient as you wait for the coming of the Lord. Consider the farmer who waits patiently for the coming of rain in the fall and spring, looking forward to the precious fruit of the earth."

Homily

"The cracks are important. It's where the yam fruits are hidden."

—*Anselm Williams, Lowe River United Church, Trelawny, Jamaica*

Prayers of the People: Lowe River United, Trelawny, Jamaica

Beloved God, so many of our brothers and sisters have been hit hard by struggles, which makes us question Your presence among us. These struggles have made us broken. Sometimes we cannot get answers. Sometimes we feel abandoned. Sometimes we feel hopeless. Sometimes we are powerless. Please give us hope, dear God, so we can continue to serve you, reap the fruits of this Earth, share them with those who hunger, heal those who have fallen ill, and restore the faith of those who can no longer believe. Be our hope, our strength, our rock, oh God.
All other ground is sinking sand.

Closing Song: "My Hope Is Built on Nothing Less," by Edward Mote

Blessing and Going Forth: Heat of the Earth

To be sung with Milton Nascimento's song "Cio da Terra" (https://www.youtube.com /watch?v=qevMiA2KU3w).

Find the cracks on the ground;
Feel the pulse of earth, find the yam fruit, gently dismantle the dirt
all around, the miracle's alive.

Eucharist for Women

The community will gather in a circle to celebrate the Eucharist. In the middle of the circle will be tissues; objects representing the four elements: earth, water, air (can be represented by incense), and fire (candles, etc.); and the elements of the Eucharist, bread and wine (which can be replaced by contextual elements).

Hymn: "Song of Walking"

Dm   G7
If walking is necessary,

          Am
we will walk together,

Dm   G7
and our feet, our arms,

Am   C
will sustain our steps.

   Dm   Em   F
We will no longer be the mass,

Am   E
without place, without voice,

Am   F
without history,

  G7   C
but a church that goes

  Dm   Em G7 C
in hope and solidarity.

Dm   G7
If walking is necessary,

          Am
we will walk together,

Dm   G7
and our faith will be so great that

        Am C
we will cross the mountains.

Dm   Em F
Let's open borders

330

```
Am  E       Am   F
where there were only barriers,

            G7        C
because we are people who walk

    Dm     Em G7 C
with hope and solidarity.

Dm          G7
If walking is necessary

            Am
we will walk together,

Dm                        G7
and we will have the kingdom of God

        Am   C
as the horizon of life.

        Dm  Em  F
We will share the pain,

Am    E     Am    F
the suffering and the pain,

            G7        C
leading the force of love

    Dm     Em G7 C
in hope and solidarity.

Dm          G7
If walking is necessary,

            Am
we will walk together,

Dm                    G7
and our voice in the desert

              Am  C
will sprout new life.

        Dm  Em  F
And the new life on earth

Am E        Am    F
will be a foretaste at parties

    G7          C
it is God who is among us

    Dm     Em G7 C
in hope and solidarity.
```

Confession of Faith

I believe in a gentle God.

I believe in a gentle God who cries with us for all the ways our bodies were raped, destroyed, murdered, broken, unloved, and obliterated.

I believe in Jesus, the Incarnate, Gentle God, who takes our breath away and returns it when we no longer have the strength to keep on living.

I believe in the Soft Spirit that—from the depths—gently visits us to remind us of the sounds of our own voices, our sorrows, the cries of the earth, and the strength we still hold.

I believe in a gentle Church that hears the whispers of the Earth, that feels the pain circulating in its body, that is not indifferent to violence, that believes in the cries of those who denounce this violence at the expense of their lives. I remember those who cry silently because using their voices is not a safe option.

I believe in communities, those that are artistic and respect different bodies, communities that are beyond the walls of churches, faiths, and religions and have been organizing resistance for millennia.

I believe in the communities that continued to move forward in solidarity, Divine Softness, responsibility, integrity, and coherence to undo the violent configurations of power, patriarchy, misogyny, racism (remembering environmental racism, too), classicism, xenophobia, transphobia, homophobia, supremacy, colonialism, capitalism, pain, abandonment, indifference, and hatred.

I believe in the communion of ancestors, saints, sinners, spirits, and all of creation who have thoughts that they feel and feelings that they think, and who resist hatred and intolerance and come to the tables of communion hand-in-hand in an inclusive way, to follow gently on the path, with an incorrigible joy, with radical and blameless acceptance, in hope and in "terrestrial" coexistence.

—*Yohana A. Junker, October 2018*

Greeting of Peace

Leader: May the restless peace be with you always.
All: And also with you!

Leader: Let us greet our sisters saying:
May the restless peace be with you!

Thanksgiving

Leader: God be with you.
All: Now and forever.

Leader: Lift up your heart, your mind, your body.
All: We lift them up to God and to our sisters.

Leader: Give thanks to God.
All: God is sweetness and justice.

O God, Father-Mother,
Creator of rivers, seas, land, fruits, animals,
Creator of the diversity of bodies, colors, flavors, smells,
You are our joy and salvation.
We give You thanks
through thy son Jesus.
We learn to walk in the paths of justice,
challenging oppressive powers in the name of freedom and
the God who became a child, someone like us, who celebrated and suffered.

He suffered for striving for justice, for loving, for giving life for all humankind.
Innocent blood was shed, which is still shed in our alleys, streets, and in our
    homes,
women's blood, the blood of martyrs, blood that is shed by the hands of the
    State.
But this blood, mixed with the blood of all of us, allows hope to rise,
a resurrection of joy and love.

Your blood lives in us, as does the blood of so many others who died defending
    life.
Your holy Rûach brings life to the dry bones of despair. Wind that blows in us
    the communion of being one body in You.

Therefore, with all the animals, waters, forests, insects, flowers, clouds, and
    sunbeams,
with all our martyrs and ancestors we sing:

Holy Holy Holy
is the God of peace.
The heavens and the earth are full
of your love!
Blessed is the One who comes in the name of God!
Hosanna on earth and in the heavens!

Blessed be the Love,
power of Life!
Creator of the Universe
and blessed be Jesus,
the God-child
who smiles and plays!

Saudade

"While they were eating, Jesus took bread, blessed it, broke it, and
gave it to the disciples and said, 'Take and eat. This is my body.' He
took a cup, gave thanks, and gave it to them, saying, 'Drink from
this, all of you. This is my blood. . . . I tell you, I won't drink wine
again until that day when I drink it in a new way with you in my
Father's kingdom'" (Matt 26:26-29).

From Our Bleeding Body

*One woman passes out red string (fabric or thread) so that each woman is holding a
piece; they form a circle while another woman reads the following passage slowly.*

A woman bleeds. Every month. Every week. Every day. A woman bleeds.
This blood emanates from her body, from her orifices, from her tears
and her sweat. A woman bleeds in her heart because of the many ways
she is excluded. A woman bleeds in bed—a mark of holiness or a mark
of promiscuity. A woman bleeds by giving birth to human, divine, and
utopian existences. A woman bleeds for not giving birth: monthly blood
of destruction and renewal or blood of painful abortion. A woman bleeds
with violence, racism, and control: she bleeds to death. A woman bleeds.
Not by choice!

Then the minister says:

> The bread and the chalice, the body and the blood, the communion of bodies.

Prayer of Humble Accession

> Your grace grants us communion.
> We thank you for our grandmothers, mothers, aunts, friends
> who teach us daily amidst the nightmares and pains of being a woman.
> We ask for your mercy and your strength.
> May your Rûach make an abode in our being,
> allowing us to be one
> in You.

Sharing the Elements

> Come closer, O sisters
> and celebrate the body and blood,
> ours and Christ's.

The minister breaks the bread and serves the elements to the community, still forming a circle.

Final Prayer: The Kiss Prayer

> The community holds hands. Each person kisses the hand of the woman standing next to her.

> When they are finished, all say: "Amen."

Liturgy Honoring Indigenous People and Communities

The following rubrics were inspired by traditional Cordillera rites from Luzon Island, Philippines, and were designed for more inclusive use by indigenous and non-indigenous participants.

ACT ONE: The Call

Dancing, singing, and playing of traditional indigenous Cordillera musical instruments.

> Come you who people the villages!
> Leave your farms and gardens!
> Leave your farm implements and work animals!
> Rest your spears and machetes on the ground.
> Put the fire off your clay stoves.
> Come and be one!

Dancing, singing, and playing of traditional indigenous Cordillera musical instruments.

ACT TWO: The Planting of the Podong* Sticks

Leader: Cut from among the lively grasses, we plant anew these reed sticks, nourished by the soil, daily bathed by heaven, watered by rain...

People: **We plant the reed sticks to affirm the holiness of this place, of this gathering, and of this act of faith that we are to do together, and to affirm that God is with our families, protecting our farms, our gardens, our forests, and our dwellings.**

Leader: Cut from among the sparkling green grasses, we plant anew these reed sticks nourished by the soil, bathed by heaven, watered by rain...

People: **We plant these reed sticks to welcome our visiting ancestors...they who guard the forests and streams, the trees and rivers, the mountains and our abodes.**

Leader: Cut from among the lively green grasses, we plant anew these reed sticks nourished by the soil, daily bathed by heaven, watered by rain...

336

People:	We plant these reed sticks to welcome the spirits of our peoples' martyrs*...

We plant these reed sticks to welcome the spirits of our peoples' martyrs*...
The spirits of Ama Macliing and Pedro
The spirits of Ama Daniel and Romy
The spirits of Romeo and Pepe
The spirits of Jovito and Abelino
...of Nicanor and the Titoh and Blanco families
...of Budbud and Alice
...of Markus and James

Leader: Cut from among the lively and dancing green grasses,
we plant anew these reed sticks nourished by the soil,
daily bathed by heaven, watered by rain...

People: **Come, Creator Spirit! Welcome us to your life-nourishing, life-warming embrace!**

ACT THREE: The Offertory

Each community's representative presents an object that speaks of the life and struggles of her or his community. The representative shares the story of her or his community in a few sentences, after which she or he places the object in the ritual 'offertory' bag.

The offertory bag(s) of peoples' stories is hung on the pole(s) planted prominently on the side(s) of the assembly space. Chanted prayers of thanksgiving can be sung by the elders and cantors along with the hanging of the offertory bags.

Ayee [Kabunian]!
Come to us in our gathering and receive our offerings.
Be with us in this [dap-ay] and listen to our stories.
Sit beside each one and be warmed by the fire.
Try our sweet tapuy, see our dancing, and listen to our singing.
Teach us new steps and new tunes, and new words.
Ayee [Kabunian]!
Our legs are tired, and our voices are failing us.
Our ancestors and nature-spirits are fleeing our balding mountains,
our vanishing forests and dying rivers.
Come to our rescue and keep your people strong.
Like the beating of the gangsa, come and rouse us to life.
Like the warrior of old, come and lead us to [Pulag's] summit
and preside over our rites of triumph.

ACT FOUR: Acknowledgment and Celebration of the Gathered Community

This is the statement of the purpose of gathering and the acknowledgement of the gathered community by the presiding officers or elder.

This may be followed by solidarity dancing or by community singing, led by the host community. Many indigenous communities in the Philippines have dances and songs that welcome people and celebrate community-building. This would physically and festively express the spirit of community and inter-national and inter-community solidarity.

Ayee [Kabunian]!
Teach us the best dance steps,
that the land may rejoice in our dancing
and yield more abundantly this season.
May our women glide like the proud fowls on the ground
and swing like the free birds in the sky.
May our men stomp their feet like the mighty boar
and chase like the giddy rooster.
Ayee Kabunian!
May our dancing bring us together,
reunite us with the spirits
and all that dwell in our forests.
May the banging of our gangsa
and the *sapol* prayers of our elders
forge our resolve:
to resist;
to live.

The dancing, singing, and playing may transition into an act of festive preparation for the people's liturgical conversation with God's word.

The Good News from the Scriptures may be received with much festivity through upbeat singing, dancing, and the playing of musical instruments. Even the Bible can be danced to in courtship dance-like movements to celebrate the love story between God and the people of the world.

ACT FIVE: *The Word Proclaimed*

The Word Sung (chanted) . . .
and Interpreted

This is an occasion for the gathered community to reflect on the concerns of their communities, that is, for the peoples' struggle for self-determination— from bilical-theological perspectives.

How do we view our humanity and our becoming (from our cultural anthropology and the Judeo-Christian understanding of the human being and peopling)? How do we relate our struggle for self-determination with our imaging of divinity? What good news do these reflections communicate to our communities in their everyday life and struggles?

ACT SIX: *Statement of Faith*

This is based on the text of the "Indigenous People's Collective Rights," sourced from the Cordillera Women's Education Action Research Center and the KAM people.

Leader: WE BELIEVE that we, indigenous peoples, are created in the image of our Creator.

People: **Blessed by God with the capacity to manage and develop our assigned spaces in the garden of our Maker: our ancestral lands and all that dwell therein.**

Leader: WE BELIEVE that we, indigenous peoples, are created in the image of God.

People: **Blessed with the creativity to develop and practice our own systems of relationship and governance, our own ways of knowing and believing, and to maintain who we are and whose we are.**

Leader: WE BELIEVE that we, indigenous peoples, are created in the image of God.

People: **Blessed with the will and natural capacity to chart our own paths and destinies as peoples and communities, to participate actively in the ecumenical work of bringing about a just world, and to reject impositions by imperial powers that are detrimental to the well-being of our peoples and our parent earth.**

339

Leader: WE BELIEVE that we, indigenous peoples, are created
in the image of our Maker.

People: **Blessed with an image and being that make us an
integral part of the Body of God-in-Christ.**

Leader: WE BELIEVE that we are all created in the image of
our Creator; that our indigenous sisters and brothers
are part of us and that we are part of them.

ACT SEVEN: *The Cup of Covenant*

*This includes another round of solidarity dancing and singing. At this point, too, a cup
of wine is passed around or given to able participants to further forge the Eucharistic
and covenantal spirit of the event.*

Ayee [Kabunian]!

[Anian a nagsam-iten tay tapuy]

It warms the body and strengthens our knees.

It kindles the fire and lights our rage.

It makes us remember

what our pastors [Apo Padi and Apo Pastor]

say when they pass around the [ungot] of wine

in their chapels and cathedrals:

'Do these in remembrance of

me breaking my body and shedding my blood for you . . .

that you may have life and have it to the fullest.'

Ayee [Kabunian]!

May he come to us

may this man, Jesus, come to us

and we shall dance around the fire

the feast of justice . . .

the feast of life

(*and the assembly sings*)

**GOD OF LIFE
LEAD US TO JUSTICE AND PEACE
MARANATHA
COME, LORD, COME**

ACT EIGHT: The Blessing

*The elders of the community, with the priest or pastor, may take the hand
of each one, tightly and warmly, and place on his or her palm a fresh
green leaf and say these words: either "May the spirits come back to our
mountains and rivers and forests soon," or "May a grand feast follow these
long days of struggle," or "May the day of feasting come soon," or some
other appropriate lines that express not only the hopes of peoples but also
the call for the ecclesia's commitment to this struggle.*

Glossary of Terms for This Service

*IGOROT or *Y-gollotes*, meaning, "people from the mountain," is the
collective name for the approximately 1.5 million people from at least
eight major ethno-linguistic groups that populate the Cordillera mountain
region in the Northern Philippines.

*THE *PODONG* STICKS are stalks from a grass variety common in
the Cordillera region and the rest of the Philippines. The leafy ends of
the stalks are knotted and are planted at the entrance of a village with
the prayers of the elders. It may not be a visibly prominent feature in the
entirety of the ritual performance, but the *podong* rite is always essential to
the ritual's efficacy.

When one sees a *podong* stick stuck in the ground, it means that a ritual
act is being performed in the place and that everyone in the village is
expected to respond and act accordingly. The planting of the *podong* is
accompanied by prayers bidding everyone, both seen and unseen, to look
after the houses, gardens, swidden farms, livestock, properties, and all
that the villagers have left behind for the gathering. The standing *podong*
sticks give the villagers the assurance that no dwelling will be trespassed
throughout the duration of the ritual performance because all these are
under divine protection. Any infringement on those under the watch of
Kabunian, or the spirits, will have to suffer their wrath.

Furthermore, the *podong* provides the passageway through which the ancestral spirits come by to commune with the living. It is this communion
of the living, the ancestral spirits, the earth, and all that dwell therein (that
is, nature spirits) that calls on everyone to observe with solemnity. When
the *podong* sticks are standing the whole earth and all life rest.

Reintroducing the *podong* in context, and in this case the continuing
Igorot struggle and vigilance against development aggression, emphasizes

the significance of the rite in the development of a spirituality of struggle among Cordillerans. When done or performed in mining grounds, *podong* planting is an act of resistance. It is a statement that these lands belong to their ancestors and that they enjoy God's protection.

*Peoples' MARTYRS are those community leaders who fought and died for the rights of indigenous peoples. Most of them became victims of political killings or extra-judicial killings. Some disappeared and have not been found to this day.

Rite for Sending Leaders

As we prepare to leave this place, let us remember our commitment and our collective.

A brief silence for centering.

Family in the struggle, let us go forth, strengthened by one another and ignited by love.

On our way, may our desire for a just and liberated world
outweigh our inclination toward complacency.

May our shared plans become shared action

and may our bodies, filled with hope, and encouraged by these people who surround us,
march toward the promise of a better tomorrow,

knowing, together, that the path becomes wider and that we never march alone.

As we go from this place, will you commit to your family here?

We will! And we will not do it alone.

Will you march with them, side by side, toward the hope of a better world?

We will! And we will not do it alone.

Will you encourage them when they get tired, care from them when they are wounded and all the while carry on, carrying them if you have to, that we all might arrive in hope together?

We will! And we will not do it alone.

On the way, will you agitate one another in Love? Will you hold one another accountable, reminding one another that the system that caused your pain and gave rise to your oppressions is the same system that afflicts each person in this room, and that together that system is the common enemy that we engage?

We will! And we will not do it alone.

Will you fight all forms of oppression, engage the principalities and powers, knowing that without struggle, without power, without uprising, the world gets worse, or simply stays the same?

We will! And we will not do it alone.

Will you care for one another here and now, seeking to live out the justice and liberation we work for in this community and in your relationships, that this collective might be a glimpse of that for which we hope: imperfect, yet proof that a better world is possible?

We will! And we will not do it alone.

Will you build power to fight powers and instigate the desire for liberation in the world, inviting your friends and neighbors to join in this work, trusting that together, united, we will rise victorious?

We will! And we will not do it alone.

Trusting then that, together, united, no barricade, no blockade, no principality, or power is going to stop our movement, our motion, our march toward a liberated world, a Reign of Love and Justice, where all hold value and everyone is able to eat?

Let us be bound together, for the sake of Justice, and in the Spirit of Joyous Rebellion.

May the Spirit of Joyous Rebellion inhabit our hearts and fill us with an unending desire for liberation, knowing as we go forward together, we go forward in love, we go forward in power, and we widen the path that those who love justice and desire liberation have marched for centuries before us, marching toward the hope of a liberated world.

And as we go, we go together, in power and in love,
nobody,
nobody,
nobody,
will ever be able to turn us around.
Amen.

Song: "Ain't Gonna Let Nobody Turn Us Around," a spiritual
from the Civil Rights era

A Liturgy of Joyous Rebellion: A Rite for Rededication to the Cause

Family in the struggle, gathered together in the Spirit of Joyous
Rebellion,
I invite you to confess your commitment to the Liberation of all people
and the restoration of the planet; and to renounce all obstacles that stand
in the way.

Do you renounce greed, the love of wealth, and all of capitalism's empty
promises?
(*If so, please say "WE RENOUNCE THEM!"*)
WE RENOUNCE THEM!

Do you renounce oppression, structural and internal, and all the forces
that keep us from living liberated lives, dedicated to the liberation of all?
WE RENOUNCE THEM!

Do you renounce the fear that dwells in you, all its insecurities—those
things that draw you away from confronting your own oppression, loving
your own neighbor, and building power for the sake of a liberated world?
WE RENOUNCE THEM!

Do you renounce all answers to the cry of the oppressed that would
belittle and chastise, like the saying, "Pull yourselves up by your boot-
straps," knowing that when we've been stripped of our boots, the answer
is never isolated, individual acts, but structural, communal, and organized
change; and knowing that, together, we are never alone?
WE RENOUNCE THEM!

Do you renounce all ideologies that would claim that some deserve to
thrive while others, based on culture, class, creed, or nation of origin,
deserve a prison or a grave, a deportation or a desert wall?
WE RENOUNCE THEM!

Do you renounce the destruction of the earth and its resources, the de-
valuation of nature, and the denial of climate change, as the planet is sacrificed for human greed, leading to pending and unimaginable calamity?
WE RENOUNCE THEM!

Do you renounce racism and nationalism?
WE RENOUNCE THEM!

Do you renounce sexism and ableism?
WE RENOUNCE THEM!

Do you renounce xenophobia and elitism?
WE RENOUNCE THEM!

Do you renounce homophobia, classism, and religious sectarianism?
WE RENOUNCE THEM!

Do you renounce the structural manifestations of all these things (promising to fight them within and all around us)?
WE RENOUNCE THEM!

Do you renounce any society or economy structured around the purpose of benefiting a few, while the many at the bottom are sacrificed for a bottom line?
WE RENOUNCE THEM!

Do you renounce all these things?
WE RENOUNCE THEM!

With all your heart, soul, strength, and mind?
WE RENOUNCE THEM!

While we have your back and you have ours?
WE RENOUNCE THEM!

As we march toward liberation and life for all of Creation?
WE RENOUNCE THEM!

Do you renounce them?
WE RENOUNCE THEM!

Do you renounce them?
WE RENOUNCE THEM!

Do you renounce them?
WE RENOUNCE THEM!

Do you renounce them?
WE RENOUNCE THEM!

Then in the Spirit of Joyous Rebellion, and in the presence of one another, may we work together as a collective to fight oppression in all its forms, to build power with each other in configurations and coalitions yet unimagined. May we fight together, for one another, never alone. May we end oppression, empower the powerless, and lift the lowly in Love so that together we might tear the tyrants from their thrones and create a world where the earth is alive, and all people are able to eat. Amen.

Song: "Keep Your Eyes on the Prize," a folk song influential during the Civil Rights era

345

A Liturgical Observance of Indigenous People's Month

From the Philippines

We Prepare Our Liturgical Space.

During the Indigenous People's Month, the parishes or congregations may hold at least one Sunday worship in the 'open church or chapel' or outdoor—in the *dap-ay*, the *abong*, or any open or roofed place outside of their traditional houses of worship. This is to 'free' the worshipping community from its literal confinement to the four walls of Euro-American Christianity into celebrating the suffusion of all spaces by the divine.

Surround or fill the spaces with images, symbols, and objects that we use to offer in our indigenous religious rites in the Philippines. This is an occasion where we weave together our stories with the story of our Christian faith in a visual way.

We Gather the People.

Telling our stories and laying out the life-setting of our worship:

Commence the act of worship with the singing of the story of the faith, that is, with the Eucharistic narrative, using traditional music forms with the appropriate congregational or people's responses. Others may creatively extend and expand the story by telling the love story between God and the communities in their indigeneity.

This may be concluded by a 'call to worship':

Listen to the flapping of the winged creatures,
and the loud choruses of the small ones in every grass, leaf, and branch.
Listen, the birds are humming a tune!
LET THE WHOLE EARTH SING OF GOD'S REALM!

Listen to the soft whispers of the pine-scented wind,
to the music of the streams cascading into the river.
Feel the joyous heartbeat of the earth!
LET THE WHOLE EARTH SING OF GOD'S JUSTICE!

Listen to the *uggayam* [chanting] of our elders,
to the *bagbagto* [singing] of the young and youthful.

346

Let the villages of the first nations sing their praises!
LET THE WHOLE EARTH SING OF GOD'S GLORY!

And a prayer of invocation:

Come, Great Spirit and awaken the mountains.
Rouse the forests from their slumber.
May their shadows conceal us from our enemies.
Sharpen the blades of our spears
and sweeten our wine.
These are long days, O Great Spirit.
Come and lead us on.

We Listen to the Word.

The Sacred Scriptures. An alternative to the traditional reading from
the Hebrew-Christian scriptures is the act of sketching or drawing some
doable images and symbols, or even keywords and phrases, on fabrics,
or on the ground with a stick, or with the fingers, that is, if the assembly
space allows for it and is not paved. Or some may do it on prepared dried
bamboo cuts or also on some earthen objects and pieces of stones. This
can be done while the chosen texts or lectionary texts are being chanted
and read or immediately following this as a meditative act of responding
to the word 'read.'

The 'texts' on fabrics, bamboo, stones, and earthen objects are then laid
on the ground or on an altar (like a patpatayan or a Eucharistic table, or a
dulang), or hung on posts or traditional installations. A homily, a com-
mentary, or an exposition of the text by the clergy, the community priests,
or an elder may follow.

We may respond with this statement of faith or other appropriate response:

On this song of faith, we stand:
that we are the peoples and communities of these
living and pulsating mountains, valleys, and plains—
lands shared with and suffused by eternal spirits
and watered by the sweat and blood
of our ancestors and martyrs.
From these lands we define
and proclaim who we are
and where we are going.

On this song of faith, we stand:
That we are free and self-determining peoples,
made to speak, resist, and build
by the very cry of the God
of the high places;
that in our struggle against those that impose
their truth, their rule, and greedy money over us,
we become our self-identified and self-determined selves:
the *umili* (people) of these mountains,
tillers of our Creator's garden,
guardians of this planet's last frontiers,
partisans for the new world,
daughters and sons of the merciful God of justice.

On this song of faith, we stand.

We partake of the Eucharistic meal.

A feast of dancing and singing follows the homily, underscoring the fact that the Eucharist or the Communion service is a banquet celebrating the new heavens and the new earth where God is in full reign (what the contemporary ecumenical Church calls 'the feast of life'). This 'eschatological movement or performance' suffices for some ecclesial communities as a full 'textual' preface to the breaking and sharing of the bread and wine. The bread and wine may be distributed following the Ibaloi's—the indigenous people from the Benguet Province of the northern Philippines—way of sharing and distributing food to all people, including strangers, during their feast days. Here the bread (wafer or regular leavened bread) and wine (grape wine) may have their local counterparts.

We prepare for the long day: the moment of "panakidangadang" (resistance).

Ayee Kabunian!

This feast is for us a moment of atonement,
a moment of being one with your Spirit,
that Great Spirit who hovers and flies the sky above us,
who waters and resides in our forests,
who breathed life into our ancestors,
who formed these mountains that cradled our race;
the Great Spirit who reinvigorated our knees with [bread]
and nourished our spirits with wine;
the Great Spirit who now calls us to defend the homeland,

348

to drive away those who bow not to the guardian spirits;
the Great Spirit who now calls us to invite the divinities
back to our streams, rivers, mountains, gardens and valleys.

This feast is, for us, a receipt of your blessing.
AyeeKabunian,
These are long days.
Come and lead us on!

The Blessing

The final act of blessing may use the Ibaloi's Wasiwas Rite. The rite involves plenty of water in big basins and thick bundles of full-length reeds. The elders or the administrators of the rite dip or immerse the reed bundles into the basins of water and shower the crowd with water. The more exaggerated the showering and the more plentiful the water the better. The wasiwas is an act of both exorcism and blessing.

. . . as we continue in our faith journey may, the
Spirit of God descend upon us like the refreshing
waters of streams, river, and sea.

May this sprinkling free you from your ailments.
May this sprinkling heal you of your blindness.
May this sprinkling free you from your fears.
May this sprinkling liberate you from cowardice.
May this sprinkling release you from your bondage!

**MAY THIS SPRINKLING REFRESH OUR BODIES.
MAY THIS SPRINKLING ALLOW US TO SEE AGAIN.
MAY THIS SPRINKLING WAKEN THE COURAGE IN US.
MAY THIS SPRINKLING ROUSE
THE TRANSFORMER IN US.
MAY THIS SPRINKLING KINDLE OUR FREE SPIRITS!**

May the cool streams refresh you.
May the mighty rivers empower you.
**MAY THE SPIRIT OF GOD,
LIKE THE POWERFUL WAVES OF THE SEA,
LEAD US FORWARD!**

Stations of the Cross: Good Friday

Suburban Station Philadelphia, Pennsylvania

We gather outside the Women's and Men's bathrooms in the train station.

Brief History and Introduction to the Stations

• This is a way to enter into the mystery of the gift given to us by Jesus.

• This began with early pilgrims wanting to follow the footsteps of Jesus to the cross. In the 1500s, small replicas or shrines were made depicting the story. The hope is to fill us with a sense of deep gratitude for what God has done for us in Jesus.

• Why the Station? Because it reminds us that God is here with us, in this place, right now.

• This is a reminder to move from station to station as quietly as possible.

So let us pray . . .

The First Station: Jesus Is Condemned to Die

The gathering spot is outside the bathrooms. This is the place where I first met women washing up, changing clothes, and using hand dryers to dry their hair. In spite of ongoing efforts to maintain these restrooms, it is rare to have a hand dryer that is not broken. A broken system, broken hearts. And so we turn to Jesus, our alpha and omega.

> Then Pilate called together the chief priests, the rulers, and the people. He said to them, "You brought this man before me as one who was misleading the people. I have questioned him in your presence and found nothing in this man's conduct that provides a legal basis for the charges you have brought against him. Neither did Herod, because Herod returned him to us. He's done nothing that deserves death. Therefore, I'll have him whipped, then let him go."
>
> But with one voice they shouted, "Away with this man! Release Barabbas to us." (Barabbas had been thrown into prison because of a riot that had occurred in the city, and for murder.)
>
> Pilate addressed them again because he wanted to release Jesus.
>
> They kept shouting out, "Crucify him! Crucify him!"

350

For the third time, Pilate said to them, "Why? What wrong has he done? I've found no legal basis for the death penalty in his case. Therefore, I will have him whipped, then let him go."

But they were adamant, shouting their demand that Jesus be crucified. Their voices won out. Pilate issued his decision to grant their request. He released the one they asked for, who had been thrown into prison because of a riot and murder. But he handed Jesus over to their will. (Luke 23:13-25)

The journey begins. An innocent man wrongly sentenced to death. Jesus stands with all who have been wrongly accused, harshly judged, knowing what it is like to be part of an unjust and broken system. His hands are literally tied. We follow the story as Jesus is broken and given for us.

We adore you, O Christ, and we bless you . . . because by your holy cross you have redeemed the world.

The Second Station: Jesus Carries His Cross

The gathering place is the doors to the Comcast Center where people are coming and going all day long.

Then Pilate handed Jesus over to be crucified. (John 19:16)

Jesus is forced to carry the cross on which he will die. He carries the cross of all that each of us will have to carry. Those places of pain and worry that are visible and invisible. Look around. Some folks are carrying bags holding everything they own. Bags that have to be carried and watched everywhere throughout the day. Others carry briefcases or shopping bags.

What is the cross that you carry? On this day, we remember that Jesus came so that we might never bear any burden alone.

We adore you, O Christ, and we bless you because by your holy cross you have redeemed the world.

The Third Station: Jesus Falls the First Time

Gather at the steps going down to tracks three and four.

This year, the Southeastern Pennsylvania Transport Authority has added gates and turnstiles to prepare for the change in the fare system. These gates will also serve as a way to separate those in the station who can pay for fares from those who simply use the station to stay warm, dry, and safe.

The weight of the cross knocks Jesus to the ground. He fully enters our lives, as Jesus experiences those things that knock us down. Can he move another step? The strength comes and he continues the journey.

We adore you, O Christ, and we bless you because by your holy cross you have redeemed the world.

The Fourth Station: Jesus Meets His Mother

> When Elizabeth was six months pregnant, God sent the angel Gabriel to Nazareth, a city in Galilee, to a virgin who was engaged to a man named Joseph, a descendant of David's house. The virgin's name was Mary. When the angel came to her, he said, "Rejoice, favored one! The Lord is with you!" She was confused by these words and wondered what kind of greeting this might be. The angel said, "Don't be afraid, Mary. God is honoring you. Look! You will conceive and give birth to a son, and you will name him Jesus. He will be great and he will be called the Son of the Most High. The Lord God will give him the throne of David his father. He will rule over Jacob's house forever, and there will be no end to his kingdom." (Luke 1:26-33)

Mary knows the pain of a mother watching her child be murdered. It is a pain that so many mothers know in our own city. It is the pain of having a part of you die with your child. Jesus looks into the mirror of his mother's eyes and sees how she is suffering. It is the pain of loss and grief, a pain that he cannot take away from one that he loves so much. It is the pain of watching a loved one suffer. They look at each other and stand together in the suffering, when it would be so much easier to look the other way.

We adore you, O Christ, and we bless you because by your holy cross you have redeemed the world.

The Fifth Station: Simon Helps Jesus Carry His Cross

The gathering is at SEPTA's customer service and information center. This is a place for the lost and the found, a place where folks offer help to those on the journey. At this time of year, we also note and give thanks for those offering free help with tax returns. Let us remember to pray and give thanks for all in this station who are here to offer help.

> As they led Jesus away, they grabbed Simon, a man from Cyrene, who was coming in from the countryside. They put the cross on his back and made him carry it behind Jesus. (Luke 23:26)

Jesus is one with us; he needs help. He knows dependency and enters into the struggle to receive help. He did not ask Simon to help carry the cross; still he received the help that was offered. This is not so easy for many of us to do.

We adore you, O Christ, and we bless you because by your holy cross you have redeemed the world.

The Sixth Station: Veronica Wipes the Face of Jesus

In the past we have gathered at the wall of the Dollar Tree. For many who sleep in the station, Dollar Tree is a place to buy food. At some point, the glass was replaced, making it so much harder to look at ourselves. So today, we stop in this hall to reflect. This is an in-between place that also reminds us of so many who are in-between jobs, housing, or even relationships.

We notice our reflections in the glass. Do we see ourselves in the eyes of Jesus?

By now, the face of Jesus shows the brutality of the journey. He is dripping with dirt and sweat and blood. His lips are beginning to crack from dehydration. His vision is clouded by the pressure on his neck and back.

Veronica, a woman in the crowd, offers Jesus her veil and wipes his face. His gift to her is the imprint of his face on her veil; it is a reminder of the God who not only created us in God's own image but also became flesh and lived among us in a very real way.

We adore you, O Christ, and we bless you because by your holy cross you have redeemed the world.

The Seventh Station: Jesus Falls the Second Time

We gather at the elevator, a place of assistance for those needing extra help in getting around.

In spite of the help Jesus receives from Simon, he falls again under the weight of the cross. Here, Jesus knows what it is like to be disabled . . . to be physically weak . . . to grow old and have the body break down. There is no pain that Jesus does not know.

We adore you, O Christ, and we bless you because by your holy cross you have redeemed the world.

The Eighth Station: Jesus Meets the Women of Jerusalem

We gather at the women's accessory store in the concourse. Jesus looked into the heart of all he met. There are so many things we do to adorn, cover-up, or make ourselves look pleasing to others. Jesus meets us in our total vulnerability and says, "You are beautiful, precious in my site, and I love you!"

> A huge crowd of people followed Jesus, including women, who were mourning and wailing for him. Jesus turned to the women and said, "Daughters of Jerusalem, don't cry for me. Rather, cry for yourselves and your children." (Luke 23:27-28)

Jesus stood with those considered to be "the least" in society. He broke all kinds of social conventions when it came to women. Now, it was their turn to show Jesus their support. What would happen to them when he was gone? His promise was to be with them and all who were oppressed always. The women stood by his side even unto his death.

We adore you, O Christ, and we bless you because by your holy cross you have redeemed the world.

The Ninth Station: Jesus Falls the Third Time

For many in The Welcome Church, the station became a place of nightly refuge. This year, the corridors were again filled with folks lined up on the floor with their gear. The weight of homelessness can sometimes feel unbearable.

Jesus is broken. The last fall is crushing. There is no humanly possible way for him to continue, but he depends on the Divine. His executioners come to move him up the hill where he will die. He is spent, poured out for each one of us.

We adore you, O Christ, and we bless you because by your holy cross you have redeemed the world.

The Tenth Station: Jesus Is Stripped

We gather at the entrance to the subway. Sadly, this is a place where many have been assaulted.

> They also led two other criminals to be executed with Jesus. When they arrived at the place called The Skull, they crucified him, along with the criminals, one on his right and the other on his left. Jesus said, "Father, forgive them, for they don't know what they're doing." They drew lots as a way of dividing up his clothing. (Luke 23:32-34)

When we began this journey with Jesus to the cross, we saw that Jesus stood with all who were wrongly accused. As Jesus hangs on the cross, we see that Jesus also reaches out to those who have done wrong, offering mercy and forgiveness. He knows the pain of all who have been stripped, violated, raped, and humiliated. Still, Jesus shows us that love is stronger than hate.

We adore you, O Christ, and we bless you because by your holy cross you have redeemed the world.

The Eleventh Station: Jesus Is Nailed to the Cross

We gather in the courtyard where Ash Wednesday service was held. It is a gathering place for many. Three crosses were inscribed with cigarette ashes. This past year, even with the chaos of construction going on and having the space cut in half, we were given the unexpected blessing of a street musician playing our service. Jesus always shows up, even in the midst of chaos!

The weight of all that Jesus carries pulls against the nails in his hands and feet.

We adore you, O Christ, and we bless you because by your holy cross you have redeemed the world.

The Twelfth Station: Jesus Dies on the Cross

See this sign in the tunnels (now painted over); look at the ways the cross is breaking through!

> When he had received the sour wine, Jesus said, "It is completed." Bowing his head, he gave up his life. (John 19:30)

For Jesus, death was not passive; it was an active gesture of surrender and love. Upon breathing his last he says, "Into your hands I commend my spirit."

We adore you, O Christ, and we bless you because by your holy cross you have redeemed the world.

The Thirteenth Station: Jesus Is Taken Down from the Cross

Further into the tunnel, woman hands over her heart.

> After this Joseph of Arimathea asked Pilate if he could take away the
> body of Jesus. Joseph was a disciple of Jesus, but a secret one because
> he feared the Jewish authorities. Pilate gave him permission, so he came
> and took the body away. Nicodemus, the one who at first had come to
> Jesus at night, was there too. He brought a mixture of myrrh and aloe,
> nearly seventy-five pounds in all. Following Jewish burial customs, they
> took Jesus' body and wrapped it, with the spices, in linen cloths. (John
> 19:38-40)

Joseph and Nicodemus tenderly cared for Jesus after his death, though
they had some fear in showing their love for him while he was alive. As
the broken body of Jesus is carried down from the cross, we remember his
words at the Last Supper: "This is my body, which is given for you" (Luke
22:19). For us.

Jesus died for us.

We adore you, O Christ, and we bless you because by your holy cross you
have redeemed the world.

The Fourteenth Station: Jesus Is Laid in the Tomb

We are still in the tunnel . . . and we know Jesus did NOT loiter in the tomb.

> There was a garden in the place where Jesus was crucified, and in the garden was a new tomb in which no one had ever been laid. Because it was the Jewish Preparation Day and the tomb was nearby, they laid Jesus in it. (John 19:41-42)

Jesus enters all the places of our lives, even the tomb. The places of death, the places of absolute loneliness and pain. Jesus is there, ready to hold us and to love us back to life.

Sing two verses of the spiritual, "Were you There?"
(Verse 1, "Were you there when they crucified my Lord?" and Verse 3, "Were you there when they laid him in the tomb?")

We adore you, O Christ, and we bless you because by your holy cross you have redeemed the world.

The Fifteenth Station: Jesus Gives Us Glimmers of Hope

This year we celebrate the new Hub of Hope, offering services, rest, showers, laundry, meals, and welcoming folks experiencing homelessness.

The Hub of Hope, a joint effort between Project HOME, SEPTA, and the City of Philadelphia is a glimmer of what can happen when folks come together. We ask God to bless all who enter its doors. Even as we reflect on the death of Jesus and enter the lonely tomb, we know we are never without the hope of resurrection.

Please visit www.reimaginingworship.com, to find prayers and liturgies not included in this book. You'll also find reflections and testimonies from participants, visual art, songs, and theater compositions created as part of this project, plus photos and videos from the locations. You're invited to engage with all the content, to write your own prayers and liturgies, and to share them in your faith community and social networks.

Printed in the USA
CPSIA information can be obtained
at www.ICGtesting.com
LVHW030730110724
785126LV00006B/24